GARDEN
DIY MANUAL

GARDEN
DIY MANUAL

Great step-by-step projects for a complete garden makeover

Peter Bishop • Jenny Hendy

Bath · New York · Singapore · Hong Kong · Cologne · Delhi · Melbourne

First published by Parragon in 2010
Parragon Books Ltd
Queen Street House
4 Queen Street
Bath, BA1 1HE

Conceived and produced by **Focus Publishing**, Sevenoaks, Kent
Project directors: Guy Croton; Caroline Watson
Designers: Neil Adams; Heather McMillan
Editors: Guy Croton; Vicky Hales-Dutton
Note: The authors and publishers disclaim any liability, loss,
injury or damage incurred as a consequence, directly or
indirectly, of the use and application of the contents of this book.

See page 288 for photograph copyright details

ISBN 978–1–4075–5634–5

Printed in China

Contents

Transforming your garden

Few people are fortunate enough to inherit a garden in exactly the state they would like. The patch of land adjacent to your home has the potential to become your ideal 'outdoor room', but chances are that it does not have all the features you would like.

Whether you are starting from scratch or keen to renovate and re-model an existing garden, the scope for do-it-yourself improvements is unlimited. However, before you decide what it is that you want to plant, landscape or construct, you need to consider practical matters such as budget, the time you have available for building and maintenance and exactly how you plan to use the garden. The following pages offer some ideas on how to get started.

your garden

Whether you have just moved into a new house or have taken over an existing garden, you need to have a good look at what you have before making any design or planting decisions. A bit of initial detective work avoids costly mistakes, and remember positive features or problem areas may not be immediately apparent.

Some authorities suggest waiting a full growing year before making alterations to an established garden but in our fast-moving world, this is a luxury we may not be willing or able to afford. Continue mowing lawns and weeding borders until you are confident you are ready to implement changes. Working your way through an overgrown jungle requires time and patience. Resist the temptation to rip everything out all at once as you could inadvertently remove choice plants or mature specimens that would take years to replace.

Brand new gardens often have some 'landscaping' supplied by the builders such as turf, a few paving slabs and perhaps fencing panels, but this veneer can hide a multitude of potential problems such as poor drainage caused by soil compaction, buried rubble and an inadequate depth of topsoil.

BELOW: *At first sight a badly overgrown garden might just look like an eyesore and you could be tempted simply to rip everything out. Take your time, though – you never know what treasures might be hidden by the overgrowth.*

Sunlight and shade

How much light the garden receives differs from the depths of winter to summer when the sun is high in the sky and the days are longer. As the sun moves round from east where it rises, to west where it sets, parts of the garden will be shaded by buildings, walls, fences and trees. North-facing walls receive little direct light. Plot the passage of the sun around the garden to work out where to position elements like patios to make the most of the site at different times of day.

A garden with a southerly aspect usually has sunshine casting over it for most of the day and will tend to be warmer, with drier soil than a garden that is predominantly in shade. You can grow a wider range of plants here because winters, even in colder latitudes, will seem less severe and the majority of plant varieties prefer good light.

BELOW: *These tall irises and verbascum are protected by the white wall behind, which also reflects the sun to make a warm, sunny, protected spot for them.*

Soil and moisture

Before adding new plants to your garden, find out what type of soil you have. Are any areas prone to waterlogging, particularly in winter? Dig a few test pits to see how deep the topsoil is. This fertile layer, which is capable of supporting plants, will be darker in colour and of a different texture to the underlying layers of relatively poor subsoil. Thin topsoils overlying stony or sandy ground drain freely but may be low in nutrients and sufficient moisture. Clay soils are the most fertile but are usually poorly drained and can be difficult to cultivate for much of the year. They are sticky and wet in winter and if low in organic matter such as garden compost or manure, dry like concrete in summer. Fortunately, each of these extremes is able to support groups of plants that are adapted to tolerate and even thrive in the conditions.

Plants also have preferences for more alkaline or more acid soils, so carry out some pH testing around the garden using a kit or pH meter. The pH scale runs from 1 (most acidic) to 14 (most alkaline), with pH 7 representing neutral. Most soils have pH levels that are around the neutral mark, but to grow acid-loving or ericaceous plants such as rhododendron, camellia and pieris, you need soils with a reading of pH 7 or below, as these plants will not tolerate lime.

Exposure

Strong winds can damage plants, strip moisture from the leaves and prevent insects from pollinating fruit and vegetable flowers. Windy gardens are also unpleasant to sit out in, so some form of shelter or wind filtering is necessary.

Gardens at higher altitudes can be much colder with a shorter growing season than those down in the valleys or closer to sea level. Ask local gardeners and staff at garden centres about the conditions you can expect. Shelter from cold winds and a warm southerly or westerly aspect can create microclimates within apparently inhospitable areas. Seaside locations may be relatively frost free because of the warming effect of the water and urban plots are also mild because of the heat radiated by buildings.

do you want?

Planning your garden

Having worked out what conditions you have in terms of soil type, sun and shade, drainage and exposure to wind and cold, you can start to decide how to design the garden from scratch or adapt an existing space. Bear in mind the garden's strengths and weaknesses. You may, for example, have a pleasant view beyond the boundary, which could be enhanced, or an eyesore that needs camouflaging. A sloping site might seem like a problem at first but steps and terraces add drama and provide opportunities for introducing striking water features. In urban areas and on housing estates it can be hard to find parts of the garden that aren't overlooked but there is plenty you can do to alleviate the problem, to attractively screen off sitting and outdoor dining areas and filter views of surrounding buildings. Mature trees may cast a lot of shade and be difficult to underplant but they also add an air of maturity to the garden and should not be disposed of lightly. Be aware that some trees and hedgerows carry preservation orders and cannot be removed or pruned without permission from the local council.

What to keep

If there are existing elements such as patios, lawns, water features and garden buildings, decide whether to retain them as they are, modify or remove them. You may need to fill in ponds if you have young children or secure boundaries to keep in family pets. It may be possible to recycle some materials resulting from dismantling patios and so on, including bricks, paving slabs and timbers. This helps to keep down costs and is more environmentally friendly than buying and transporting new products.

Mature or overgrown shrubs and climbers as well as hedges can be given a new lease of life with radical pruning and this will also help to open up the space. Herbaceous perennials that are lifted and divided in autumn or spring can easily be moved to new borders if reworking the design requires it, and most will benefit from the treatment in any case.

RIGHT: *There is much that could be done to transform and improve this big, sloping garden. Steps could be introduced to break up the long slope, and the large area of lawn might benefit from a terraced area to reduce what is presently a rather dull and open expanse. A review of the many mature trees and shrubs in this garden would also be worth undertaking.*

ABOVE: *If you have pets, you need to consider their needs as you plan your new garden. Perhaps boundaries need securing, or some pets require protection from others, as here!*

Practicalities

Make a list of all the things that you and your family require from your plot and the way you envisage it being used through the year. Don't forget to factor in the amount of time you might actually have to garden and think carefully about undertaking projects such as a vegetable garden, that might create more work than you can actually manage.

Gardens have many functions apart from being a place to grow flowers, especially if you have children. They provide somewhere to play in the fresh air; to hang washing; to exercise and even to work. You can use them to store bulky items and tools; to make compost, store recycling and waste bins. Messy jobs such as cleaning off mountain bikes or washing the dog may be done outdoors and the garden may also house pets like rabbits, be part of a cat's territory or home to egg laying chickens.

More and more of us are growing our own fruits, vegetables and herbs, even if this is just in a few containers on the patio. A greenhouse might be a necessary part of the propagating and overwintering process and concerns about water wastage have persuaded many gardeners to install water butts.

All of these elements and functions need working in to your overall design.

The outdoor room

Today's gardens are often extensions of the internal living space and function as alfresco dining and kitchen areas, incorporating elements such as barbecues and fire pits. Whilst growing plants is still a major use for the garden, the space frequently doubles as a relaxation and entertainment area. Here you will find elements that strengthen the room-like feel, including overhead structures, walls and screens; decorative flooring; furniture, cushions and throws; lighting and ornaments. Styling decisions depend on personal preferences, perhaps mirroring the interior design of your home, but the look and feel of the house exterior and surrounding landscape should also be taken into consideration.

BELOW: *Many people consciously set out to make their garden an extension of their house – an outdoor room. In this case, a low-maintenance style has been adopted, with few plants, no grass and not much to be managed and maintained. Rather, the sheltered terrace pictured here looks more like a second living room.*

styles of garden

Most of us have an idea of what our dream garden might look and feel like, even if only in relatively abstract terms such as colourful and exciting or cool and serene, contemporary or traditional. When planning a new garden or updating your plot, it helps to make a wish list and even a mood board covered with clippings from magazines, sketches and colour swatches. If your idea of heaven is a grand country house estate but your plot is the size of a postage stamp, the situation may seem irreconcilable. However, adding signature plants like roses, clipped box and lavender, decorative elements such as an ornate stone vase or traditional structures including a trellis obelisk or an arbour seat might create the atmosphere you have been looking for.

Dealing with difficult plots

As well as the limitations of size, odd-shaped plots and sloping sites can present other challenges. A long narrow site usually benefits from being divided into a series of partially enclosed gardens. A more informal approach would be to wind a sinuous path from top to bottom and to use plants, hedges and structures to block off views around each bend, drawing the onlooker forward to explore.

Gardens that are wide and shallow look best when the axis is on the diagonal or the lawn or patio shaped into a broad arc or semi-circle. This takes the eye away from the close boundary opposite, forcing it to follow a longer track across the garden and fooling the brain into thinking the plot is larger than it actually is. Use a strong focal point at the end of the diagonal to hold the attention.

Sometimes the answer for a very small or odd shaped plot is to camouflage the boundaries by deepening the borders, making the plantings lush and providing a central space such as a round lawn, pool or patio. A triangular plot, tapering to a narrow point could work well with this treatment but here you might also try a series of connecting lawn or gravel circles edged in brick that reduce in size towards the tip.

Disjointed plots that go round corners, for example, are best divided into interconnecting and clearly defined spaces. But if the garden seems too small as a result, you could also try drawing a long diagonal axis across from one garden to the other, setting up a strong sight line using a pergola walkway, for example, or straight pathway lined with obelisks or topiaries. Position a seat or garden building at the far end to draw the eye and allow views in the opposite direction.

ABOVE: *Personally selected ornaments and statuary immediately lend the garden a unique quality. Combine these with imaginative plantings to create the look you are after.*

LEFT: *This very narrow garden has been cleverly divided into several different areas. This both breaks up the elongated, uniform shape of the space and offers the owners lots of different options, from decking for sitting on to a sun-drenched gravel garden beyond the trellis that divides the garden halfway along its length.*

Sloping gardens

If your garden slopes down towards the house you will probably need a retaining wall with added drainage to keep water from the garden pooling round the walls. This arrangement creates sufficient usable flat ground around the building to accommodate patio furniture, for example. Make the steps up into the garden wide and shallow to lessen the feeling of the wall being a barrier and consider building a wall fountain or water cascade into the retaining wall.

Relatively gentle slopes often suit an informal garden layout, with winding pathways, ribbon-like lawns and perhaps some island beds. Steep gardens usually require terracing and you can use heavy wooden railway sleepers or their modern equivalent or walls made from breeze blocks faced with brick or stone to hold the soil back. Hire a building consultant if you are considering doing this work yourself as it can be tricky to calculate the necessary load-bearing capacity of retaining walls. There is also a health and safety issue to bear in mind, in that if you get it wrong the wall might collapse. Don't forget that terracing provides opportunities for impromptu seating using smooth paving slabs or sanded wood to top the walls.

Simple proportions

Whatever style of garden you decide on, keep the underlying footprint as strong and simple as possible without unnecessary flourishes that may prove hard to maintain when they are transferred from paper. Pathways should have a reasonably logical route as otherwise people will be tempted to bypass them and walk across lawns or flower beds, especially in front gardens. Borders need to be as wide at some point as the fencing or hedging is high, in order to feel in proportion with the space. Lawns are much easier to mow if curves are kept broad and if corners aren't too tight to turn the mower in one sweep. Incorporating a mowing edge of bricks or stone lessens the need for time-consuming edging. And make terraces and patios deep enough to accommodate people and furniture with ease. Even if your main sitting area is elsewhere, a broad flat piece of hard landscaping between the house and main garden helps to connect the vertical walls with the horizontal space and keep things in proportion. Add planting beds against the walls and around the patio area to soften the effect.

Alternative layouts and
styles of garden

ABOVE: *A formal garden need not be an old-fashioned garden. In this case, geometric shapes, minimalist use of materials and un-fussy plantings have created a pleasingly formal yet ultra-contemporary overall effect.*

Choosing your style

The kind of garden you choose might be dictated by the type or historic period of your house, but the beauty of garden design today is that just as with interior design, you can mix and match styles and influences with more freedom than you could in the past. There is no reason why you shouldn't create a cottage garden around a contemporary brick building. You just need to keep the layout simple and use modern paving and fencing alternatives that link more closely with the architecture and fabric of the house.

Look at your neighbourhood, particularly when designing a front garden, and see if there are any vernacular materials that you could incorporate or general themes that you could build on or modify. This helps create a more harmonious feel. Most people are comfortable with either a formal or an informal garden layout but once you have a theme in mind, try to carry that right through from the choice of paving, fencing and hedging to the planting, furniture and garden buildings, pots and ornamental detailing.

Schemes may start out ambitiously but are invariably modified by budget. Keep costs down by doing as much of the hard landscaping

yourself as you possibly can, saving money for special pots or plants. However, as before, be careful not to overestimate the amount of work you can realistically take on. Family gardens need to be able to be adapted over time as the children grow and elements like sand pits and play equipment might be replaced with a water feature and a vegetable garden, for example. Dividing family gardens can create areas for the children to run around on the grass and play ball games away from precious flower borders. These rough lawns could later be made more formal or replaced with gravel or paving for a low-maintenance surface.

Formality

Elements of formal garden design include symmetry and a rectilinear or geometric footprint of straight lines, squares, oblongs and circles. Formal gardens often feature rectangular lawns, broad decorative pathways or canal-like pools that lead the eye to a strong focal point. The effect may be strengthened by lining the axis with pleached lime trees, regularly spaced columnar conifers such as Iris yew (*Taxus baccata* 'Fastigiata'), or perhaps a wisteria-covered pergola walkway. At the end of the sight line you might find an attractive garden building, a piece of sculpture or topiary, an urn on a plinth or a bench seat.

Formal gardens are often associated with period properties but with some adaptations, formality also suits contemporary spaces, the crisp geometric lines creating a sense of space and minimalist simplicity. The use of plain, modern materials such as square concrete paving slabs laid on the diagonal, decking and galvanized metal planters creates an entirely different atmosphere to that of a garden paved in random stone and filled with period details such as Italianate terracotta vases, Victorian cast iron seats and ornate fountains. Use your imagination and adapt as you see fit.

A relaxed approach

Although the style of informal gardens is altogether more relaxed and free-flowing than the formal, you still need to pay attention to getting the underlying footprint of the garden right. Elements of scale and proportion matter just as much here, although this might not be so obvious to the naked eye as in a formal garden. Informal gardens tend to mirror the natural landscape. Paved areas often have margins that are randomly staggered, fingering into lawns and beds. Retaining walls, borders and lawns are gently curved and undulating while pathways take a lazily meandering rather than a direct route. Water features are also reminiscent of those found in the countryside – perhaps a small pebble stream or pond margined with water plants. Again, what you choose to include in an informal garden and the way you choose to interpret the 'look' is limited only by your imagination.

LEFT: *This very relaxed, informal garden might look relatively unkempt, but thought has nevertheless gone into the scale and nature of the layout and the plantings.*

Style influences

Many people get inspiration for their gardens from international travel, by witnessing different styles and alternative uses of plants in foreign climes. In this case a Mexican-style terrace features agaves and other exotic plants in terracotta urns.

LEFT: *The garden pictured here represents a more traditional interpretation of formal design, with its sculptural topiary, use of giant terracotta urns, symmetrical layout and the classic use of gravel for a clean surface finish.*

preparation

Making a feature of your lawn

Our view of lawns tends to be restricted to grass turf, but you can use several kinds of plants for soft surfacing the garden. The shape of a lawn also has a tremendous influence on the design of the garden and even a few simple changes can make a dramatic improvement.

Lawns form clear, flat open areas that create a feeling of spaciousness. The colour and texture of a lawn makes a pleasing contrast with other kinds of garden surfacing, and in winter, when the garden has largely died down, the emerald green of a lawn is a cheering sight. Lawns act as a foil for the plants and features contained in the garden but can also become features in their own right.

ABOVE: *Lawns can help to lead the eye through the garden. Here a series of stepping stones adds further emphasis as the green continues beneath the rose arch to a hidden area beyond.*

BELOW: *This circular lawn is edged in brick, which emphasises the shape of the lawn and separates it from the gravel area. The stone bench reinforces the circular theme.*

Transforming lawned areas

Sometimes all you need to do to transform the whole look of a garden is to change the shape and layout of the lawned areas. For example, if you have the traditional long rectangular lawn with straight-edged flower borders, you could superimpose two or three interlocking or 'kissing' circles over the rectangle and cut the new lawn edge making the borders curved. The circles could be defined more clearly by edging them with bricks set just below the cutting height of your mower. A circular or semi-circular lawn that replaces a square one can also make a small garden feel much larger because the eye follows the perimeter of the lawn in an uninterrupted ark. The circular lawn is also a useful solution for irregularly or awkwardly shaped gardens such as triangles. Once the borders are planted up and the boundaries disappear, the pleasing shape of the lawn becomes a central focus.

Lawns can be used to subtly guide a person through the garden along the route you wish them to take. It is hard to resist following a long, sinuous ribbon of green as it winds through the planting revealing previously hidden aspects of the garden. If you have a long narrow garden, a serpentine lawn such as this can create exciting design possibilities. Remember, circles and broad, gentle curves feel restful; wiggly lawn edges are too 'busy'.

Alternatives to grass

Variations in height and texture are an all-important part of good garden design. Unrelieved lawns covering a large area can be rather boring, but if you create new island beds or flower borders, will you have time to maintain them? This question is particularly important in front gardens, which tend to be more public and therefore less pleasurable to work in. In a small garden, it may be impractical to have a lawn, especially where access for the mower is difficult, but you may still want a relatively low expanse of greenery to contrast with paving and surrounding plantings. Low-growing, spreading evergreens such as certain hebes and *Vinca minor* varieties can also be used as an alternative ground cover to lawns. For larger areas, the many types of prostrate or spreading conifers – for example, junipers – can be used to spread and cover the ground quite quickly, creating a pleasing evergreen tapestry of greens, blues, greys and gold. Heathers are traditional partners, and interesting effects can be achieved by filling gaps in a mixed conifer/heather planting with a cobble mulch and the occasional larger boulder, or by placing taller, jagged rock specimens in small groups to give height amongst surrounding plants.

Such borders would be easy to maintain once the plants had matured and covered the ground but to be sure that you are really keeping your work to a minimum, you could also plant through a weed-proof membrane.

ABOVE: *A thyme lawn makes a very pretty feature in a decorative 'edible garden'. Plant a mixture of creeping varieties in a random pattern. Well-drained soil and a sunny spot are essential.*

Grass sculpting

In a very large lawn you can experiment by mowing different areas with the blades set to different heights. This technique will create curving abstract ground patterns that you can change periodically.

Try this

■ Consider changing the shape of your lawn to improve the garden's design.
■ Keep the design simple with straight lines or broad curves.
■ Emphasize the shape with a decorative lawn edging of brick or stone.
■ Use circular lawns as a solution to awkwardly shaped sites.
■ Contrast areas of lawn with other surface textures for year-round interest.
■ Replace very small areas of lawn with other surfaces.

Avoid this

■ Don't create difficulties with mowing or maintenance of lawns by growing in shady or inaccessible areas.
■ Don't allow gravel to be walked onto the lawn. Small stones can ruin mower blades.
■ Don't forget to maintain a clean-cut edge in more formal gardens or where the lawn shape is geometric.
■ Don't use grass under trees or in the shade of buildings.
■ Don't use overly vigorous ground-cover plants.

Choosing features and selecting
projects to make

Selecting which features are suitable for your plot will depend partly on your particular circumstances – for example, whether or not you have youngsters and how much time you have to garden. You also need to consider how you use your outdoor space, whether it is primarily to relax and entertain; as a playground for the children; to grow ornamental plants, fruits and vegetables; or perhaps to get closer to nature. Consider what projects could enhance the different parts of the garden, improving their various functions – cooking, eating, relaxing, playing, exercising, storing and recycling, providing a wildlife habitat – and how any new additions might facilitate greater enjoyment and satisfaction for you and your family.

There is no doubt that it is cheaper to build your own garden features than to hire someone to do it for you or to buy them off the peg. For example, children's outdoor play equipment can be very expensive, and if you consider how quickly little ones can grow out of something like a sand pit or a Wendy house, it makes sense to build such items yourself. Project managing from start to finish also allows you to select quality materials and to check that everything is constructed and planted to a high standard.

BELOW: *This ornamental vegetable garden has been cleverly incorporated into a small space in a border, brightening up a dull space in a practical way.*

ABOVE: *A treehouse for the kids makes a lovely garden feature, but for how long will they actually use it and will it ultimately become an eyesore? Think carefully before embarking on expensive and ambitious projects.*

Adapting to circumstances

The size of garden or areas within a plot will inevitably affect which projects are possible. For example, a small courtyard might not have room for a garden building or large compost bin. Conveniently though, you will find that many of the projects featured in this book can be adapted and scaled up or down once you have the basic techniques and designs to hand. Small spaces, whether a postage stamp-sized plot or a discreet area within a larger garden such as a patio or deck, often benefit from extra detailing or even a complete facelift because they are under greater scrutiny. You could brighten a corner with a stylish planter, say, or add something that is both ornamental and functional, such as a dovecote, sundial or mosaic-paving panel.

Another key issue to consider is whether you are starting from scratch and therefore have carte blanche to incorporate numerous new projects, or whether you are adapting and altering what you already have. Even when

the latter is the case, you will still have room to work in new elements and to update the garden, possibly by demolishing outmoded or ramshackle features and reworking the shape and size of existing lawns, borders and terraces. Cracked, discoloured and worn paving mars the appearance of the garden as a whole and there are a number of practical solutions within these pages that you can follow to upgrade your plot.

Style matters

The architectural style of the house and surrounding buildings and the overall theme selected may exclude the incorporation of some projects detailed in this book but also make others more attractive. If your house is quite modern and urban and you have opted for a contemporary theme, you are less likely to be able to work in rustic seating, post and rail fencing and so on, but you might want to swap a lawn for a smart deck or drought-busting Mediterranean gravel garden. Or you may

decide to build a barbecue and pebble pool in a paved outdoor 'room' designed for entertaining. The walls could be made from trellis panels and the 'ceiling', a climber-clad pergola.

If your house is in a more rural setting, features such as picket fencing, a tree seat or a rustic rose arbour should fit in perfectly. A more carefree design and interest in wildlife makes features like a bog garden or a natural pool a likely proposition and most gardeners will enjoy attracting wild birds with a birdbath.

ABOVE: *This characterful roof garden might be tiny but it offers a wealth of distinctive features that delight the eye and reflect the owner's style and personality.*

RIGHT: *In this photograph the rich, colourful plantings in the foreground perfectly complement the style and colour of the old house in the background.*

projects to make

Large and small-scale projects

Some of the projects included in the forthcoming pages require several days to complete and a certain level of DIY skill and physical energy. These projects need a little more planning than others and with something like a larger-scale paving or decking project you will also need to consider ease of access for materials and equipment as well as your budget. Other features could be created for relatively little outlay and in a matter of hours once all the materials and plants are to hand. Small-scale activities such as laying a pebble mosaic, planting a window box or rigging up a hammock don't require any special skills and can provide virtually instant gratification!

Although many of the smaller projects can be worked into your garden scheme without the need for planning, larger constructions are likely to have more impact and may affect the rest of the garden in ways you hadn't considered. Take time to visualize any new additions and to work them into the garden as a whole.

A working plan

It always helps to have a scale drawing of the garden and a few spare photocopies, so that you can try out your ideas in pencil and work new features into the overall scheme. Having an accurate plan on which to sketch in new additions such as pathways, patios, seating or children's play areas helps you to work out the size and proportions of proposed projects and to calculate what materials will be required. Draw on grid or squared paper and incorporate as much detail as possible. For most compact domestic gardens, a plan on A1 paper with a scale of 4cm to the metre (1½in to the yard) is ideal. For reasonably large gardens, 2cm to a metre (¾in to a yard) will suffice.

Visualizing new ideas

If your skills at graphic design or technical drawing are reasonably developed, you may be able to work up three-dimensional, isometric views of your garden plan that allow you to bring additions and alterations to life. Most garden design programmes made for use on home computers will do these graphics for you and even allow you to 'walk' through the garden and look at it from a variety of angles. However, if this all seems too complicated, just take a whole series of snapshots of your garden in its current state and draw on the photos or printouts with felt pens. You will be amazed at how effective this is as a way of seeing how something like a new, built-in barbecue, pond, flight of steps or garden shed might look in the chosen location.

ABOVE: *A new garden feature might be something as simple as a decorative container, which will not require any special planning.*

FAR LEFT: *If you are planning a complete garden makeover – or, for that matter, the introduction of a few large, significant features – it is always a good idea to plan out on paper first.*

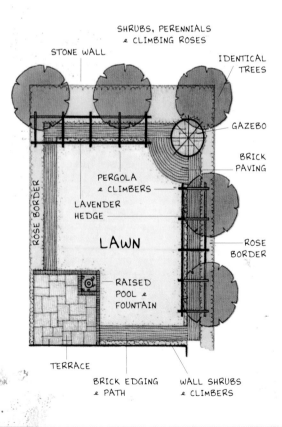

SHRUBS, PERENNIALS & CLIMBING ROSES

STONE WALL

IDENTICAL TREES

GAZEBO

BRICK PAVING

PERGOLA & CLIMBERS

LAVENDER HEDGE

ROSE BORDER

LAWN

ROSE BORDER

RAISED POOL & FOUNTAIN

TERRACE

BRICK EDGING & PATH

WALL SHRUBS & CLIMBERS

Building mock-ups

If you aren't sure how something large such as a new terrace, pergola or trellis screen will look, mark out the 'footprint' with tent pegs, 15cm (6in) nails or wooden posts and string or use a can of white, line-marking paint. A hosepipe, warmed in the sunshine to make it more flexible, is also useful for marking out the margins of a natural pool, say, or the curve of a lawn. These life-size representations will enable you to walk round and gauge if the space is large enough and also to see how well it connects to other features and to check that it is in proportion. Don't forget to view from upstairs windows, as well. Flesh out three-dimensional constructions using bamboo canes, if necessary lashing these together to create longer verticals and horizontals. Variously sized cardboard boxes and even plastic dustbins can be substituted for medium-sized elements such as shrubs, pots and planters or an obelisk.

For projects that include planting, either as an integral part or helping to soften hard landscaping, bear in mind how much shoots and branches are likely to grow – across paving, out from walls and trellis panels or down from the overhead cross bars of a pergola or arch. Allow space for these living elements to develop over time. New features such as pathways may seem too wide and out of proportion initially, but plants will soon grow and you will be grateful for having accommodated them at the start.

considerations

Your choice of plants and the way they are used has a marked effect on the feel of a garden. Contemporary plots tend to feature architectural specimens such as New Zealand flax and ornamental grasses, coupled with bold blocks or swathes of just a few types of flowering plant. It is interesting that the underlying layout of the traditional cottage garden is formal, with beds divided into a grid criss-crossed with straight brick pathways. However, overlaid with an exuberant jumble of plants – herbs, traditional flowers, fruits and vegetables – this type of garden doesn't appear to have much structure and the effect is romantic and old-fashioned.

Regardless of style, plants well suited to their environment and which are coping with the maintenance regime you can afford to give them, will make the garden look good. Choose wisely in the first place and you will remove much of the hard work and heartache associated with failing displays. Nothing is worse for a gardener than seeing lovingly nurtured plantings not work out.

BELOW: *For a contemporary look and feel, try combining ornamental grasses with boldly coloured blocks of flowering plants.*

Bulk buys

You will create more impact and drama in the garden by planting in bold swathes. However, if you don't have the finances to buy flowering and foliage perennial plants in the recommended groups of threes, fives and so on, buy one of each type in spring, cosset them and grow them on to a size where they can be divided and replanted to cover a wider area – usually by early autumn. Alternatively, if a plant is not suited to division – for example, penstemon, fuchsia and many herbs – take summer cuttings instead. A surprising number of hardy perennials can also be grown from seed and if you sow in early spring some even flower in their first year.

Choosing the right plant

Trips to the garden centre or nursery can be quite confusing since plants having different requirements in terms of sun, moisture levels and soil type tend to be mixed together. Having observed your garden and made notes on the various habitats – for example, damp and shady or dry and sunny – you should be able to put together a targeted shopping list. Avoid the temptation to simply buy what catches your eye unless you know it will suit the position you have in mind. Information on plant labels tends to be minimal, so do your homework in advance and always take a handy reference along with you or dip into the garden centre's customer copies.

Some plants are one-shot wonders, in bloom for just a couple of weeks and then lacklustre for the rest of the year. Unless you have a large garden and can afford the space to accommodate such plants, avoid them in favour of reliably hardy varieties that bloom for several months or which have other attractive qualities such as ornamental seed heads and fruits, variegated or coloured foliage, bright winter stems or a striking habit.

ABOVE: *Hostas offer striking variegated colour and are excellent choices for shady areas.*

RIGHT (CLOCKWISE FROM TOP LEFT): *Glory of the snow; 'Emerald Gaiety'; daffodil; Japanese anemone.*

Planting for shade

Don't despair if your garden appears to be predominantly shady. There are many beautiful plants that thrive in shade and with some simple design tricks and cultivation techniques, your garden can be turned into a tranquil haven. In a sun-drenched south- or west-facing plot it can be refreshing to deliberately create areas of dappled shade. These spots introduce contrast and make cool retreats when summer temperatures reach a peak. Shade also lets you try different kinds of plants – ferns, hostas and hydrangeas, for example, and other lush large-leaved specimens – that might not fair so well in strong sunlight.

Shade with reasonable moisture is fairly easy to plant, especially if the soil is neutral to acid (pH 7 and below). Many woodland types evolved on acid, humus-rich soil and are ericaceous or lime-hating for example, rhododendron and azalea, skimmia, camellia, pieris and leucothoe.

Dry shade is much more of a problem and this situation is often found under mature trees where the ground is also impoverished and full of roots or in the rain shadow of walls. Apply large amounts of well-rotted manure, ground-composted bark and garden compost in late winter when the ground is relatively moist and plant through this mulch in spring and early summer or early to mid-autumn.

Plants for dry shade

The following ground cover plants, ferns, flowering perennials, shrubs and bulbs will tolerate dry shade, especially where soil has been improved and heavily mulched, but young plants are best watered in their first summer until established.

- *Anemone* x *hybrida* (Japanese anemone)
- *Bergenia cordifolia* (elephant's ears)
- *Carex pendula* (pendulous sedge)
- *Chionodoxa luciliae* (glory of the snow)
- *Cyclamen hederifolium* and *C. coum*
- *Dryopteris filix-mas* (scaly male fern)
- *Epimedium* species and forms (barrenwort)
- *Euonymus fortunei* 'Emerald Gaiety'
- *Euphorbia amygdaloides* var *robbiae* (wood spurge)
- *Galanthus nivalis* forms (snowdrop)
- *Geranium nodosum* (cranesbill)
- *Geranium phaeum* 'Album' (mourning widow)
- *Hedera helix* cultivars (English ivy) – use white rather than gold variegated types which tend to revert
- *Iris foetidissima* and *I. f.* 'Variegata' (Gladwyn iris)
- *Lamium galeobdolon* (yellow archangel)
- *Luzula sylvatica* 'Aurea' (golden wood sedge)
- *Mahonia aquifolium* (Oregon grape)
- *Narcissus* (cyclamineus types) – daffodil
- *Pachysandra terminalis* and *P. t.* 'Variegata'
- *Saxifraga* x *urbium* (London pride)
- *Vinca minor* (lesser periwinkle)

Planting
considerations

ABOVE: *This* Santolina chamaecyparissus, *planted up in a bed covered in pinkish pebbles, is perfect for a hot sunny spot and will immediately convey a Mediterranean feel to any garden.*

RIGHT: *Here a basket of rocket has been suspended from an olive tree in a conscious attempt to mimic the classic Mediterranean style.*

Hot spots

Parched, sun-baked areas of the garden can be almost as problematic as dry shade. Free-draining sandy or thin stony soils dry out quickly in summer and especially tricky areas to plant are borders at the base of hot, sunny walls or south-facing hedges, raised beds and permanent planters. Fortunately, many shrubby Mediterranean herbs and aromatic plants, silver-, grey- or blue-leaved species and succulents have remarkable drought tolerance. With our changing climate and likely future restrictions on watering, it makes sense to major on such plants if your garden is in a relatively dry area or a suntrap.

Follow the Mediterranean way of planting, establishing new additions in spring, soaking the plant and the planting hole, backfilling with soil and mulching with gravel, pebbles or flat stones to keep the ground cool by reflecting sun and heat and trapping moisture. This type of mulch also sets the plants off to good effect.

To continue the Mediterranean theme, you could create a false perspective by using tall trees planted at a diagonal to make your garden look longer. The best trees to use for this effect are Italian cypresses and Juniper. The Italians actually clip these trees to make them look more compact. However, if you choose to do this you must clip only on the green, as cutting on the brown will prevent re-growth.

For a more low-level perspective, but one with just as much of a Mediterranean feel, plant hedges of sun-loving lavenders. These look beautiful in flower and offer the added advantage of smelling fantastic. When they have finished flowering, cut them back because if you don't, they quickly become straggly and ugly. You can also use rosemary for a hedge.

Finally, consider planting a grapevine. It is almost impossible to kill a grapevine, making them great for covering up the garden and creating a shady space.

LEFT (CLOCKWISE FROM TOP LEFT): *Blue oatgrass; Thyme; Ballota; Cistus.*

Plants for hot dry areas

Many of the plants listed here could be used to colonize cracks in paving, as a ground cover alternative to lawns as well as for low-maintenance planters. Combine broad-leaved types with spiky or grassy-leaved plants to create interesting textural contrasts. Water during dry spells until established.

- *Artemisia* (includes shrubby forms as well as herbaceous)
- *Ballota*
- *Carex buchananii* (leatherleaf sedge)
- *Cistus* (hardy species and cultivars)
- *Convolvulus cneorum*
- *Erigeron karvinskianus* (fleabane)
- *Festuca glauca* (blue fescue)
- *Gaillardia* (blanket flower)
- *Gaura*
- *Helianthemum nummularium* (rockrose)
- *Helictotrichon sempervirens* (blue oatgrass)
- *Heliopsis helianthoides* (false sunflowers)
- *Jovibarba*
- *Lavandula* (lavender)
- *Oenothera* (evening primrose – alpine species and forms)
- *Ophiopogon planiscapus* 'Nigrescens' (black mondo grass)
- *Oreganum* (flowering and foliage varieties as well as herbs)
- *Perovskia atriplicifolia* 'Blue Spire' (Russian sage)
- *Rosmarinus* (rosemary)
- *Salvia* (herbs as well as flowering species and cultivars like S. x sylvestris 'Mainacht')
- *Sedum* (especially low-growing alpine species and cultivars)
- *Sempervivum* (house leek)
- *Stachys byzantina* 'Silver Carpet' (lamb's ears)
- *Stipa gigantea* (golden oats grass)
- *Thymus* (thyme)
- *Yucca*

Tips for busy gardeners

• Self-supporting
Look for plants that are compact and don't require staking. Some taller plants such as ornamental grasses and *Verbena bonariensis* are self-supporting and create useful contrasts amongst lower-growing types.

• Slug-free
On damp clay soils that harbour slugs or near to a snail roosting site such as an ivy-clad wall, use plants that are resistant to these troublesome creatures. Those with furry, felted, bristly or strongly aromatic leaves, and tough shrubs such as berberis and potentilla tend to be left alone.

• Water-wise
Use drought-tolerant plants where conditions allow but remember they don't like waterlogged soil!

• Lean diet
Avoid any that need frequent feeding, though you could use slow-release fertilizer granules, especially in containers, to make life easier.

• Troopers!
Plants that continue to look good through the seasons are a bonus, especially those that don't require dead-heading, as you will probably only have to deal with them once a year in spring.

• Well-mannered
Some plants are thugs that quickly outgrow their allotted space or have other weed-like characteristics such as nuisance seeding. Look for tell-tale comments on plant labels such as 'quick ground cover' or 'rapid climber'. Plants with a fast growth rate often need a lot of pruning or division to keep them under control and flowering consistently.

irrigation systems

Saving and re-using water

As the population of the world increases and the planet gradually warms up, it is incumbent on all of us to find ways of conserving water, which in many places is becoming an increasingly valuable commodity. Gardeners use more than their fair share of water, so perhaps they have a greater responsibility than most in this regard.

Many plants are not especially fussy about the state of the water they receive, so apart from saving rainwater, the opportunities for recycling water from the home and spreading it around your garden may be greater than you think.

TOP RIGHT: *Not only is this water butt saving rainwater, it also provides a sanctuary for wildlife, with a cleverly designed frog ladder resting on the edge and reaching down to the ground.*

Water conservation

Nature has designed plants to like rainwater best of all, so it makes sense to collect as much of the stuff as you possibly can. A plastic water butt is an inexpensive purchase from any garden centre or DIY store, which can make a huge difference to the successful and economic irrigation of any garden. With an accessible top and a tap on the side, it is easy to fill smaller receptacles from a water butt and then distribute water where it is needed around the garden. Some higher-tech models come with rain-saving devices that can be hooked up to guttering and downpipes to maximize their water-collecting efficiency. You don't strictly need a water butt to catch and conserve water, though; any open-topped container left outside will do the job.

RIGHT: *This water butt is teamed with a rain-saving device to give it maximum water-conserving efficiency. The butt is attached to the guttering downpipe so that the maximum amount of rainwater passes directly into it. Smaller receptacles such as watering cans can then be filled from the tap at the base so that water is then easily distributed where it is needed around the garden.*

Recycling water

Next time you do the washing up, don't just pour the contents of the bowl down the sink – take it outside and give it to your plants! We all waste huge amounts of water every day, water that might be dirty and used as far as we are concerned but that could help to sustain a plant that is missing the rain. Soap suds and food deposits don't bother many plants and will soon soak away without leaving an unsightly mess around your flower borders. If you make the effort, there are myriad opportunities to recycle water and make it go that little bit further. Think water-wise and do your garden and the environment a favour.

Sprinklers

Garden sprinklers are great for quick and easy watering of plants and particularly lawns. They can be set up and turned on in no time and are light and portable, making them easy to move around the garden. The only problem is that they do use a surprisingly large amount of water and need mains pressure via a tap in order to work efficiently. During hot, dry weather they are often also subject to government or local council bans, which means that it is not a good idea to rely upon them during summer months. It is possible to buy pumps which can be rigged up to water butts and sprinklers in turn, but these are fiddly to operate and relatively expensive.

Seep hoses

Seep hoses are rubber or plastic pipes with hundreds of minute holes along one side of their length. They can be positioned so that the holes face upwards to produce a fine spray over a designated area – for example, a lawn – or with the holes facing downwards so that the water seeps out of them to gently saturate the surrounding area. This makes them ideal for running through beds and borders, where they can water plants and vegetables unobtrusively and without fuss. Seep hoses can deliver water to plants slowly, evenly and efficiently.

Soaker hoses and subsoil systems

A soaker (or weeping) hose is a variation of the seep hose, made from a network of porous hoses. It offers a controlled method of watering that reduces evaporation and run-off and uses up to 70 percent less water than conventional watering methods. As the water fills the hose, pressure builds up and expands the hose wall, opening the tiny holes that slowly seep water. A system like this may be positioned on the surface of the soil or buried at a depth of 10–15cm (4–6in) below the surface as a permanent irrigation system. It is ideal for fruit and vegetables.

ABOVE: *A network of border sprinklers connected by seep hoses is a most efficient way of ensuring that your plants get the irrigation they need.*

BELOW: *Sprinklers are useful but very wasteful of water, as they require mains pressure to operate.*

in the garden

ABOVE: *Spotlights come in all shapes and sizes and can be put to any number of uses in the garden. Ensure they are always correctly and safely wired.*

Power among your plants

The whole subject of electricity and electrical safety in the garden must be treated with extreme caution. Electrical wiring outdoors is far more likely to become damaged than wiring hidden inside the walls, floors or roofs of houses. Classic examples of accidents involving electricity in the garden are cutting through a flex with a hedge trimmer or lawnmower, or digging through a buried electrical cable. Electricity is also dangerous outdoors – especially in and around a pond – because it does not mix with water, which tends to abound in the average garden. If you are in any doubt at all, do not wire electrical items yourself but instead consult a qualified electrician.

BELOW: *The coloured lighting on these spiky plants is very atmospheric and the uplighting on the side of the house emphasizes the texture of the stone.*

Safety RCDs

What makes electricity dangerous to you in the garden is that you could provide a perfect earth connection if you touch a live wire – particularly if you are standing on damp ground – and the short circuit that then passes through you could prove fatal. A residual current protection device (RCD) can overcome this problem. One of these monitors the currents flowing in the live and neutral wires of a flex or cable and acts like a switch to cut off the electrical supply if it detects even a tiny difference (for example, if some of the current is about to flow through you rather than a cable). RCDs have saved the lives of countless people who have, for example, cut through

ABOVE: *These tiny lights on decking will help guide the diners to and from their chairs after dark.*

the flex of a lawnmower. It is fair to say that an RCD should ALWAYS be used in conjunction with outdoors electrics. If in doubt, consult a qualified electrician.

Electrical wiring and fuses

The function of 'fusing' is to protect the wiring, not you. In particular, fusing prevents wiring from overheating and, possibly, causing a fire. A big fuse protects the whole house (and all the circuits); medium-sized fuses protect individual circuits; small fuses protect the flex leading to electrical appliances and, sometimes, tiny fuses within the appliance protect its own wiring.

Garden and aquatic lighting

Lighting can bring the garden alive at night, particularly during warm, summer evenings.

Simple lighting can take the form of garden candles and torches, but a strong spotlight directed at a fountain or waterfall, causing the water droplets to sparkle against a dark background, is fairly unbeatable.

Interesting effects can be created by using coloured lights to illuminate water descending down a waterfall or cascade, or on the upward and downward flow of a fountain. Modestly priced kits, which often feature different coloured lights, can be bought from most garden centres. Sophisticated versions even change colours, with moving discs travelling across the bulbs.

Remember that you want the lighting to produce an effect – you do not want to see the source of the light. Therefore, try to keep the light fittings as unobtrusive as possible. Many are available in matt black for this reason.

ABOVE: *These aluminium torches are somewhat utilitarian in style, but they match the minimalist feel of their surroundings perfectly.*

ABOVE LEFT: *There is nothing more dramatic than aquatic lighting in the garden – especially when the lights are actually located underwater – but careful wiring is absolutely essential.*

Running electricity to your garden and pond

Unless you are planning on using solar-powered lights and torches, if you want some garden lighting, or to run a fountain or a waterfall in your pond, you will need access to a source of electrical power. To ensure safety with electricity wherever you live, installations must comply with the local wiring regulations, which vary from country to country. Although a professional electrician will be fully familiar with these regulations, if you carry out any installation yourself, for reasons of safety it must still comply in every respect. You may find that your insurance is invalidated if it does not.

RIGHT: *Outdoor power sockets should always have waterproof protective covers.*

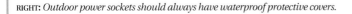

with what you already have

Elements such as driveways, paths and steps as well as patios and decks are part of the overall footprint of your garden. They are the means by which you travel round the plot and live within its boundaries. When drawing up a plan or sketch of the garden, try to ensure there is a logical progression around the site and don't leave sitting areas, gazebos and so on marooned. Lawns also provide access during the summer months but visually too, they connect sections of the garden such as terraces, flower beds and pools, flowing between and around the different elements.

ABOVE RIGHT: *This garden path has been well planned to lead visitors past elegant borders to a seating area at the far end of the garden away from the house.*

BELOW: *Here, there is a strong colour link between the green door and surrounding plants and the red brick of the house with that of the terrace.*

Linking house and garden

Designers use simple tricks to create a seamless connection between house and garden and to help knit together the various parts of the plot. A broad terrace of paving, gravel or decking, connected to the house, balances the strong vertical lines of the building and makes them seem less dominant. A climber-festooned pergola attached to the house has a similar effect. Softening the edge of the terrace with planting, particularly including bold, architectural forms, begins the process of merging house and garden. Staggering the margin of your patio or using sweeping curves also helps blend the architecture and hard landscaping into the more natural garden environment.

When designing a building, architects use repeating measurements to create a visual rhythm and pleasing proportions. You can borrow some of these same lines to divide up the plot and form a grid into which your various DIY garden projects fit, making them appear part of the overall design. For example, the position and width of a set of French doors could give you two perpendicular lines, or two sides of a square. Complete the square, take a line from the side of the garden and then repeat this shape to create a grid over the whole plot. The grid may also be rotated through 45° for a more dynamic feel. When drawing in the position of lawns, paths, play areas, borders and so on, you can sub-divide the squares of the grid or add them together forming larger squares, L-shapes and rectangles or superimpose circles or curves.

Keep it simple

Limit the use of different materials in the construction of the garden to avoid a bitty, fragmented look. If you are adding to existing features such as a paved patio, either find a perfect match for the slabs or use a contrasting material and make a clearly defined separation between the two sections. An almost-but-not-quite match will niggle more than using a different element altogether.

Repeating the same materials throughout the garden creates a strong design theme. If, for example, you have used a combination of brick pavers and natural stone for the main terrace, use the same materials, either in combination or singly, to create paths and additional areas of paving. Gravel and pebbles can also be used to visually tie in different areas and to work around random paving.

The same applies to building fences and screens. For example, with trellis, stick to one style – diamond or square – and if trellis panes have been used to screen off outdoor rooms or to camouflage utility areas, consider a boundary treatment that combines solid fence panels with a topping of the same trellis. Alternatively, you could add shaped trellis panels to a pergola or arbour – to ring the changes a little without going over the top. The key lies in subtlety and consistency.

ABOVE: *This garden shows the interesting use of a repeated shape, with its square plant, gravel, decking and borders.*

BELOW LEFT: *For strong colour ties, paint features and furniture the colour of plants.*

Colour ties

Plantings of small trees, climbers, evergreens, shrubs and perennials dress the garden. Their height and form soften raw new constructions and make them appear 'bedded in'. Stick to a broad colour scheme for a more unified look. As well as colour provided by foliage and flower, you can also use exterior quality paints and stains. These come in vibrant contemporary shades as well as more muted 'period' hues. To link elements together, try picking a colour like cornflower blue or sage green and apply it sparingly to highlight certain features. However, keep some of the wood, such as that used for decks or raised beds, natural, in order to retain balance in the overall look and feel of the garden.

Paths, patios and terraces

Hard landscaping in the form of paths, patios and terraces is an integral part of most gardens. It is these elements which connect and delineate the different areas of an outdoor space, while offering practical access to leisure activities and providing a firm surface for displays of plants or any number of other garden features.

Paths, patios and terraces can take on many forms and may be constructed from a wide range of different materials. The options are unlimited and need not involve great expense or complexity in construction. This chapter offers a host of ideas for pathways and hard surfaces that you can construct yourself, with plenty of scope for adaptation. Only basic DIY skills are required to create any of the following features, together with a little enthusiasm.

paths, patios and terraces

A pathway should not merely be a means of getting from 'A' to 'B' and neither should a patio or terrace simply be a place to sit, eat and entertain. They present an opportunity to add to the beauty and style of the garden and can enhance the outlook from the house, especially during the winter months.

RIGHT: *In the depths of winter, when the rest of the garden is not looking its best, an attractive paved area can really stand out as a visual feature.*

BELOW: *This unusual coloured path, winding its way through the garden to the gazebo in the background, makes a powerful statement as well as serving as the main route through the plot.*

Blending in

The choice of hard landscaping materials and the way they are used has a strong effect on the look and feel of the garden. Each type – whether modern concrete paving slabs, dressed stone flags, brick pavers and setts, decking or gravel – has its relative merits.

When buying for a path or patio be guided by the colours and building materials used in the construction of the house and boundary walls. For example, a building of grey stone could be toned with a dark slate paving whilst the rendered, whitewashed walls of a country cottage provide a backdrop for brick and gravel or stone and stone-effect paving. Around a modern red or buff brick house, you could floor the garden with gravel and lawns edged in a brick that matches the wall or roof colour or use a square grid of crisp contemporary paving slabs in a light, neutral shade.

It's also worth looking at what buildings in the general area use, since vernacular materials often have a pleasing resonance and help to 'settle' new buildings and gardens into the surrounding landscape. It may be that a local stone or gravel from a nearby quarry is available, helping to cut down on transport costs.

Creating design features

Straight pathways direct the eye to key parts of the garden and highlight features such as an arbour, gazebo or fountain. Direct paths tend to be used in gardens with a symmetrical or formal design and typically form a central dividing axis. But for a more contemporary look, use an asymmetric layout where the pathways are offset and perhaps kink or dogleg around rectangular lawns, pools, decks and paved terraces.

A curving path that winds through the plot creates an informal feel and can introduce an element of surprise and intrigue, with hidden corners and features awaiting discovery around each bend.

LEFT: *These grand and imposing steps clearly serve a useful purpose by connecting the different levels of the garden, but also look fantastic in their own right. The broader and more sweeping the steps, the more dramatic the effect.*

Changes in level

A sloping site offers plenty of opportunity for design and a well-planned flight of steps could become a major focal point. Making steps wider and deeper than they need to be, with relatively shallow risers, looks wonderfully theatrical in a period style or formal garden. Enhance the symmetry further with a matching pair of urns or topiaries.

Steep, narrow steps aren't very user friendly but made from natural stone or logs, could suit a wild or woodland garden where obviously man-made features are kept to a minimum. Another approach with naturalistic, rocky gardens is to blend the steps and different levels with the natural stone outcrops. Stepped and offset terraces, wide enough to put a small table and chairs on, can slow the meandering pace up a gentle slope. Try combining shuttered concrete sections with the natural stone or make stone-faced steps and terraces backfilled with gravel or slate.

Pattern and texture

Too large an area of unrelieved paving, especially when using the same colour and size of material, makes the garden feel more like a bland, public space than an intimate and private outdoor room. If you need to create lots of hard surfaced areas for ease of access or to minimize maintenance, try to break them up with a matrix of borders, hedges and pools and introduce paving patterns.

Create the illusion of room-like divisions, each having a different function or mood by sectioning off areas floored with the same paving unit. Try contrasting bands of brick pavers or granite setts as your dividing lines. Laying random stone paths and paving within larger areas of gravel, pebbles and cobbles also works well.

Additionally, when paving randomly using a mix of square and rectangular slabs of at least four different sizes, try working in small groupings of bricks or setts. Or, if you are feeling adventurous, insert a pebble mosaic panel (see pages 82–5).

BELOW: *This large area of paving is broken up both by the use of different coloured slabs and the inclusion of an unusual curved stone wall to one side.*

paths, patios and terraces

Practical considerations

Calculate the space needed for patios and terraces by imagining how you will use the area. What size of table do you require and how many chairs and loungers do you need to accommodate family and extra guests? What about other items such as a chiminea, barbeque or a collection of pots and planters? If you plan to incorporate lighting or powered water features, liaise with an electrical contractor about the layout of cables and ducting that might run beneath paving.

Some pathways are mostly functional. Test out whether access pathways – for example, running to the compost heap – will work practically. It is difficult to negotiate tight corners with a full or heavy wheelbarrow. Bear in mind how much planting along the margins of pathways grows; you do not want to be constantly cutting back or staking.

BELOW: *This patio area with seating, pots and an adjacent pond offers easy access both to and from the house and conservatory.*

Concrete paving

Concrete paving slabs of varying finishes and colours include budget options as well as top of the range 'designer' paving and natural stone look-alikes. For a surprisingly upmarket feel, try mixing medium range paving slabs with more expensive elements such as granite setts. Paving designed for modular construction allows you to create abstract curves with contrasting colour bands or even elliptical patios. Circular features of varying sizes and finishes often include 'squaring off' sets that enable you to incorporate them into rectangular designs. Circles surrounded by gravel provide a level surface for garden furniture. Miss out the central unit if you want to incorporate something like a water feature or a mosaic panel.

Some stone effect pavers are moulded from original stone slabs including slate and sandstone. These are uniform in thickness and usually lighter in weight than the genuine article, making laying easier. Concrete pavers finished to look like handmade clay or slate tiles are ideal for achieving a seamless transition from indoors to outside. Be aware, though, that the surface veneer can chip away to reveal an ugly interior and colours may also fade in sunlight unless sealed. Contact your manufacturer for advice.

To avoid having to cut too many slabs, plan out your design carefully on grid paper marking what size slab you plan to use where. You can also download designs from paving manufacturer's websites and some will even do the planning for you if you give them your dimensions.

Natural stone

Relatively inexpensive imports of sandstone and slate from India and China have made natural stone a real option for many households. Buy from companies and merchants which guarantee the materials are ethically sourced. Stone flags are available in an even greater range of sizes than the concrete look-alikes but be aware that pieces larger than 45x45 cm (18x18in) can be very heavy indeed. The variable thickness of stone also requires some skill in laying. Before buying, check the colouring of sandstone when both dry and wet.

Bricks and setts

Invaluable for paths and hardwearing drives as well as small courtyard areas, bricks and setts also provide valuable textural contrast amongst larger paving units. Being small allows flexibility with design. Use to create curving and circular patterns as well as traditional designs such as herringbone and basket weave bonds.

Reclaimed and antique style bricks are ideal for older properties and cottage style gardens but check that they are frost proof otherwise they may disintegrate. Concrete block pavers come in a wide range of finishes and ones that have been artificially aged work well with sandstone and other natural paving. Robust engineering bricks have a smooth, almost glazed finish. Use to contain gravel areas and pathways and to create mowing edges.

LEFT: *Formal paving often looks most effective when combined with equally regimented plantings like these clipped buxus balls.*

ABOVE: *A mixture of antique brick, different coloured paving slabs and cobbles can be particularly effective for a small courtyard garden or similar.*

Drainage

Wherever possible when building new drives, patios and paths consider the effect of heavy downpours or days of persistent rain. Extensive areas of paving with mortared joints can lead to flooding as a sudden influx of water overwhelms the drainage system. Divert water via a gentle gradient into flowerbeds, borders and lawned areas or to gravel overlaying landscape fabric. Brick pavers laid on sand drain reasonably well and so can areas of paving provided the slabs are laid on sand and stabilized with just a few blobs of cement.

LEFT: *Plantings in the middle of paving will assist with drainage.*

Making a gravel path

SKILL LEVEL
- This is an easy project to attempt, although some general DIY experience would be useful.

BEST TIME TO DO
- A gravel path can be laid at any time, so long as the ground is dry and not frozen. Avoid areas which are perennially wet or which do not drain well.

TOOLS REQUIRED
- Garden roller (ideally, but not essential); garden or lawn rake; shovel; mallet or pound hammer; hammer; saw.

MATERIALS REQUIRED
- Wooden pegs; preservative-treated gravel boards; semi-permeable membrane; gravel or stone chippings.

TIME REQUIRED
- Depending on the width and length of the path, normally one to two days' labour time will be required.

A gravel path can make an attractive feature in any garden, especially when it is used to provide contrast alongside flat paving materials and low-growing plants. Gravel is available in a range of mixed natural-earth shades that look particularly good when wet, while crushed stone, which is rough-edged rather than smooth, is sold in a range of colours from white through reds and greens to grey and black (see the image at the bottom of this page). Although both gravel and crushed stone are attractive and relatively easy and inexpensive to lay, they do have several practical drawbacks. Firstly, they need a solid edge to prevent stones from straying onto lawns and flowerbeds. They may also need weeding fairly regularly, although a semi-permeable membrane beneath the gravel will help in this regard. Avoid fine gravel, which gets easily dispersed and might attract the unwelcome attention of cats.

1 Excavate the area over which you want to lay the gravel until you reach solid subsoil. Set out preservative-treated boards around the perimeter of the excavated area.

2 Hammer in wooden pegs to hold the gravel boards in position.

LEFT: *If you are not keen on gravel, you could always make your path out of red stone chips, like these, or something similar.*

3 Secure the boards to the pegs with galvanised nails. Add more pegs at roughly 1m (39in) intervals along the boards all round the area to prevent the boards from bowing.

4 Rake over the whole area to level it and tamp it down to ensure the base for the gravel is stable. For extra stability, lay 50mm (2in) of hardcore over the firmed soil.

Variations on the theme

Gravel looks good in most settings, but it is not the most stable of materials and will easily get spread around the garden. It also adheres to muddy boots, which can be a nuisance if you are a keen planter and need to use the path whilst walking between beds and borders. For a variation on the theme, try bigger, more solid stones.

5 The best way of preventing weeds from growing up through gravel is to lay a semi-permeable, porous membrane. Fold the edges over and tight against the gravel boards.

6 Pour gravel on top of the semi-permeable membrane. A thickness of at least 50mm (2in) is required, and possibly more, depending on traffic.

7 Spread the gravel out evenly using a rake. Draw a wooden straight edge along the tops of the boards to even out high spots and rake again. If you have a garden roller, roll flat.

ABOVE: *This path created from scalpings of Welsh slate makes an attractive alternative to the gravel path shown above. The blue-grey colour of the slate contrasts beautifully with the lawn that the path meanders through and the materials used are relatively big and stable.*

PROJECT

Making a tile-inlaid path

Tips, tools and materials

SKILL LEVEL
- Some DIY, craft or design experience would be useful but is not essential for this project.

BEST TIME TO DO
- The project can be attempted whenever the weather is reasonably fine and there is no chance of frost.

TOOLS REQUIRED
- Tools to lift paving slab (as necessary); bricklaying trowel and/or pointing trowel (depending on size of tile holes); tile cutter (as necessary); tile squeegee.

MATERIALS REQUIRED
- Sharp sand; ready-mix mortar/cement; frost- and water-proof tiles (for example, ones suitable for outdoor pools); exterior grade tile adhesive and applicator; exterior grade tile grout.

TIME REQUIRED
- 1 day-plus, depending on extent of path.

You do not need to be artistically gifted to create a tile-inlaid path. The simplest designs can be striking and will give any path a lift. The best way to proceed is to combine plain or patterned tiles with bricks or block pavers, as shown here. You can do this by constructing a path from scratch or by lifting some of the bricks or pavers out of an existing path and simply replacing them with tiles, cobbles, pebbles, or just about any other solid material that takes your fancy. Sometimes all you need to do is to use bands of tiles in contrasting colours, or maybe change the way that tiles or pebbles in different areas are orientated. Start with something quite modest in size and design until you develop the skill and confidence to go onto more complex and challenging pieces. Keep your design simple and, if possible, mark it out on squared paper before you begin.

1 If you are starting from scratch and building a new path, level the ground and spread a layer of sharp sand over the area to be paved. Position the first block paver carefully on the sharp sand.

2 Press the block pavers firmly into the layer of sharp sand. Place the tiles into their positions and mark out the area that they will take up. Place them face-side down to prevent scratching.

3 Having worked out and marked the positions of the tiles, remove them and then check the levels of the pavers using a spirit level.

4 Use a rubber mallet to tamp the pavers firmly into place while checking the levels again. Ensure that no high spots or hollows remain across the run of pavers.

5 Pour extra sharp sand into the holes left for the tiles in order to bring them up to the same level as the pavers.

6 Spread the sand out evenly and add mortar mix to it, working it into the sand with the trowel. Use a watering can and rose to wet the sand and mortar mix.

7 Position the tiles on top of the dampened mortar.

8 Place the last tile carefully into the remaining space, ensuring that the tiles abut one another without excessive gaps. Brush a fine sand and mortar mixture into the cracks between the tiles to finish off.

ABOVE: *The finished effect. Wash the pavers down to get rid of any excess sand and mortar and wipe over the tiles thoroughly with a squeegee to give them a polish. If the tiles you have used are unglazed, you could paint them with varnish for a brighter finish. This will also help lengthen the tiles' lifespan, as even frost- and waterproof tiles which are designed for outdoor use and heavy wear and tear will weather over time. Replace any tiles that become cracked.*

Making log steps and risers

Setting log steps into a lawn or a sloping or steep bank is a simple process that can create an attractive feature in your garden. In most cases the steps can be made from just about anything. On flat or slightly sloping ground, discs cut from a fairly large log offer an easy way to create a stepping stone effect. These can usually be found in your local garden centre or DIY supplier. If not, cut them yourself or find a friendly timber merchant who is willing to cut them for you. For banks and steeper gradients, you may have to build something slightly different. Half-round poles provide a simple solution when cut and jointed to create level steps. Alternatively, if you have access to large enough log slices, you may be able to overlap the discs to create the steps on the incline. Extend the life of your log steps by applying a liberal coating of preservative, or buy them ready treated.

Tips, tools and materials

SKILL LEVEL
- Basic DIY skills are ideally required for this project. You will also need to be reasonably strong to cut the log steps, depending on the hardness and thickness of the wood.

BEST TIME TO DO
- This project can be undertaken whenever the ground is not too wet or frozen.

TOOLS REQUIRED
- Spirit level; saw; spade; pound hammer or mallet; clamps.

MATERIALS REQUIRED
- Log blocks and stakes; nails.

TIME REQUIRED
- Depending on the size of the area to be covered, allow at least a weekend for this project.

1 These round, sawn-through chunks of log are usually laid out like stepping stones. They can be used on gentle slopes and flat ground. The first thing to do is to drop them roughly into position. Try walking on them to make sure the spacing is right.

2 Once you are satisfied that each log step is in the right place, simply cut all the way round each one with a spade. A narrow one is best.

3 Lever out the first layer of turf and soil. Your spade cut should be no deeper than the depth of the log step.

4 Check the log step for depth of fit. Make final adjustments so that the log step sits firmly and flush with the adjacent grass level. The objective is to have a solidly placed log step that allows your mower to pass over without disturbing it.

5 Use a mallet to firm the step into place. Backfill any gaps and tamp in the soil to prevent the log step from moving. If you are not happy with the way the step is sitting, lift it and make adjustments.

Variations: alternative risers and treads

There are plenty of variations on this theme that would work well in the projects described above and below. For example, in a wild, woodland style garden, why not try rugged rock treads with round log risers, or, in a more formal setting, straight-edged wood and gravel in combination?

RIGHT: *The rustic look and feel of logs might not suit your garden. Improvise with straight-edged, preserved wood and pink gravel instead.*

1 On steeper slopes and banks, simple steps made from half-round poles are quickly erected. Two short posts are driven into the ground to start and then the front, top rail is levelled and attached.

2 Fit a further rail on the front, if necessary, and some short return rails on the sides. Line out the step cavity with a weed inhibiting membrane and backfill with bark, stone chips or gravel.

ABOVE: *Log risers can be randomly positioned and used in conjunction with other materials.*

Paving on sand

Tips, tools and materials

SKILL LEVEL
- Basic DIY skills are ideally required for this project. You will also need to be reasonably strong to handle the paving slabs, depending on their size.

BEST TIME TO DO
- This project can be undertaken whenever the ground is not too wet or frozen.

TOOLS REQUIRED
- Spirit level; club or pound hammer; rubber mallet; rake; spade or shovel; broom or hand brush.

MATERIALS REQUIRED
- 45cm (18in) square paving slabs; hardcore; concreting sand and fine sand; straight-edged batten; wooden spacers; ball of string or twine.

TIME REQUIRED
- Depending on the size of the area to be paved, allow at least a weekend for this project.

Most gardens need a certain amount of hard landscaping, to provide areas for eating and drinking, other leisure activities, or simply somewhere level and stable on which to stand pots and containers. Concrete paving is a relatively cheap and widely available option, which comes in a wide range of 'natural' shades. These paving slabs often also feature riven or textured finishes that give them a softer look which is more suitable for the smaller garden. One of the easiest ways to pave an area is to lay small square paving slabs on a base of sand. There is no cement to mix, which keeps the job well within the capabilities of most gardeners, and if you do need to lift a slab later on, it is quite a simple task. Paving slabs measuring 45 x 45cm(18 x 18in) are relatively light and easy to handle, so most people could lay slabs of this size without assistance.

1 Dig over and grade the soil thoroughly, using a garden fork. Rake the broken up soil and ensure that the site is level and even.

2 Spread and compact a layer of solid material over the site. Spread the hardcore out to an even, level base.

3 Drive in pegs to which you can attach a levelling string.

4 Tie the string to the first peg.

5 Make sure the pegs are set level so that the string guide will run level along the top of the paving slabs when they are set in place. Tie the string between the level pegs and use this as your guide as you set down the paving slabs.

6 Spread out the bedding sand on top of the compacted filling and rake it out evenly to a depth of 25–50mm(1–2in) across the whole site.

7 Working to the string level at the edge of the area to be paved, spread the sand so its surface is just less than the slab thickness below the top of the string.

8 Place the first slab. The paving should have a slight fall (away from the house if this is adjacent) to help rainwater to run off it. Use a batten and spirit level to check the direction of the fall.

9 Lay four slabs in one corner of the site, setting small wooden spacers between adjacent slabs to ensure an even gap for the pointing. You can

remove the spacers as soon as each slab is surrounded by other slabs.

10 Lay a batten across the slabs and check the direction of the fall, which should be away from the house. If necessary, tamp the slabs further into the sand bed using the handle of a club hammer.

11 Continue laying slabs across the site, kneeling on a board on the sand bed if you cannot reach right across the area from the edge. Be sure to check the fall. Remove the last spacers and spread some fine sand across the surface. Brush it into all the joints and then sweep off the excess.

Tip

To avoid cutting too many slabs – particularly at the edge of the area to be paved – plan out your design carefully on grid paper, marking what size slab you plan to use where. (This is very important if you intend to mix different-sized slabs.) You can also download designs from paving manufacturers' websites and some will even do the planning for you if they are given your dimensions.

PROJECT
Paving for areas of heavy use

Tips, tools and materials

SKILL LEVEL
- You will need some DIY experience to undertake this project.

BEST TIME TO DO
- This project can be undertaken during any dry, non-frosty period. Summer is the ideal season for a job like this.

TOOLS REQUIRED
- Club hammer; spirit level; brick-laying trowel; pointing trowel; shovel; cement mixer for large areas.

MATERIALS REQUIRED
- Ready-mixed concrete; polythene sheeting or damp sacking; wooden shuttering; hardboard expansion joints; mortar (masonry cement and chemical plasticizer); water; wooden spacers.

TIME REQUIRED
- Depending on the size of the area to be paved, this project will normally require at least two weekends or four days.

If a patio surface is intended to support a considerable weight it will be necessary to prepare a concrete base on which to lay the paving slabs. Excavate the site to a depth of at least 150mm (6in) – more if the subsoil is unstable – and lay a concrete base a minimum of 100mm (4in) thick. You can use ready-mixed concrete or mix your own with one part of cement to five parts of combined sand and 20mm (¾in) aggregate. Set up wooden shuttering around the area, tamp the concrete down well, level the surface with a long straight edge laid across the formwork and remove any excess material. Give the base a slight fall across its width, and incorporate full-width vertical expansion joints of hardboard every 3m(10ft) to prevent cracking. Cover concrete with plastic to protect it from rain or frost, or damp sacking if it is hot and sunny. Leave for at least three days.

1 To give the slabs adequate support, place the mortar on the concrete base in a square beneath the edges of the slab and add more mortar beneath the centre of the slab.

2 Lower each slab gently onto its mortar bed and press in place.

3 Tamp the paving slabs down using a rubber mallet or the handle of a club hammer to compress the mortar. Ensure that you tamp evenly across the whole slab so that no corners sit up.

4 Check that the slabs are level using a spirit level and tamp down any unevenness with the rubber mallet.

5 After placing the slab, bedding it down and setting it to the correct fall, insert small wooden spacers between it and its neighbours to ensure an even pointing gap.

6 Grout in the slabs using a mortar mix and a pointing trowel. Ensure that you push the mortar right down into the joints and compress it with the tip of the pointing trowel.

7 Brush off any excess mortar using a soft brush or a broom if a large area has been paved.

8 To prevent the slabs from staining, remove any excess mortar before it drys, using water and a brush.

RIGHT: *It is vital that all your joints are even and smooth. The paving will last much longer if care is taken in this regard.*

Patio designs with block pavers

Tips, tools and materials

SKILL LEVEL
- Good DIY experience is ideally required for this project.

BEST TIME TO DO
- This project can be undertaken whenever the ground is not too wet or frozen.

TOOLS REQUIRED
- Spirit level; hammer; rubber mallet or club hammer handle; garden rake; shovel; soft brush.

MATERIALS REQUIRED
- Pegged gravel boards, kerbstones or path edging tiles; hardcore for soft ground; a length of fence post to consolidate hardcore or subsoil; concreting sand and fine sand; brick pavers.

TIME REQUIRED
- This project will take up to a weekend or two days to complete, depending on the size of the area to be covered.

Block pavers are relatively new additions to the world of garden building, but they have rapidly become extremely popular because they are small and easy to handle, are designed to be dry-laid on a sand bed and do not need pointing. Unlike other dry-laid paving, they can even withstand the weight of motor vehicles thanks to the way they interlock once laid, so they can be used for all hard surfaces around the garden. However, for large areas you must lay the sand bed with a continuous edge restraint to prevent the sand from leaching out. Be sure to use concreting sand for the bedding layer, as building sand is too soft and may stain the blocks. If you need to cut many blocks, hire a hydraulically operated block splitter to cut through cleanly. You can split them with a bolster chisel and club hammer, but they may not break so successfully.

1 Place edge restraints – pegged boards or kerbstones – all round the area you intend to pave.

2 Check that your edge restraint boards or kerbs are level using a spirit level.

3 Fill the area to be paved with sand. To get the blocks level with the top of the edge restraints, measure the block thickness and tamp down the sand to this depth, with a slight fall across the area.

4 Check that the tamped down sand is perfectly level across the entire area to be paved before you begin laying the block pavers.

5 Decide on the pattern you intend to follow and start placing the first blocks at the edge of the sand bed.

6 For a path or patio, tamp down the pavers with a rubber mallet.

7 Build up the paving by adding more blocks, working away from the first corner.

8 After completing a small area, check for level once more and tamp down any rises in the pattern. If there are any hollows, lift up individual pavers and distribute more sand beneath them as necessary.

9 Spread fine sand over the surface and brush into all the joints. Sweep off excess. Hire a plate vibrator to settle in areas of heavy usage.

RIGHT: *The finished block paver design. Once again, tight joints are the key.*

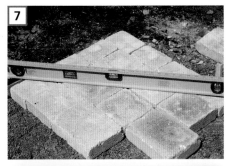

Random stone terrace paving

Tips, tools and materials

SKILL LEVEL
- Some DIY experience is ideally required for this project.

BEST TIME TO DO
- This project can be undertaken whenever the weather is dry and not frosty. Summer is the ideal season for this type of garden DIY.

TOOLS REQUIRED
- Club hammer; spirit level; wooden straight edge; brick-laying trowel; shovel; cement mixer for large areas.

MATERIALS REQUIRED
- Random assortment of stone or broken paving; ready-mixed mortar or sand and cement; brick-laying trowel; pointing trowel; spirit level; club hammer.

TIME REQUIRED
- Depending on the size of the area to be covered, this project will normally take at least a whole weekend or two days.

Random stone or 'crazy' paving, is made from randomly shaped stone pieces or broken concrete paving slabs that fit together like pieces of a jigsaw. The gaps between the pieces are pointed with mortar which bonds the stones to a stable base layer. Random paving can look very attractive if you fit the pieces together carefully and neatly detail the pointing. An old concrete surface would make an ideal foundation for a driveway or parking place; well-rammed coarse aggregate is suitable for light-duty areas such as a patio or garden path. Start laying the stones at the perimeter, using pieces with one straight side and use a long wooden straight edge as you lay down more stones to ensure that they are level. If necessary, check that the stones are laid to a slight fall to allow surface water to drain off. Only spread as much mortar as you can cover with paving pieces within the time it takes for the mortar to set.

1 To break up a stone or improve the fit, lodge it between two stones and crack it cleanly with a firm hammer blow. Practise on a few old bits of stone first, to avoid shattering good stones later on.

2 A solid foundation is essential for crazy paving. Spread a bed of wet mortar over the concrete base layer, using a brick-laying trowel. Level it out carefully with the trowel.

Colour contrasts and more formal designs

If you are not a fan of crazy paving but would like to create something similar yet a little more formal, manufactured pavers in random shapes are available at many stone merchants. These are designed to fit together in a multitude of ways. They are also often available in different colours, so with a little thought and imagination a range of effects can be easily created.

RIGHT: *These manufactured stones look smarter than standard crazy paving* (see below right).

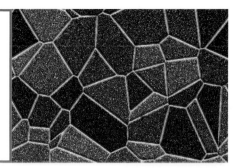

3 Create a pattern with the stones, selecting sizes and shapes that will fit together well and trying to keep the edges straight on to one another from stone to stone. As you lay the stones down, try to keep the gaps between them as uniform as possible.

4 Apply extra mortar to the area where you are going to lay the stones, immediately prior to setting each stone in place. This makes it easier for the stone to bed in, once it has been tamped into the extra blob of mortar.

5 Spread the mortar out evenly to the width of the stone using the point of a bricklayer's trowel. If you apply too much mortar and the stone sits up when it is laid, simply lift the stone and remove some.

6 Tamp the stones down into the mortar using a rubber mallet. It is easy to break some stone, even with a rubber mallet, so take care and tamp evenly across the stone as a whole.

7 Check the level across the stones as you work, using a spirit level. Continue to tamp down all the stones, lifting them and adding or removing mortar as necessary until you have an even surface.

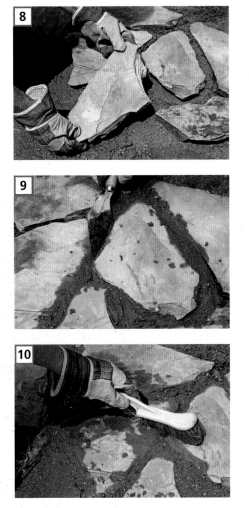

8

9

10

Planting in and around random stone paving

If you want to soften or break up an area of random stone terrace paving or steps, consider planting some ground cover plants immediately beside and around the stones. These are easy to incorporate into your design and will help with water run-off and drainage. Another option is to leave small gravelled areas in the midst of the design which can then be planted with spring bulbs to create a stunning seasonal display at the heart of an area of hard landscaping.

To plant bulbs under gravel, first scoop out a depression in the soil and scatter the bulbs at random. Then press the bulbs in and twist them firmly to ensure contact with the soil. Cover the bulbs and level the soil to match the surrounding area. Add a thin layer of stone chippings as a mulch and decorative finish. When the bulbs are not in flower, the gravel areas will serve to add extra visual interest to the terraced or stepped area in their own right.

8 Continue laying the stones down and creating the pattern. As the area covered by stones extends, use a long wooden straight edge in conjunction with a spirit level to ensure levelness across the entire design.

9 Allow the mortar bed to harden overnight before filling the gaps between the stones. Fill and point between the stones using a mortar mix. Try to create a bevel in your pointing with the tip of the trowel, to assist with water run-off and drainage.

10 Brush the excess mortar off the stones using a soft brush to prevent stones from staining and discolouring.

OPPOSITE: *The most effective areas of random stone paving are always planned with plants firmly in mind. They both soften and complement the hard surface.*

Lawns, decking and decorative surfaces

This chapter explores alternatives to hard surfacing in the garden, with the emphasis on 'soft' and organic materials, from the grass of a conventional lawn to alternative plantings for garden surfaces and wooden decking.

Some of the best garden effects can be achieved through the clever mixing and matching of materials, including a range of plants. The differences between adjacent areas of the garden can also be given a contrasting feel by simply changing the flooring effects. Lawns can be shaped and edged to make them both more aesthetic and practical and decking can be introduced to maximize the potential of an area or to hide a multitude of sins.

for decorative surfaces

Lawn design

The contrast between vertical elements – border plantings, trees, potted specimens – and horizontal surfaces – paving, decking, pools and lawns – creates an exciting visual dynamic. Most commonly, lawns are used to form a plain open area at the heart of the garden, engendering a feeling of spaciousness. To enhance this effect, keep the shape very simple, either geometric, for example, circular, rectangular or perhaps an 's' shape using bold curves. Avoid wiggly margins. They look fussy and are difficult to maintain. Style an existing shapeless lawn by superimposing a strong design, such as interlocking circles or rectangles, and adding a mowing edge for extra definition.

To avoid wear and tear, ensure access is reasonably wide and use stepping stones to cut across lawns or to set round the edge for all weather access. A grid pattern of square paving slabs works in contemporary plots.

TOP RIGHT: *These exotic looking succulents in a small gravel garden make an instant feature and provide alternative ground cover.*

BELOW: *Why not grow your lawn long and let wild flowers proliferate? It makes a pleasant change.*

Lawn options

Lawn grass types vary and include hardwearing 'family' mixtures, ones tolerant of shade and even drought, the latter including special small-leaved clovers.

Allowing so-called weeds or native plants to infiltrate a general-purpose lawn, helps to keep them looking green during dry spells. To reduce work and minimize mowing, try letting sections of larger lawns grow long and flower, perhaps adding spring bulbs. Deliberately sowing a flowering meadow mix creates an even richer habitat for insects.

Gravel gardens

In smaller gardens, gravel laid over weed-suppressing landscape membrane makes an easy-care alternative to turf. Shingle, flint and river gravel has a pleasing natural look that works well in the garden. Crushed stone or stone chippings can look rather harsh but may suit some contemporary designs. For most situations choose muted tones of mottled greys and browns. Golden gravel and flint tends to work best in Mediterranean style gardens. Select a large grade gravel around 19mm (¾in) diameter that will bed down easily and won't 'travel'.

Like lawns, gravel or slate can be used to make a flat, uniform surface or void at the heart of a garden in contrast to the undulating shapes of surrounding plants. In Japanese dry gardens, very fine gravel substitutes for water. The surface may be raked into ripple patterns and the margins are contained by an edging made from short sections of bamboo pole or rocks. The Japanese 'pool' effect works well in shady areas with a surround of plants like evergreen ferns, elephant's ears (bergenia), bamboos and variegated sedges.

Sunny gravel gardens feature carpeting alpines and herbs as well as more substantial Mediterranean shrubs and architectural plants such as tall ornamental grasses, yuccas and phormiums. On flat ground, consider working in groups of large stones or boulders or add one or two giant vases such as Greek olive jars. Confine most of the planting to islands made up of just a few varieties in bold clumps. For example, use a couple of low carpeters such as thymes with mound-forming, daisy-flowered osteospermums or rhodanthemums. For vertical contrast add a swathe of medium-sized tussock-forming grasses, for example blue oatgrass (*Helictotrichon sempervirens*) or the coppery-coloured sedge (*Carex flagellifera*). Add a single large architectural specimen such as cabbage palm (*Cordyline australis*) or New Zealand flax (*Phormium*) to anchor the arrangement. Avoid nuisance self-seeders such as lady's mantle (*Alchemilla mollis*) which can still manage to germinate. Flow the gravel around these islands to create interconnecting walkways but keep at least one area clear of planting.

Alternatives to grass

Other plants can also be used to create green carpets, especially in areas where it is difficult or impractical to maintain a lawn – for example, in shade under trees, in very dry areas or where access for mowing is restricted. Very small conventional lawns hardly warrant the regular care regime necessary. Consider replacing with a herb lawn.

For shade

- *Cotoneaster adpressus* (creeping cotoneaster)
- *Cotoneaster dammeri* (bearberry cotoneaster)
- *Hedera helix* (English ivy)
- *Mentha pulegium* (creeping pennyroyal)
- *Mentha requienii* (Corsican mint)
- *Ophiopogon planiscapus* (mondo grass)
- *Soleirolia soeirolii* (helxine, mind your own business)
- *Vinca minor* (lesser periwinkle)

For sun and drained soil

- *Acaena microphylla* (New Zealand burr)
- *Chamaemelum nobile* 'Treneague'
- *Festuca glauca* (fescue)
- *Juniperus squamata* 'Blue Carpet'
- *Sedum spurium* (Caucasian stonecrop) and others
- *Sempervivum* spp and cultivars (house leek)
- *Thymus serpyllum* 'Pink Chintz'

ABOVE, CLOCKWISE FROM TOP LEFT: *Creeping pennyroyal; house leek; caucasian stonecrop; lesser periwinkle.*

LEFT: *In this Japanese-style zen garden, carefully raked fine gravel is intended to look like water, with the rocks forming an island at its heart.*

for decorative surfaces

Pebbles and cobbles

Like some forms of natural stone paving, pebbles darken when wet revealing an array of colours, mottles and stripes. Their rounded form is very pleasing and adds textural interest to surfaces of gravel, natural stone and timber as well as smooth concrete pavers, hi-tech metals and glazed ceramics.

Picking pebbles

Pebbles are expensive to buy but it is illegal to collect them from beaches, so look for the best deal locally. Ordinary brown and grey pebbles work in most garden settings and come pre-graded by size, giving you the option of creating naturalistic beach-like effects. As well as 'natural' pebbles you can also buy more decorative types, including shiny black, pure sparkling white and mottled granite. Use these in contemporary or oriental-style gardens to create striking ground patterns or mosaics.

Varied effects

Cobbles and pebbles may be banked up in the corners of a gravel patio, say, to create a beach effect, as if water has deposited bands of different sizes from shingle to small pebbles, larger cobbles and the occasional boulder. You can use the same technique around a shallow, butyl-lined pool, flowing the pebbles under the water surface. Pebbles are also useful for camouflaging the underground reservoirs of water features, such as bubbling millstones and geysers. Use cobbles to 'mulch' raised beds or planted islands within a paved patio or simply to create visual contrast with a smooth surface of decking or tiles. Either lay them loose over membrane to prevent weeds springing up or set them in a dry mortar mix. Loose cobbles are difficult to walk over but you could lay sleepers (railway ties) as a pathway, working the pebbles in between, or use flat-topped stepping-stones set proud of the pebbles. A slightly raised boardwalk brings the seashore to mind and works well connecting decking with other parts of the garden.

LEFT: *Pebbles are an attractive and versatile garden floor material that can be used to create myriad effects. They can be laid loose, lightly set in dry mortar or formally cemented and grouted into decorative patterns, as shown here.*

BELOW: *When pebbles and cobbles are wet they reveal patterns, mottles and stripes which are not always visible when they are dry. For this reason they are good materials to use in conjunction with water features.*

Pebble mosaics

Using simple designs and techniques such as those demonstrated on pages 82–85, you can create impressive decorative elements for paths and terraces. Mosaics featuring figurative designs like a flower, sun or star suit cottage and period-style gardens as well as Mediterranean-inspired terraces. For contemporary plots, try abstract or geometric designs, perhaps using black and white pebbles. As well as making square or rectangular floor panels within paths and patios, you can also work mosaics around features like sundials or fountains or make a decorative border around the base of a gazebo.

Decking designs

Decks are a great way to acquire usable space in a sloping garden and to create interest through varying levels in a flat, featureless plot. Raising part of the garden immediately gives that area prominence. Decks built at the same level as door sills encourage barefoot access into the garden in summer and seamlessly link indoors and out. Decks set over a pool create the illusion that water flows underneath.

Change the orientation of deck boards to create textural interest and lead the eye. A square or rectangular deck is the easiest to build but for a designer look, try combining shapes, for example creating an 'L' on two levels. For an introduction to the art of laying decking, see the project featured on pages 70–73.

Avoid siting decks in shady areas as they become slippery with algae and can be hazardous to walk upon.

BELOW: *This deck is fairly basic in terms of the materials used and its construction, but its circular shape sets it apart. The circle is emphasized by the curving wall at the back and the water feature at the front.*

Plants and pebbles

The rounded form of pebbles and cobbles is the perfect foil for plants with grassy or strap-shaped leaves. Avoid broadleaf deciduous plants, as leaf litter will mar the display. Try the following plants:

ABOVE: *Ferns combined with pebbles and water will bring a forest-like quality to your garden, brimming with natural-looking beauty and elegance.*

- *Agapanthus* (African lily)
- *Astelia chathamica* (silver spear)
- *Calamagrostis* x *acutiflora* 'Overdam'
- *Carex buchananii* (leatherleaf sedge)
- *Fargesia murielae* and forms (bamboo)
- *Iris* (bearded and Siberian)
- *Libertia grandiflora*
- *Miscanthus sinensis* forms
- *Pennisetum alopecuroides and form*s (fountain grass)
- *Phormium* (New Zealand flax)
- *Phyllostachys* species and cultivars (bamboo)
- *Stipa gigantea* (giant feather grass, golden oats)

Laying and shaping a lawn

Tips, tools and materials

SKILL LEVEL
- No special skills are required in order to undertake this simple project.

BEST TIME TO DO
- This project is best undertaken in fine weather, when the turf for the lawn will be dry and easy to work.

TOOLS REQUIRED
- Garden rake; sharp border spade or half-moon edging iron; wooden straight edge; spirit level; wooden board for working off; broom or hand brush.

MATERIALS REQUIRED
- Turf — carefully measure the area to be covered and then consult your local dealer for the amount required.

TIME REQUIRED
- Depending on the area to be covered, this project will normally take 1–2 days or a weekend.

Making a lawn from turf creates an instant effect in the garden, although it will need a few weeks to establish itself and bed in properly before it can be used. Laying the turf is actually the easy part – it is the ground preparation that takes the most time and which it is vital to undertake thoroughly in order for the lawn to thrive and last. The great advantage of a turf lawn over one prepared from seed is that you do not have to wait for turf to grow – you buy it when the grass is already established. This is by far the more expensive option, but if you are in a hurry to transform brown earth into a lush green lawn, laying turf is the best way to go. Creating curves and shapes at the edges of a lawn adds visual interest and immediately makes a lawn more of a feature. This is easily achieved with the use of a few basic gardening tools and a little patience.

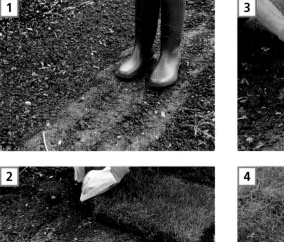

1 Level and firm the ground thoroughly with a garden fork, spade and rake prior to laying any turves. Tread the area down with your boots. It is vital that the ground is well prepared.

2 Begin by laying a row of turf around the perimeter of the lawn, ideally using a path or string line as a guide. This forms a solid edge to the lawn and is better than an edge made of small pieces of turf.

3 Stagger the joints of the adjoining turves to make the bonds between them as strong as possible.

4 Where pieces of turf join, make sure that the ends are tightly butted together. This will prevent weeds growing up in any gaps that are left between turves.

5 Use a garden fork to push down any humps in the turves. This will improve the joints between the turves, ensures they will be in contact with the soil below and will keep everything level.

6 Fill in any gaps between turves using handfuls of soil. Use a soft brush to brush and press soil into any cracks between the turves.

7 Use a half-moon edging tool to shape the edges of the turves as desired.

8 When all the turves have been laid, filled, cut and shaped to your satisfaction, water everything in thoroughly with a watering can or hosepipe.

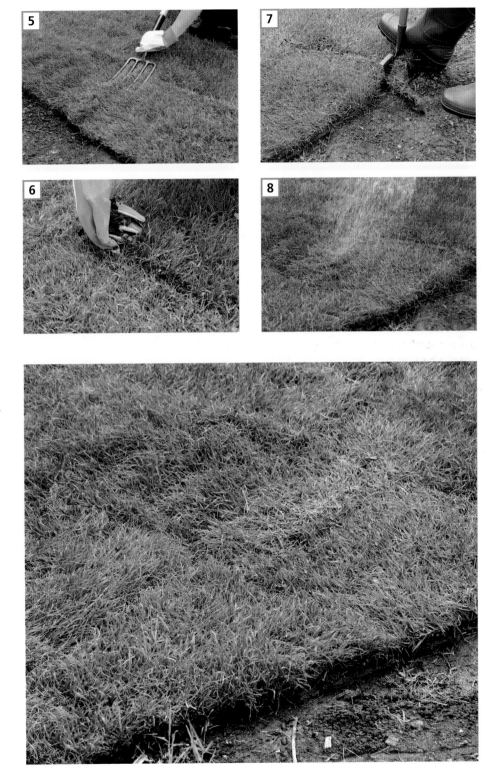

Setting stepping stones in a lawn

Tips, tools and materials

SKILL LEVEL
- No special skills are required for this simple project, but you will need to be strong enough to handle the slabs.

BEST TIME TO DO
- This project can be undertaken whenever the weather is fine and the ground is dry. Avoid wet, muddy ground which will result in a difficult, messy job.

TOOLS REQUIRED
- Sharp border spade; brush or broom, depending on size of stones.

MATERIALS REQUIRED
- Fine gravel or sand to make up levels; small paving slabs or alternatively random pieces of flat stone such as slate; quantity of fine dry soil; small amount of grass seed to cover gaps.

TIME REQUIRED
- Depending on the number of stepping stones to be laid, about 1–2 days.

Some garden lawns look pristine all the time – usually as the result of the huge amount of work that their owners put into looking after them and because they are not often walked upon. However, the reality for most gardeners is that they need to cross their lawns on a regular basis, which makes for unsightly wear and tear. Comparatively speaking, small lawns get much heavier wear than large ones. In a tiny garden you have no choice but to use the same route across the lawn to the washing line or shed, so no wonder it soon starts to look patchy and worn out. In winter, worn areas of grass turn to mud which gets trodden indoors. In summer, heavily used grass cannot grow fast enough to replace itself, and thin patches let in moss and weeds, which makes the lawn look scruffy and ill-kempt. So, how can you deal with this problem? Set your own path made of stepping stones.

1 Instead of wearing a track through a small lawn, sink a few 'stepping stones' into the lawn to walk on. Rest the slabs on the grass and cut round them with the back of a sharp spade.

2 Remove the slab and lift the turf. (If you leave the slab for a few days, the grass underneath it turns yellow and leaves a shape for cutting round.) Remove all the turf, leaving clean vertical cuts.

3 Offer up the slab. If it is proud of the surrounding turf, make the hole deeper by digging out more soil as evenly as possible. If the hole is already too deep, add a layer of gravel to raise the level of the slab. However, bear in mind that the mower needs to pass directly over the slab, so it must be slightly recessed in the lawn.

4 Press the slab down well into the hole so that it sits securely. The snug fit and vertical sides of the hole help to hold it in place. If necessary, press the slab down by pushing down with the heel of your boot or shoe.

5 Fill narrow gaps around the slabs with fine dry soil or potting mix brushed into the cracks.

6 Allow the slabs to bed in naturally and any grass to grow back thoroughly before using the stepping stones.

RIGHT: *As an alternative to manufactured paving slabs, you could lay your own stepping stones, made from flints or cobbles.*

Decorative edging for lawns

Tips, tools and materials

SKILL LEVEL
- No special skills are required in order to undertake this simple project.

BEST TIME TO DO
- This project is best undertaken in fine weather, when the edge of the lawn is dry and easy to work.

TOOLS REQUIRED
- Club hammer; sharp border spade; wooden straight edge; spirit level; broom or hand brush.

MATERIALS REQUIRED
- Bricks, pavers or paving slabs; sand and/or ready-mix dryish mortar for bedding the edging units onto; sand or dry mortar mix to brush into the joints between the slabs and any gaps at the edge of the lawn.

TIME REQUIRED
- Depending on the area to be covered, this project will normally take 1–2 days.

Mowing and lawn edging are two of the most time consuming jobs in the garden, but the latter can be almost completely eliminated by the installation of a mowing strip. This consists of an edging of brick or flat stones set just below the lawn so that the mower can run freely over the surface. A formal brick or paved mowing strip defines the lawn beautifully and looks well in a contemporary urban setting where the lines are crisp and neat. Brick pavers, which are normally laid on concrete foundations, are ideal for edging circular or curving lawns. The curve is easily accommodated by leaving wedge-shaped mortar gaps between the blocks. Even wider mowing strips made from stone or concrete paving are useful in less formal situations, in which summer herbaceous plants and shrubs are planted to spill out over the lawn.

1 Lay the slabs, bricks or pavers out on the edge of the lawn and mark out around them using a sharp border spade or a half-moon edging tool.

2 Pull back the cut turf and remove it completely, leaving as neat an edge as possible.

3 Spread a layer of sand over the exposed earth. This serves as a bed for the edging stones.

4 Mix a dry mortar mix into the sand using a hand trowel or fork. Ensure that plenty of mortar mix remains on the surface of the sand.

5 Tamp the edging slabs down using a rubber mallet. Then check that the slabs have been positioned correctly using a spirit level.

6 Fill any spaces at the edge of the slabs with sand, packing it in around the slabs as tightly as possible.

7 Brush the excess sand into the gaps between the slabs to finish off. The dry mortar mix will go off after a few days.

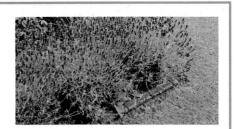

LEFT: *The finished effect. This formal stone edging is an expensive option but it looks fantastic and provides a broad, even surface for a lawn mower to run over. A cheaper option is to use bricks or block pavers instead.*

Maintaining an edge

To neaten up the edge of the mowing strip and to prevent lawn grass from encroaching too far over it, periodically run over the edge of the strip with a nylon-line trimmer. Alternatively, use a half-moon cutter or sharp border spade to re-cut the edge next to the pavers or rectangular paving pieces. If the edge pieces degrade or become dirty, replace them or give them a clean.

ABOVE: *This two-tiered lawn edging strip made of old bricks also serves as a retaining border for the flower beds in this garden.*

Chamomile and thyme carpets

SKILL LEVEL
- No special skills are required to undertake this simple project.

BEST TIME TO DO
- Whenever the ground is not too wet or muddy.

TOOLS REQUIRED
- Garden or lawn rake; spade or shovel; hand trowel; watering can.

MATERIALS REQUIRED
- For sun and sharp drainage, creeping plants, for example *Thymus* 'Doone Valley', *Chamaemelum nobile* 'Treneague'. For shade, *Soleirolia soleirolii*, *Mentha requienii*; rounded cobbles and boulders; grit or gravel to lighten heavy soil for sun-lovers; organic matter to retain moisture for the shade plantings.

TIME REQUIRED
- 1–2 days, depending on the size of the area to be planted.

Variations in height and texture are an all-important part of good garden design. Unrelieved lawns covering a large area can be rather boring, but if you create new island beds or flower borders, will you have time to maintain them? This question is particularly important in front gardens, which tend to be more public and therefore less pleasurable to work in. To create contrast in large areas of paving, creeping evergreen herbs such as thymes and non-flowering chamomile can be grown singly to create the effect of a lawn without the need for mowing. Many of these plants thrive on relatively poor dry soil where grass would suffer. Grass also has a tough time under trees, where the ground is not only shaded but often very dry and full of roots. Lawns also suffer in the shade cast by buildings. For shade ground-cover, choose any of the plain green or white-variegated ivies.

1 Dig over the ground as necessary and then rake it to a level tilth using a garden rake or fine-tined lawn rake, as shown.

2 Add a layer of compost to the prepared soil and work it well in. This will help the plants to become established.

3 Add some gravel or grit to the mix by hand. This will help with drainage, which is important for many of these plants.

4 Gather your plants together, ready for planting. Dig a hole for the first one with a hand trowel.

5 Take the first plant out of its pot and test for depth in the hole. Dig out more soil or backfill as necessary.

6 Place the plants in evenly spaced holes and firm them in with your fingertips, pressing the soil back around the rootball.

Alternatives to grass lawns

Some forms of chamomile and thyme are resilient enough to be planted as an alternative to a grass lawn, not just in and around cobbles to break up paving areas, as demonstrated in the project above. Well-drained soil and a sunny spot are essential. Dig in plenty of gravel for good drainage.

ABOVE: *Select one hard-wearing form of chamomile or thyme or mix creeping varieties.*

RIGHT: *The raised texture and lustrous green of this chamomile lawn contrast beautifully with the surrounding lakes of gravel.*

7 Water the plants in thoroughly, using a watering can fitted with a rose. Newly planted chamomile and thyme can be vulnerable until they become well established, so give the plants plenty of care and attention in the days immediately after planting.

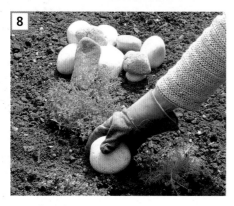

8 Spread cobbles and pebbles in and around the plants. These make an attractive decorative feature but also serve a useful purpose as a mulch, preventing weed seeds from germinating.

The versatility of thyme

Thyme is an incredibly useful and versatile garden plant which comes in many different varieties and colours. Its tiny leaves and dense habit create a carpet (above), low hedge (below) or cushion (bottom), depending on the variety.

Thyme is ideal for softening harder landscaped features, such as walls, paths and the edges of containers. Creeping thyme roots wherever the stems touch the soil, so plants are extremely resilient.

ABOVE: *This scheme could be walked upon once the plants have become established and have spread over the cobbles.*

OPPOSITE: *This thyme and chamomile feature has been allowed to grow tall and bushy, so that some of the cobbles and rocks have become obscured. The gravel sets off the design perfectly.*

Constructing wooden decking

Tips, tools and materials

SKILL LEVEL
- Intermediate. You will require some fairly advanced DIY skills in order to undertake this project successfully.

BEST TIME TO DO
- This project can be undertaken at any time, although spring and summer are the best seasons to build a deck.

TOOLS REQUIRED
- A basic set of woodworking tools, including a saw and hammer.

MATERIALS REQUIRED
- Preservative-treated softwood; bearers can be made from pieces measuring 50 x 75mm (2 x 3in) up to 75 x 75/100mm (3 x 3–4in) (Choose a size of decking to suit the project. Wide material for large areas, narrow for small.) Galvanized nails.

TIME REQUIRED
- 2–4 days minimum.

Decking offers a very flexible alternative to the harder landscaping materials such as patio slabs. With sub-structures constructed from load-bearing wood, decking levels can be built in single or multiple stages out and over banks, around ponds and streams and so on. If you can imagine it, there should be no reason why it cannot be built! The key to any successful decking project is to get the sub-structure right. It should be substantial enough to bear the foot traffic and numbers of people likely to be using the deck above. It also needs to be laid level and consistent across the area to be covered. The sub-structure joists should be set at no less than around 375mm (15in) through to 600mm (24in) depending upon their cross-sectional size and the thickness of decking laid onto them. The decking boards themselves are usually available in a variety of thicknesses and widths.

1 Select the area to be covered by your decking and mark it out with chalk, a can of white spray paint or simply string and pegs. In this case, a triangular deck is to be built into the corner of a garden. Work out the total surface area to be covered and then order the joist and decking boards accordingly. It is a good idea to order at least 10 per cent more material than you need, to allow for inevitable wastage.

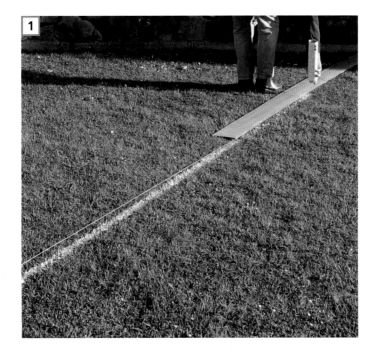

2 The key to a tidy job is to get the first run of joist straight. A slight run-off, as long as it is not too obvious, can help water drain off. If you are using grooved boards, make sure the run-off is in line with them.

3 A semi-permeable membrane below the decking will prevent weeds from growing through. Ideally, remove the turf or use weedkiller before laying. Spread the membrane out and pin it to the ground.

4 Set and fix in place all the perimeter joists to start with. The outer joist edges can be faced up with some of the decking board to tidy them up.

5 The joists should be laid evenly spaced across the area to be covered. Before settling on the actual distances apart consider the thickness and length of the decking material. Support any gaps between the joists and the ground with offcuts at regular intervals.

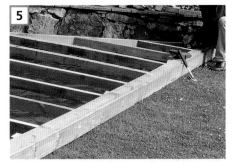

Hardwood or softwood?

The most important consideration for wood used out of doors is that it is durable enough to resist fungal decay. This means using a hardwood which is classified as naturally durable or a softwood given extended durability through pressure treatment. Over 90 per cent of all decks are made from suitable pressure-treated softwoods because of their availability, ease of working and cost-effectiveness.

ABOVE: *Most decking is built from pressure-treated softwood in one yellowish colour.*

RIGHT: *Hardwoods come in a range of colours but are more expensive and harder to work.*

6 To speed up the laying process, a number of loosely laid boards can be cut to length to start.

7 Work consistently laying one run of boards at a time. Be sure to stagger any joints in the length.

8 Don't be afraid to use short lengths. Decking is costly and waste should be minimized.

9 There may be corners of buildings or structures to cut round. Lay some loose offcuts on the surrounding joists to establish the spacings of the boards and the depth of cut required.

10 Even in small areas of decking the joists need to be laid level and off a key point. The front bearer is used here as the index point.

11 When laying decking on odd shapes, try to work from a straight edge at the front and cut the odd shapes to fit at the back.

OPPOSITE: *The finished deck. Even gaps between the boards are the key to success.*

Decorative effects with decking

Tips, tools and materials

SKILL LEVEL
- Intermediate. You will require some fairly advanced DIY skills in order to undertake this project successfully.

BEST TIME TO DO
- This project can be undertaken at any time, although spring and summer are the best seasons to accessorize a deck.

TOOLS REQUIRED
- A basic set of woodworking tools, including a saw and hammer.

MATERIALS REQUIRED
- These depend on the accessories or effects that you opt for, but these pages feature border logs, balusters and yule posts, as well as paving slabs and decking boards used as decorative trim.

TIME REQUIRED
- The time it takes to accessorize your decking depends on the size of the deck and the scale of your creative ambitions.

Pick up a decking brochure and prepare to be surprised by the variety of finishing options open to you. Ready-made posts and rails, balusters and hand rails, log edging and chains can all be added to your decking to provide a special effect. Remember it is not only the smaller accessory that can be used with decking. If the space permits, building a larger structure such as a pergola, arbour or gazebo on the decking creates a great feature. Don't forget the decking itself. If you have a corner to fill, why not shape the front with a series of curves to add a different effect to the whole thing? Alternatively, the sub-structure may be set in a straight line but the ends of the decking boards could be cut or staggered to create a special effect. Finally, in addition to straight deck boarding, there are a variety of ready-made decorative decking tiles available.

1 Some decking accessories can be a structural necessity and require a degree of preparation. Always try to cut back any soil beyond the area you will be working in.

2 This type of 'log', which is regularized and flatted on two faces, needs to be laid before the decking joists are put down. The logs create an attractive border and act as a barrier against the encroaching garden.

3 Often you will need to create your own accessories. Once more it is important to ensure that any sub-structures are solid enough to support the facing materials.

4 Some harder landscaping may be involved with some projects. When laying slabs in lawns, cut away the turf and use some weak mix mortar to bed them in level.

5 The decking boards can be cut and utilized as facing materials or features such as steps.

6 Notched posts like these can be used to finish off the edge of some laid decking.

7 When the posts are used in conjunction with low height panels, they can produce an enclosed, private area within the garden.

RIGHT: *Most decks are constructed from pre-treated wood which will resist decay for many years. However, any wood will age and fade with time. At this point, stain or paint your deck to restore it to its former glory.*

Planting a Mediterranean gravel garden

The great advantage of a Mediterranean-style gravel garden is that it will remain largely weed-free and will require little in the way of day-to-day maintenance. This is because the gravel acts as an effective mulch which helps to obviate the need for routine weeding. Mulching works by starving germinating weed seedlings of light. It also reduces moisture loss and insulates roots from extremes of heat and cold. Gravel can be used to form an area of sharp drainage around alpines, silver-leaved plants and other subjects like herbs that can be sensitive to winter wet. It is also one of the most attractive mulching materials. To be effective, spread gravel to 5cm (2in) deep. It will not prevent strong perennial weeds growing through, so these will have to be spot-treated with systemic weedkiller or dug out beforehand. An even more effective alternative is to lay a membrane beneath.

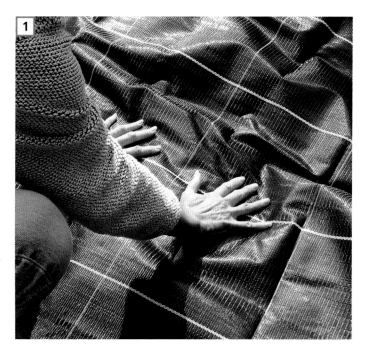

1 Cover the soil with a semi-permeable membrane made of landscape fabric. Spread the membrane down as smoothly as possible and weight down the corners with bricks or stones to prevent the wind from lifting it.

2 Secure the membrane to the soil using pegs which are sold for the purpose or bent wire prongs. Space the pegs out evenly along the perimeter.

2

Planting bulbs under gravel

Flowering bulbs such as irises (see above) and tulips can be naturalized to add spring interest to any well-drained area in the garden that is fairly dry in summer, such as gravelled areas in a patio.

To plant bulbs under gravel, first scoop out a depression in the gravel and soil and scatter the bulbs at random. Next, press the bulbs into the ground and twist them to ensure good contact with the soil (see below, top image). Cover the bulbs and level the soil to match the surrounding area. Finally, add a thin layer of stone chippings or gravel as a mulch and decorative finish (see below, bottom image). In time, the flowers will emerge through the gravel.

Ideally they should be positioned about 30cm (12in) apart.

3 Spread gravel out evenly over the secured membrane to a depth of about 5cm (2in). It is better to use too much rather than to leave too thin a layer over the membrane.

3

4 Use a hand trowel to clear a space in the gravel which is big enough to take the plant you intend to locate.

4

5 Cut a cross in the membrane using a pair of scissors or a sharp craft knife. Do not be concerned if the membrane tears as you cut it – it won't make any difference to the final planting.

5

6

9

6 Carefully dig out the soil through the cut in the membrane to a depth sufficient to take the rootball of the plant.

7

7 Remove the plant from its pot and carefully place it in the hole. If the hole is too shallow or too deep, remove more soil or backfill as necessary.

Alternatives to gravel mulch

Your choice of decorative mulch need not be confined to gravel. If you want a more unusual look, you could try slate, as pictured below, coloured stone chippings or even glass beads. All are now widely available and will work as an effective mulch. These are all more expensive options, however.

8 Secure the plant by backfilling all around its base with soil.

8

9 Water the plant in thoroughly, using a watering can and a rose if the plant has very delicate foliage.

OPPOSITE: *A fine, well-established Mediterranean-style gravel garden.*

Laying pebbles and cobbles

Tips, tools and materials

SKILL LEVEL
- Some DIY experience is advisable if you plan to undertake this project.

BEST TIME TO DO
- It is not a good idea to lay pebbles and cobbles during a frost or if the ground is very wet, but any other time is fine.

TOOLS REQUIRED
- Spirit level; rubber mallet; builder's trowel; pointing trowel; wooden straight edge.

MATERIALS REQUIRED
- Builder's sand; ready-mixed mortar or cement; edging material to outline path – for example, brick pavers; pebbles and/or cobbles.

TIME REQUIRED
- Depending on the size of the area to be covered, it is a good idea to set aside two days or a whole weekend for this project.

A relatively easy way to introduce varieties of shape and texture to your paving is to lay inset sections of naturally rounded pebbles and larger cobblestones. You can use these materials to create paths and patios from scratch, but they are not the easiest things to walk upon and so are more commonly used as a visual counterpoint to flat surfaces – perhaps as a border or to highlight a garden feature, such as a sundial or statue. Their advantage over other garden paving materials is their relatively small size, which makes it easy to fit them round curves and irregularly shaped obstacles. However, because they are small, they do take much longer to lay than other materials. You can buy pebbles and cobblestones from builders' merchants and garden centres, in a range of sizes and colours. Small quantities – enough for an individual garden feature – are usually sold in bags.

1 Either outline a pebble path with a row of bricks or pavers, or, as shown here, lift a section of stones in an area of existing paving to create an inset area for the cobbles. Fill the area with sand.

2 Spread the sand out across the area to be filled with cobbles, using a builder's trowel.

3 Work a layer of cement or ready-mixed mortar into the bed of sand.

4 Wet the mixture using a watering can and then press different sized and coloured pebbles into the wet mortar.

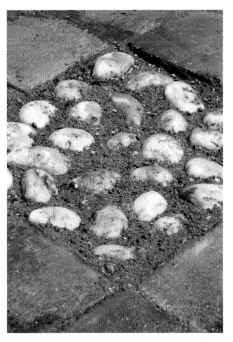

5 Tamp each of the cobbles firmly into place using a rubber mallet. Try to make the cobbles sit as evenly as possible with one another so that they can be easily walked upon.

6 Brush more sand and mortar mix around the pebbles to secure them.

Zen dry gardens

Japanese-style zen dry gardens often feature pebble and cobble designs. An imaginary stream like the one pictured below is a traditional element of the Zen dry garden or *karesansui*. Such a design is normally created with a combination of differently coloured, sized and shaped gravel, pebbles, cobbles and boulders. Flat slate shards can also be used to create the impression of a flow of water. A simple wooden bridge is often added to a design like this to complete the illusion. This clever dry stream effect works well in just about any kind of garden.

Useful tips

Pebbles and cobblestones are usually fixed in a bed of mortar, especially if they are going to be walked on or are used to line a watercourse. However, loose pebbles can be used to discourage weed growth and prevent soil erosion in areas of the garden that are in permanent shade. For large areas it is more economical to buy stones loose by weight. Ask your supplier for advice about coverage and have large quantities delivered; otherwise, more than two or three sacks of heavy stones could wreck the suspension of your vehicle.

PROJECT

Creating mosaic and pebble patterns

One of the great things about transforming your garden is that it is such a personal process. You decide what comes out and what goes in. If you like, anything goes! One way to bring a truly unique flavour to your garden is to create a terrace, patio or maybe just a small path of stepping stones made from mosaic tiles combined with pebbles. Using these materials, even the simplest designs can be striking. To emphasize the garden theme, you could incorporate a simple tulip or daisy motif. A heavenly theme could also work well, with panels showing a stylized sun, moon or star. Or you could go for something more symbolic, such as the Chinese yin and yang symbol. Give these mosaic features the prominence they deserve, siting them at the junction of two pathways, to focus attention on a garden ornament, pool or fountain, or to enhance a seating or outdoor dining area.

Tips, tools and materials

SKILL LEVEL
- Some DIY experience would be useful for this project.

BEST TIME TO DO
- Laying mosaics and pebbles is best undertaken when the weather is warm and the ground is dry and firm.

TOOLS REQUIRED
- Pad, pen and ruler for a plan; spade; plastic bucket or trug; brick layer's trowel; pointing trowel; tin clippers; tile cutter; tile squeegee; paint brush.

MATERIALS REQUIRED
- Ready-mix sand and cement; frost- and water-proof mosaic/ceramic tiles – for example, those suitable for outdoor pools; a selection of pebbles and/or cobbles; wire mesh.

TIME REQUIRED
- Depending on the size of the area to be covered, 1–2 days or a weekend.

1 It is always a good idea to draw out your design on paper before starting to set down your mosaic tiles and pebbles.

2 Wipe around the bottom and sides of the plastic bucket with washing up liquid. This prevents the design from adhering to the bucket.

3 Spread a 25mm (1in) thick layer of mortar across the bottom of the bucket.

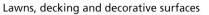

4 Trim the wire mesh to fit the bucket and lay it over the mortar. This will help strengthen and bind the design together. Spread a second 25mm (1in) layer of mortar over the wire mesh.

5 Select a number of evenly matched pebbles, ideally in an assortment of colours, and press them into the mortar around the edge of the bucket.

6 Take some miniature mosaic tiles or broken pieces of larger tiles and press them carefully into the mortar, following the plan you drew up in step 1.

7 Add a second colour of tile, ideally in different shapes, and alternate these pieces with the first colour.

8 The mortar will cure quickly, particularly in fine weather, so make sure all your pebbles and mosaic pieces are close to hand before you start and press them into the wet mortar without delay. Leave the design to set, ideally overnight.

Formal vs informal designs

There is no limit to what you can achieve with mosaic tiles and pebbles – it all depends on how much time you have available. A very formal pattern like the one below, featuring a cockerel on a roundel of brown pebbles, will take considerably longer to create than the more random patterns pictured opposite.

ABOVE: *In order to work effectively on the ground, a pattern like this needs careful planning and measuring on paper beforehand.*

RIGHT: *These colourful flower pots feature a mosaic design made up from a variety of tiles.*

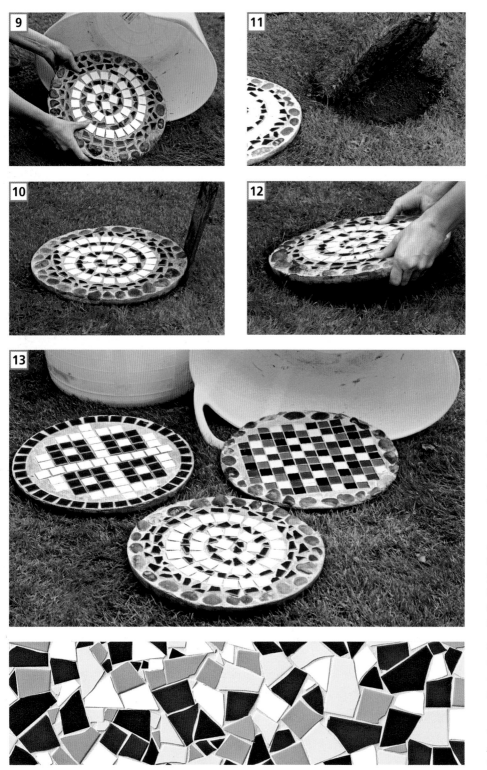

9 Once the design has set, carefully remove your pebble and mosaic circle from the bucket.

10 Lay the pebble and mosaic circle on the ground and cut around the outline with a sharp spade.

11 Cut out the turf to the depth of the circle, ensuring that the ground is as even and as firm as possible prior to receiving the circle.

12 Carefully place the pebble and mosaic circle into the prepared hole in the ground. Make adjustments for level as necessary, digging out more soil or sprinkling it back under the circle to even out any bumps or hollows.

13 If you make up a number of circles in different designs, you can then set them in the lawn as a stepping stone path (see opposite).

LEFT: *Mixing lots of different colours together will always give your designs a lift.*

OPPOSITE: *Three finished circles arranged as a path.*

Fences, arbours and pergolas

The fences, trellis panels and hedges that surround a garden form the boundaries of the property and offer shelter, privacy and security. Within this space, additional vertical structures such as a climber-covered trellis obelisk, pillar-trained rose or an archway add instant height and interest. They are particularly useful in new gardens where the shrubs and flowers are only just beginning to grow or where the plot is too small for trees.

Larger elements including trellis screens, pergolas and walkways help to create a room-like feel, encouraging you out into the garden and extending the living area, especially during summer. Surprisingly, dividing the plot up into sections, each with a contrasting function or design treatment, makes the space feel larger. It is also potentially more exciting visually.

garden structures

Boundary treatments

Garden walls and fences form a backdrop to the garden and act as a foil for planting and other features. Selecting the right material, design and colour is critical as boundaries are likely to be on show both inside and outside the garden limits. Take a look at the character of the house and discover what materials are in common use in the neighbourhood before deciding which type of fence, wall or screen to construct. For example, a cottage would look charming with a picket fence or hazel hurdles surrounding a traditional flower-filled plot, while a ranch-style post and wire fence would suit a country garden amid fields or woodland.

ABOVE: *Rustic fencing or panels suit cottage and country gardens in which informality is the order of the day. Select complementary plants carefully.*

Fencing and trellis

Fence panels and hazel or willow hurdles offer virtually instant privacy at a fraction of the cost of brick or stone walls, though rendered, breeze block walls are relatively economical. The style and quality of fence panels varies tremendously. Buy the best you can afford and attach them to pressure-treated wooden posts or slot them into concrete fence posts. The latter are a less attractive option but are useful on heavy, moist ground where fence posts tend to quickly rot off at the base. Both the posts and the concrete gravel boards that run along the bottom can be camouflaged by painting the same colour as the panels. Use one of the modern timber paint/stain treatments. To delay the rotting of fence posts, also consider mounting posts above ground in prefabricated metal sockets. These are not always the most aesthetic choice, but they are very practical.

Manufactured trellis panels come with a square or diamond infill, the latter having a

ABOVE: *This white trellis screen-cum-fence gives a visual lift to what is otherwise a very utilitarian-looking and rather unattractive area of the garden.*

prettier, more elegantly feminine feel that can suit period and country-style properties. As well as rectangular pieces, you can also buy sections with curved tops or with window-like apertures. Making your own trellis allows for greater flexibility in design. Trellis lets in more light than solid panels and still provides a degree of privacy, especially when combined with a foreground of evergreen shrubs, bamboos and other large grasses or a tracery of climbers. It is ideal for internal garden room dividers, creating a sense of enclosure without making the space feel claustrophobic.

Fence make-over

If you have inherited a mismatched array of fence panels and boundary treatments, especially when the garden is bordered by several properties, it might be best to cover the panels with rolls of screening material such as willow twigs, brushwood or split bamboo, the latter adding a distinctly oriental feel. Attach

these materials with a heavy-duty staple gun. You can also buy rigid panels made from these same materials which could be mounted onto the existing posts. Another option to create uniformity is simply to paint the fences with an exterior paint/stain and to use plants to provide further camouflage.

Tall fence panels may cut out too much light in small gardens and so consider using a lower base panel and replacing the top section with a plain or shaped run of timber trellis panels. This treatment can look very decorative, especially if the fence posts are also topped with ball- or acorn-shaped finials, ideal for adding a period flavour. You can extend the height of low fence panels with narrow trellis sections attached to post extension brackets.

garden structures

Growing up

Where space is at a premium, the vertical boundaries of your garden provide valuable growing opportunities for both ornamentals and kitchen garden crops. To make the most of walls and fences ensure that climbers and wall shrubs have adequate support so that they cover evenly and keep to their allotted space. A simple system of horizontal galvanized or plastic-coated training wires is usually sufficient for attaching climbing roses and wall shrubs such as winter-flowering jasmine. Vine eyes hold the wires a few centimetres away from the wall or fence and this gap enables

you to tie the branches onto the front of the wire, leaving space behind for air to circulate.

As an alternative to wire plant supports use plastic climbing or clematis mesh which is held in place by clips that hold the rigid mesh away from the fence or wall. Wooden trellis panels provide plant support as well as looking stylish when painted and fixed neatly to a wall. Attach using horizontal wooden battens.

Growers of sweet peas or runner beans will be well used to constructing bamboo cane wigwams to support plants but these simple structures can also be used to grow other annual climbers and late-flowering clematis such as the small bloomed viticella types (cut viticellas to 30cm (1ft) from ground level in early spring).

ABOVE: *By their very nature, vertical structures maximize growing opportunities in any garden.*

RIGHT: *A simple woven willow wigwam for sweet peas, clematis or other climbing plants can be used effectively as a visual exclamation mark or end-stop.*

FAR RIGHT: *A simple network of vine eyes and wires is all that is required to camouflage a bare or ugly wall with clematis and other climbing plants.*

Positioning decorative structures

When well situated, large 3D constructions act as focal points, leading the eye to a particular area of the garden or acting as a full stop or exclamation mark. In more relaxed and rustic situations, use shrubs and climbers to help integrate decorative structures into the garden. In a formal setting, make the building stand out even more by painting it in an eye-catching shade and by framing using a matching pair of clipped topiaries, say, or lead the eye with an avenue of sentinel-like junipers.

LEFT: *Pergolas make a bold visual statement in the garden – so long as they are correctly proportioned. For large structures, they are relatively easy to construct and maintain.*

Pergolas

These overhead structures make a wonderful addition to an outdoor dining or barbecue area, covered with fragrant climbers and, for night time magic, strung with sparkling LED fairy lights. Pergolas can be freestanding or attached to a wall using special brackets that hold the cross beams in place. They can be adapted to form covered walkways over a garden path, or to run along the side of a building, providing welcome dappled shade for a sun-baked aspect.

Models of specific dimensions as well as ones for modular construction are available in kit form and are relatively straightforward to construct with the help of an extra pair of hands. In order for pergolas to work well visually, the proportions need careful consideration. The uprights must appear substantial – either heavy wooden posts or brick or stone pillars and the main support beams also need to seem weighty – so consider using reclaimed timbers or old beams. Allow a head clearance of up to 2.5m (8ft). This will seem quite high at first but once the structure is covered in climbers which hang down between the beams, you will be glad of the extra room. If you want a relatively light overhead treatment, use galvanized training wire as support for climbers instead of wooden struts.

An open-sided timber gazebo could be positioned at the intersection of two or more pathways or to mark the boundary between one garden room and another. Alternatively, you might construct an arbour seat or climber-covered bower at the end of a long straight avenue, lawn or rectangular pool to emphasize the formality of your design. Trellis arbours have a similar vertical impact on the garden's design and covered with fragrant climbers can create a blissful retreat on warm sunny days.

Finally, a trellis obelisk planted with a rose or clematis looks well in a small courtyard garden

ABOVE: *For a powerful, formal effect in the garden, consider building an open-sided timber gazebo or a rose arbour at the end of a path or as a central feature.*

Traditional picket fence and gate

Tips, tools and materials

SKILL LEVEL
- A picket fence is relatively easy to construct, but some DIY experience would be useful for this project.

BEST TIME TO DO
- Whenever the weather is reasonably fine and the ground is not too wet or muddy.

TOOLS REQUIRED
- Shovel or spade; spirit level; basic range of hand and small powered tools, including drill and screwdriver.

MATERIALS REQUIRED
- Fence posts; fence rails; fence pails (work out the quantity required for all these items before you start and consult your timber merchant as necessary); tee hinges; gate catch; screws and/or nails.

TIME REQUIRED
- Depending on the length and complexity of the fence, normally 1–2 days or a weekend will be required.

A picket fence and gate can provide a useful break between different sections of a garden or at the front of a house or building. However, they will not be substantial enough to restrain livestock or to keep out intruders. An ideal base material is pressure preservative-treated softwood. This should give the whole fence some extra longevity. Any fresh cuts you make into the wood should be retreated with a proprietary, clear preservative to maintain the integrity of the treatment. Once constructed, the fence can be left in its natural colour or painted if you so wish. With some care, and careful positioning of the posts, the easiest way to make a picket fence is in sections. A little thought needs to go into the pail spacing, to make sure that where the rails joint the gap is the same. However, if you are not confident enough to do this then fix all the posts in place first, then the rails and, finally, the pails.

1 The picket fence can be made up in sections. Work out how many pails you will need to cover the overall width of the fence section, allowing a gap in between. If your stock is not cut to length chop them off and then shape the top of each pail.

2 Lay a pair of pre-cut rails on a flat surface and carefully position the first pail on one end. Now use another towards the other end to ensure the rails are parallel. Working off the position of the first pail, fix all the rest in sequence, setting them carefully with equal spaces.

3 A simple gate frame can be made by using halving joints in each corner. A brace will be required to both hold the frame square and provide support from the hinge side up. This brace should be a good fit.

4 Once the gate frame has been constructed and you have fixed the pails to it, attach the gate furniture. Hinges may need extra packing in between some of the pails where a screw needs to go. Ensure that any packing blocks are cut neatly to fit and do not protrude beyond the pails.

5 On site set a line, between two pegs, stretched taut across the width to be fenced in. Mark out, put a peg in where each hole will be and then dig them out. About two spades widths square by a couple deep should do for a standard height fence.

Painting your fence

Consider having your pails planed all round prior to preservative treatment if you are going to paint them. The smoother surface will make the coating application a whole lot easier and will be less likely to retain moisture. This means the fence will look better and last longer.

ABOVE: *Use a weatherproof paint in a colour that is complementary to nearby features and plantings.*

RIGHT: *Traditionally picket fences are painted white, but you can choose any colour you like.*

6 Carefully position each post. You may need to put some additional short pegs and braces in to hold them upright. Backfill the holes tamping down each layer as you go. Use a spirit level as you work to ensure that the fence posts remain completely upright. Replace the turf on the top afterwards.

7 The fence rails are attached to the gate posts with a batten each side. These need to be set off the ground and screwed or nailed on.

8 With some help, or using 'G' cramps, fix each section of pails in place. The fence posts should be set with the wider face to the rails, which are then simply planted and fixed on.

9 Tee hinges are ideal for hanging the gate and can be fixed to it before it is mounted in the gap.

10 Once the gate is hung, the catch can be fixed to the gate and the post.

OPPOSITE: *After a few years the fence will fade and age to look something like this.*

Erecting fence and trellis panels

Probably the most difficult job you will have with this project is selecting the style of solid or trellis panel for the chosen location. Pre-manufactured panels are available in abundance and a wide range of costs. Having chosen or made your panels, and selected your post style, work out how many you will need before making a purchase. Often the width of the fence will not directly coincide with the sizes available. Some manufacturers make half panels to address this common problem. Uneven or sloping ground often cause difficulties. It may be necessary to stagger the top levels of the panels to help overcome this. Never try to tilt the panels and posts to match the ground undulations! Gaps at the bottom can be filled in with a simple, flat board cut to fit the shape required. You can leave the fence to weather naturally or colour it to suit your garden and its features.

Tips, tools and materials

SKILL LEVEL
- Fence and trellis panels are relatively easy to erect.

BEST TIME TO DO
- Whenever the weather is reasonably fine and the ground is not too wet or muddy.

TOOLS REQUIRED
- Shovel or spade; spirit level; basic range of hand and small powered tools, including drill and screwdriver. A concrete mixer would be useful.

MATERIALS REQUIRED
- Fence posts; trellis panels (work out the quantity required for both these items before you start and consult your timber merchant as necessary); metal post holders; screws and/or nails.

TIME REQUIRED
- Depending on the length and complexity of the fence or trellis, normally 1–2 days or a weekend will be required.

1 Posts can be set straight into the ground and firmed up with soil or concrete; the latter is best. However, there are a number of easy fitting devices available. The three shown here are, from left to right, for driving straight into the ground, fixing to a flat surface and, finally, concreting in.

2 There are also different options for posts. In this picture, the one on the left is square and the panels

can be fixed directly to it or with a batten attached, as shown. The one on the right is rebated to take the panel. This makes it easy to change the style of panels later on as you choose. Concrete posts are also used where a permanent, long life fence is required.

3 When concreting the posts into the ground, position the appropriate fitting on the bases of the posts before starting. This will ensure that the posts can be set vertically before any concrete is poured.

4 Calculate where the centre of each post will be located and mark out the positions of the post holes with some pegs. You will need to allow for the width of the panel plus the equivalent of two half posts for each side.

5 The post holes need to be about two spades' width square and a spade to a spade and a half deep. The flat section of the post fitting should be level with the ground surface. Remove the turf first and dig neat, straight-sided holes.

6 With the spoil removed, check the hole for depth by placing the post assembly in it. If you have gone too deep, pack out below the fitting with slivers of old brick, stone or some other hard material. If too shallow, dig deeper.

7 Set the first and last post in place and run a line up one face in between them. A useful tool to get the positions just right is a marking stick. Simply cut dead to length or scribe with pencil marks for the exact width of panel and post combinations required.

ABOVE: *Decorative overhead trelliswork like this can make a stunning visual feature in any garden.*

8 Each post should be held firmly in place. Pegs in the ground and temporary braces off at least two sides make a good start. Each post can be set with a G cramp and batten at the top.

9 Before concreting in the posts, check that each and every one is in the right position and vertical in both planes. Pour the concrete into the holes gently, to avoid disturbing the post positions, and work it all around with the end of the shovel.

10 Whilst the post concrete goes off, prepare the panels by removing any bits of packing and labels the manufacturer may have tacked to them.

11 When fixing battens, they do not necessarily need to go right from top to bottom. A forty five degree angle cut at the top will help shed water and add a small, decorative detail.

12 The panels are positioned and screws are simply driven in to secure them. If you are working on uneven ground they may

14

need to be levelled independently or in series. Make sure that the laths in the panels in the same levels line up properly, as well as the tops.

13 If necessary, use G cramps to help with the fixing process. Don't use too many screws; three or four each side should be sufficient.

14 Finally, cap out the posts with whatever detail you have chosen. These are simple bevelled blocks, but more decorative ones are widely available.

BELOW: *A decorative, wavy trellis top like the one pictured will give any basic fence a lift. If you want to re-turf over the post holes, leave a gap at the top of the holes when you are pouring in the concrete.*

Making country-style post and rail fencing

A trip to your local timber, builder's merchant or agricultural supplier will make you aware of the materials available. Anything from the really rustic through to square posts and rails should be readily to hand. Consider carefully the reason and use for which the fence is being erected. If it is to be livestock-proof then the posts and rails should be situated closer together and should be substantial. If the fence is to be a simple boundary marker between patches of ground, then less material and strength will be required. Some consideration should also be given to the 'look' you are trying to achieve. Putting up a country-style set of posts and rails need not be done with great precision. Once the materials have been chosen, simply pacing out the distance between the posts to mark their positions is fine. However, if you wish to avoid waste, use a tape measure and set everything out carefully. A good tip when using a bar to make the stake holes is to do this when the ground is softer. The other option is to partly dig out a hole before barring in the rest. If the rustic look is required, don't worry if the posts are not vertical.

ABOVE: *There are many different styles of post and rail fencing.*

using a metal sledge hammer because this will have a tendency to split the ends of the posts. Alternatively, special post rammers are also available. One of these is slipped over the top of the posts and is then lifted and dropped to drive the posts home.

3 With the posts in place, fix the top fencing rail first. Try to drive all the posts into the ground to about the same level but don't worry if you cannot; the tops of the posts can be cut off and levelled as necessary after this top rail is fitted. Place a solid item behind where the nails are being driven in to avoid loosening the post in its hole.

4 Joint rails on the centres of the posts. Cut to length to fit and drive a pair of nails into each rail.

5 The alternative to jointing on the post is to use a short length of rail behind the meeting point. If enough nails are driven in, through and bent over this will make a secure and lasting joint. It also minimizes rail waste.

1 Erecting country-style post and rail fencing is not an especially technical process! Having decided on the materials you wish to use, work out the post spaces to maximize the length of rails in the fence. Mark the positions of the post holes on the ground and drive in a hole with a metal bar.

2 The posts can be driven into the ground using a large wooden mallet called a 'beetle'. Try to avoid

Alternative styles of fencing

In this project we show you how to construct traditional post and rail fencing. However, there are many different styles to choose from and there is no reason why you should not come up with your own. In fencing designed to restrain smaller livestock, it is common to see the central rail set lower on the posts to keep the animals in (see above). For a more decorative effect, a diamond lattice of additional cross-rails makes an interesting statement (see below).

6 Some basic alternatives for jointing rails are shown here. At the top of the image a simple butt joint is demonstrated, using a piece of waste wood behind the join. In the middle a half lap joint is shown and at the bottom a scarf joint. All can be used successfully depending upon the intended use for the fencing.

7 Three rails are sufficient to keep larger animals at bay or to delineate a boundary, say against a hedge or wood. Smaller animal enclosures will need more rails and maybe some wire mesh in between the rails.

OPPOSITE: *Whatever style of post and rail fencing you decide to build – whether of rustic poles or more formal, planed wood as here – you will bring a touch of the countryside to your garden.*

PROJECT

Making a planter and wooden trellis for climbing plants

Making a planter box with an attached trellis is a fairly simple project and creates a good planting base for any location in the garden, or on a patio or balcony. This planter and trellis is suitable for growing vegetables as well as a wide range of flowering climbing plants. The basic structure is made up from overlapping 50 x 50mm (2 x 2in) timber. This can be varied to suit the size of body required. A sheet of exterior grade plywood forms the base and everything is simply built up from this. If you are using pressure-preservative treated softwood, make sure you re-coat any freshly cut ends with a liberal dose of preservative. The two main sections of the project can be made up in parts. Once the planter body is made, fix the poles to it to establish the size of the trellis frame. Make the trellis to fit, using odds and ends if you can. Both the trellis and planter body can be coloured or left to weather naturally.

Tips, tools and materials

SKILL LEVEL
- Some DIY experience and ideally carpentry skills would be useful for this project.

BEST TIME TO DO
- Anytime, as this structure can be built indoors and then located in the garden.

TOOLS REQUIRED
- Drill; screwdriver; spanner; spirit level; tape measure; stapler.

MATERIALS REQUIRED
- Pressure preservative-treated softwood and plywood; Enough offcuts, scrap or waste wood to make a suitably shaped trellis panel for the back. Four 125mm/5in x 12mm/½in coach bolts and some plastic sheeting to line out the planter body.

TIME REQUIRED
- 1–2 days or a weekend will be required, depending on extent of DIY skills.

1 The base of the planter can be made to any size you wish. In most cases at least three bearers should be fitted to the underside to raise the planter body off the ground. Make sure the ply used is exterior grade or make it up from solid sections of wood.

2 The construction is simple and easy. Cut the sections to length for the width and depth. Each layer is screwed in place overlapping and alternating the corner joints. Coat any freshly sawn ends with preservative to maintain the integrity of the treatment.

3 Choose the bolt location points carefully; two per side. Recess the holes so that the bolt heads do not protrude.

4 Colour up the different parts of the project before assembly. A couple of flat and spring washers per nut and bolt will hold the two poles in place. These may need to be adjusted annually as the wood expands and contracts.

5 The best way to make up your trellis panel is from scrap offcuts. Measure the size required and nail the pieces together separately, making evenly sized squares. Fix the trellis in place with screws. A sash clamp will help hold everything in place.

RIGHT: *Line out the planter body with some plastic sheeting. Fill it with soil and compost and plant out with a central climber and some bedding plants.*

Making a rustic sweet pea wigwam

Making a sweet pea or other climbing plant wigwam for the garden can be an inexpensive and enjoyable way to raise flowers higher up in a border or to grow produce upon. The construction process is very simple and should not take long once you get the hang of it. There are lots of different materials you can make your wigwam from. Traditionally, wigwams are made from willow and/or hazel. This material can be found in small woodlands and hedgerows, or purchased from garden centres. Always cut it when there is some fresh growth in spring. This ensures that the sap is up and the thinner stuff is more flexible. Alternatives to willow include bamboo canes or sawn sections of solid wood. If you do not like the idea of weaving the willow sticks together, which can be tough on the hands, use string, rope or wire to connect the uprights at regular intervals.

1 If they are not green and fresh, the withies will need to be soaked for a good couple of days before use. Use a heavy weight, with a ball float attached, to submerge the bundle below the surface.

2 To make the assembly process that much easier, prepare a template for the base of the wigwam. Half a dozen equally spaced holes about 38mm (1 ½in) across will do the job, set with a 450mm

(18in) or more overall diameter to the base.

3 Harvest the materials from the wild when the sap has risen in the spring. Alternatively, buy pre-prepared materials.

4 Use a chopper and a cutting block to cut a sharp point onto the thicker end of the main poles.

5 Drop the template onto the ground, preferably where it is soft enough to push the poles in, and insert each of the six uprights through the holes and on by 50mm (2in) or so.

6 Starting at the bottom, pick a spot about 150mm (6in) or so up, and start to weave the withies all the way around the uprights. Make sure that each pole is secure and that the withies are interconnected all the way round.

7 When you get to the top, weave a ball shape to finish off. The wigwam is now ready for use directly in the garden, in a large container or in a planter.

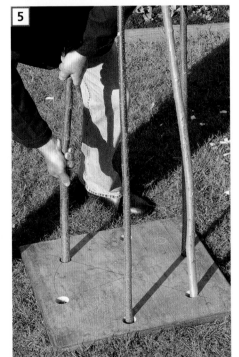

PROJECT: Making a rustic sweet pea wigwam

Making a wooden obelisk for climbing plants

Tips, tools and materials

SKILL LEVEL

■ This is a relatively easy project which can be undertaken without any previous experience or particular DIY skills. Some patience will be required.

BEST TIME TO DO

■ Whenever the weather is reasonably fine and the ground is not too wet or muddy.

TOOLS REQUIRED

■ Powered hand drill; screwdriver; saw; rule, tape measure; pencil.

MATERIALS REQUIRED

■ Preservative-treated softwood.

TIME REQUIRED

■ 1–2 days or a weekend will be required to make this project.

Making an obelisk for the garden is an easy and stylish project. It will help raise plants up above the usual levels and bring a bit of colour high in the border. This project requires two basic sizes of pressure preservative-treated softwood. The main corner posts are made from 50 x 50mm (2 x 2in) timber and the rest is 50 x 25mm (2 x 1in) in dimension. However, if you plan to make a smaller version, consider using timber with slightly smaller cross-sections. Try to maintain the integrity of the preservative treatment at the bottom of each corner post. If you have to cut the posts to length, use the original end at the bottom or treat with a good dose of proprietary preservative. When completed, the obelisk can simply be placed in a border or anywhere else in the garden. If your garden is exposed to high winds it is a good idea to anchor the obelisk down.

1 Begin by laying a couple of corner posts on a flat surface. Keeping the top close together, spread the bottoms of the posts to the desired angle/width and tack them together with some bits of gash stock.

2 Work out the positions of the horizontal rails. Ensure that they are evenly spaced.

3 With a sliding bevel, take the angle for the ends of each

rail from the first pre-assembled side. Keep this angle handy; you will need it for all subsequent marking out of the rails.

4 Take the length dimensions for each set of rails directly from the pre-assembled frame. Mark the end angles with the sliding bevel and saw to size.

5 With the temporary supports still in place invert the side assembly into a vice and start to locate and fix the rails. Use a sash clamp to hold them in place.

6 If you are going to colour the obelisk, paint the components before final assembly.

7 Join two assembled sides together with the rest of the rails. Take the dimensions for the angled pieces directly from the frame; they should all be the same. Fix in place by screwing up through the bottom and nailing through the top.

8 The final job is to fit on the finial. This can be made up from offcuts in square and angled sections.

PROJECT: Making a wooden obelisk for climbing plants

Erecting a pergola

Tips, tools and materials

SKILL LEVEL
- This is a relatively simple project which can be undertaken without any DIY skills, although these would be useful.

BEST TIME TO DO
- Whenever the weather is reasonably fine and the ground is not too wet or muddy.

TOOLS REQUIRED
- Powered hand drill; screwdriver; saw; rule, tape measure; pencil.

MATERIALS REQUIRED
- Preservative-treated softwood. (This project is based upon a ready-made kit. These are widely available, but you could construct a pergola to your own design by adapting the instructions on these pages.)

TIME REQUIRED
- 1–2 days or a weekend will be required to make this project.

A highly effective way of creating an instant garden feature is to construct a simple pergola. These striking erections are often used as walk-through structures or are simply set in a corner to create a relaxing space in which to sit. Climbers or vines can easily be trained to grow over and hang down from above and hanging baskets will add colour and look good when suspended from high on a pergola. A patio or decking area is an ideal setting for a pergola, as in this case. Make your own pergola from sawn-square materials or alternatively rustic poles. If this is not an option, there are plenty of ready-built kits available from a host of manufacturers. Some manufacturers provide a range of accessories such as screens that can be fitted to the sides or roof to form sun or wind barriers. Alternatively, you could devise and incorporate your own personal special touches.

1

2

1 When erecting a kit of any kind first check off the packing list to make sure that you have everything that you should have and then study the instructions. Never rush into assembly without preparing.

2 Depending upon the size and location of the pergola, vertical posts can be set into the ground, anchored securely with a post holder set in concrete or, as in this case, screwed down onto decking.

3 Construction of this fan-shaped pergola begins with the corner post being fixed in place. The other three posts are linked with the curved cross beam before a few of the rafters are loosely laid on. Once the positions of the components have been confirmed, and the posts are properly vertical, everything is fixed down before the rest of the rafters are spaced out and secured.

4 This kit has the connecting ends of the rafters ready shaped to fit on the corner post. They must be fixed securely to each other and the post, using long wood screws.

5 Modify the manufacturer's design if you think it is necessary. To tidy up and firmly secure this corner joint arrangement, a plywood web has been fitted to both top and bottom sides.

6 Finally, add some shaped braces for strength, even if the original kit does not specify them.

Building and planting a rose arbour

Tips, tools and materials

SKILL LEVEL
- This is a fairly difficult project for which some DIY skills are required. A helping pair of hands would also be useful.

BEST TIME TO DO
- Whenever the weather is reasonably fine and the ground is not too wet or muddy.

TOOLS REQUIRED
- Sledge hammer; spade; hammer; powered hand drill; screwdriver; saw; rule, tape measure; pencil.

MATERIALS REQUIRED
- Preservative-treated softwood. (See the cutting list on the opposite page for a detailed breakdown. Note that these dimensions can all be scaled up or down pro rata as necessary, depending on the space you have available.)

TIME REQUIRED
- 1–2 days or a weekend will be required to make this project.

An arbour set in your garden with a scented rose or roses climbing and trailing across it makes a handsome stand alone feature. Incorporating the arbour into a trellis walk or over a path are possibilities. You can even set the arbour at some outer point of your garden and build a seat underneath to appreciate the view around you. Design your arbour so that it is wide enough to walk through with ease and tall enough so that you don't get tangled up with any trailing, thorny ends. In a busy, large garden you may even need some extra room to drive your mower or small tractor through. Using pressure preservative-treated softwood affords the project protection and some longevity. Simply made with halving joints there is no need for any fancy equipment to assemble it. The four legs can be set directly into the ground and the holes backfilled firmly.

1 This rose arbour is constructed using simple halving joints. On the top of each leg these are cut out with a saw on both shoulders and cheeks of the joint. Make the saw cuts as neat and precise as possible, as this will save more work later on.

2 The top rails extend past the outside of the legs; therefore the joints need to be carefully measured and marked out in pencil on the legs.

3 Cut down the shoulders with a saw and chisel the waste away, down to the marked line, using a wide chisel.

4 To finish off the top rails bevels are cut on each end. Set a sliding square at forty-five degrees and slice off half the width of the rail as neatly as possible.

5 Check the joints out for fit and adjust them if necessary. This is 'rough' carpentry, so perfect joints are not essential. Fix all the joints squarely with some glue and a couple of large screws in each one. Temporarily fix a piece of waste across the lower part of the legs to hold them firm until they are set in the ground.

6 The trellis frame also uses halving joints in the corners. Mark these out and cut them as before. There are two frames, one for each side. The cross rails, at the top of the structure, are notched to match their width. These rails are fixed on the top of the main structure as it is erected.

Cutting list

Component:	Qty:	LENGTH nominal:	WIDTH finished:	THICKNESS finished:
Legs:	4	2.4m/8ft	75mm/3in	75mm/3in
Top rails:	2	1.5m/5ft	75mm/3in	75mm/3in
Cross rails:	5	1.2m/4ft	75mm/3in	50 mm/2in
Trellis framing:	4	1.5m/5ft	50 mm/2in	25mm/1in
	4	685mm/2ft3in	50 mm/2in	25mm/1in
Trellis:		Enough to cover two panels. 50 mm/2in		12mm/½in

7 Fix and set the trellis frames square and equal with one another. Use a couple of screws and some glue in each corner. Clean off any excess glue as you work.

8 The trellis can be attached directly to each frame. Simple square patterns normally work well or, if you are using thinner material, a woven diamond shape can be made.

9 With the structure made up the holes for the four legs need to be dug.

10 Erect the arbour and tack the main pieces together. Backfill each hole and firm down the soil.

11 Finish off by permanently fixing all the cross rails and side trellis panels in place.

12 The cross rails go in last – one each across the vertical posts and the other three evenly spaced.

OPPOSITE: *After a few years, your rose arbour will become a floral delight.*

Suitable species of roses for arbours

There are many climbing and rambling roses that will thrive when grown up an arbour. These come in a wide variety of styles and colours and many will grow very tall, once they have become well established. Rambling roses are naturally very vigorous and will produce lots of long, bendy stems. They can produce masses of small flowers in large trusses, but they only flower once a year and do tend to be susceptible to mildew. Climbing roses are the opposite of ramblers in many ways; they have larger flowers but in small trusses and they flower more than once during the season. Their stems are firmer than those of ramblers, they are more resistant to disease and their flowers are borne on old wood instead of new growth. Some of the best climbing roses to buy are the Climbing Bourbons, Climbing Tea Roses and other large-flowered climbers.

LEFT TOP: Rosa *'Blairii Number 2' is an RHS AGM plant (Royal Horticultural Award of Gardening Merit) and is a good bet for any rose arbour.*

LEFT BOTTOM: Rosa *'Masquerade' is a climbing floribunda rose ideal for arbours.*

Summerhouses, sheds and storage

If you have sufficient space in your garden, there is a wide range of wooden structures you can make which can serve both as practical items and aesthetic features. Don't be put off by the apparent scale and complexity of some garden buildings; many are now commonly available in easy-to-assemble kits from garden centres and DIY stores. However, if you are confident in your own skills, the variety of outdoor structures you can create is limited only by your imagination.

The following pages offer a series of wooden projects which are designed to offer both practical solutions for storage and garden management as well as looking good. The summerhouse-cum-gazebo that opens the chapter would grace any spacious garden, whereas the shed, cold frame and compost container offer essential practical solutions to all busy gardeners.

for practical garden structures

Working in wood

Some of the projects illustrated in this chapter are relatively simple and straightforward but once completed, they can make a big difference to the practical running of the garden. Wood is a very satisfying material to work with and provided it is protected from wet, even untreated wood resists rotting, especially hardwoods such as chestnut and oak or naturally rot-resistant softwoods such as cedar. Pressure-treated or tanalized softwood should not need further treatment after construction, but since it contains heavy metals, always wear gloves when handling and don't burn offcuts.

ABOVE: *A structure like this can serve any number of different purposes in the garden, from storage shed to home office to play house for the children.*

BELOW: *This delapidated old shed covered in plants needs some renovation work, but a structure like this undeniably adds character to a garden, as well as an invaluable storage space.*

Versatile sheds

There is no denying the usefulness of a shed in terms of providing storage, but these simple garden buildings can be put to all kinds of use. Wired up for power and with extra insulation in the roof, walls and floor, a shed can be converted into a garden study or office; a wet weather play room for the children or a peaceful retreat in which to simply get away from the pressures of modern living.

Even if your shed doubles as a workshop, you can still add home comforts such as a kettle for brewing up, a comfy chair and rug and perhaps a thermostatically operated storage heater. Try painting the interior with a light-coloured wood paint or stain – it will make the space feel bigger and more cheerful. Exterior embellishments might include fragrant climbers or a flower-filled windowbox. And rather than trying to hide the shed, you could make a feature of it by painting it cornflower blue or some other bright colour. Fix a water butt or two below the guttering and for fun, and some really green credentials, consider making a living roof of succulents like sedums and houseleeks (Sempervivum) grown on landscape matting laid over plastic sheeting. This only needs watering during

within feel more sheltered and intimate. See pages 122–127 for construction details. Using the same basic plan, you can adapt a gazebo to create a stylish summerhouse, complete with walls and doors.

Gazebos and other decorative buildings are best situated in a warm, sheltered part of the garden where you can enjoy sitting out on fine days and during balmy summer evenings. If the air turns chilly or rain threatens, you can retire under cover. Summerhouses can be as simply furnished or as luxurious as a room in the house. Pretty string lights decorating the interior or candle lanterns hung from the open facets of a gazebo create an inviting atmosphere for you and your guests. Add some evening scented plants such as those listed opposite and complete the picture with a trickling water feature or a pebble flooring mosaic.

ABOVE: *This open-sided gazebo also has no roof. This is because it is designed to serve primarily as a feature, a visual statement in the garden, and not somewhere to take shelter.*

BELOW: *Gazebos and summerhouses can serve as delightful outdoor rooms which have a particular allure on balmy summer evenings. For the ambitious homeowner, the options are limitless.*

periods of drought and will attract a range of insect life. Alternative roof coverings, which are more characterful than roofing felt, include reclaimed pantiles, wooden shingles and modular thatching units.

If you are going to use the shed principally as a potting or tool shed, fix plenty of tool racks, hooks and shelves to increase the storage capacity and maintain order and consider using stacking plastic boxes to maximize floor space. Store opened bags of different compost mixtures in mini dustbins beneath the potting bench for easy access.

Gazebos and summerhouses

Gazebos come in several different designs but essentially they are hexagonal or octagonal wooden buildings with a roof and either completely open sides or with some sections filled in using solid panels at the base and perhaps additional trellis panels on top. Extra screening can help make the sitting area

for practical garden structures

Compost bins

A large timber compost bin, or preferably a double or multiple bin arrangement that allows you to turn the compost easily, does not only process lawn clippings, weeds and other garden waste but also reduces the amount of rubbish thrown in the dustbin and therefore landfills by recycling cardboard and vegetable scraps. Once rotted down, garden compost makes a wonderfully nutritious topdressing for the productive garden and helps to maintain fertility and soil structure in flower beds. Position the bins away from the patio and shield them from view using climber-covered trellis screens, hazel or wicker hurdles or a low hedge. If you cannot hide them, make them a feature in their own right by painting them in bright colours. Leave plenty of room in front of the bins for good wheelbarrow access.

Raising and protecting plants

If you don't have room for a greenhouse and you regularly run out of windowsill space when raising seedlings in spring, a cold frame would be an ideal garden addition. As well as acting like a mini glasshouse, cold frames provide a convenient halfway house for hardening off or acclimatizing young plants before being set out in the vegetable patch or garden. They also provide a suitably humid and sheltered environment for rooting cuttings. In autumn and winter cold frames may be used to raise cool temperature salad crops or for housing more tender plants as well as alpines and succulents that dislike excess winter wet.

Though the glass-topped frame warms up quickly during the day, allowing hardy annuals and vegetables to be raised without extra

BELOW: *Compost bins serve an invaluable purpose in a productive garden but need not be eyesores. This selection of multiple bins is designed to look like colourful beehives.*

Composting tips

To make compost of the right consistency and to speed up decomposition, follow the suggestions below:

■ Compost fruit and vegetable peelings and egg shells but don't add cooked material or animal product as these are not suitable.
■ Mix with plenty of scrunched up newspaper sheets, torn up cardboard pieces, toilet roll tubes and egg boxes to stop the mix becoming too wet.
■ Include biodegradable or compostable food trays and cellulose wrappings – check packaging labels.
■ Add nettles and comfrey leaves for extra nutritious compost

as well as annual, non-seeding weeds, soft shrub and perennial prunings (chopped up), dead flowers and waste from the productive garden.
■ Layer lawn clippings with bulkier ingredients like cardboard.
■ Soiled newspaper and hay from rabbit and guinea pig hutches is an ideal addition, but don't add too many dry wood shavings.
■ Water the heap if it is dry and add more dry, bulky material if the mix is too wet and slimy. Turn several times a year to incorporate oxygen and speed up decomposition.
■ Keep heaps covered to seal in moisture and heat.

LEFT: When it comes to aesthetics, greenhouses tend to be regarded as functional-looking, necessary evils in the garden. However, they can be stylish, like this miniature, bell-shaped version.

heat, in spring, night temperatures can fall to below freezing point so layers of insulation are needed to trap accumulated warmth. Use bubble wrap or greenhouse insulation for this purpose, as well as carpet underlay. Line the bottom and sides of the cold frame with these and wrap materials around plants as far as possible, taking care not to smother the more delicate ones.

Temperature and light levels are also regulated through ventilation and by covering the glass with greenhouse shading fabric or horticultural fleece during sunny days. Shading is particularly important in summer when internal temperatures can soar in the cold frame, even with the top open, and is essential to prevent scorching or death of cuttings. Water earlier in the day to allow foliage to dry off before nightfall and reduce disease problems. Do not be tempted to overwater during hot weather as this will simply cause different problems.

Pet runs

You might start keeping hens for eggs but several breeds of chicken make delightful pets including little silkie bantams which have a fluffy appearance. Silkies produce a regular supply of smaller than normal eggs and ones with heavily feathered legs looking like pantaloons don't tend to scratch up the ground as much as other types. When allowed to run round the vegetable garden they can help to manage pests like caterpillars. To build a safe exercise run and warm and dry living accommodation, see pages 134–137. Provide a water bowl, grit and dry food.

Set on lush lawn grass a hutch and run would also suit a pet rabbit or during the warmer months, guinea pigs. Temporarily drape an old sheet over the run to give the animals confidence to come out and enjoy the fresh air and sunshine. Don't forget to fix a water bottle in the run.

ABOVE: With their hinged glass roofs cold frames offer an accessible and low-maintenance way of providing the protection that many plants need.

BELOW: Family pets are an integral part of garden life. Why not build your own pet accommodation?

Constructing a summerhouse/ gazebo

Tips, tools and materials

SKILL LEVEL

■ This is a fairly complicated project which should only be undertaken by those with good DIY skills.

BEST TIME TO DO

■ Whenever the weather is reasonably fine and the ground is not too wet or muddy.

TOOLS REQUIRED

■ Bandsaw (ideally); saw; lathe (ideally); powered hand drill; screwdriver; rule; protractor; tape measure; pencil.

MATERIALS REQUIRED

■ Preservative-treated softwood. (The finial and centre boss are made up from offcuts and odds and ends. There are also a few finishing and facing strips to be made from offcuts.)

TIME REQUIRED

■ 4–5 days or at least two weekends will be required to construct this time-consuming project.

Garden gazebos should ideally be both decorative and functional. The dictionary definition of the word 'gazebo' is: 'a summerhouse, garden pavilion or belvedere, sited to command a view'. An ideal location is a secluded corner of your garden, slightly raised if possible, where you will be able to sit and look out across the immediate and more distant landscape. You can construct your gazebo with as many sides as you like. Size and shape should reflect both the space available and the landscape in which the structure will sit. Draw out the shape, full size if possible, to enable you to take the angles directly from your drawing. This six-sided gazebo can be scaled up if you wish. It is made simply from 50 x 50mm (2 x 2in) framing with feather-edged boarding as the cladding. The manufacturing process begins with the base panel construction.

4 Once the frames are made up the panelling can be fixed to them; in this case feather-edged boarding has been selected, as it is lightweight and relatively inexpensive yet durable and good-looking. To ensure a tidy edge, each piece overhangs the solid frames by an equal amount. A loose batten at the side assists this process. On the half-panel frames, the overhang is only adjacent to the solid panels.

5 The trellis panel frames are simply made by using halving joints in the corners. A couple of screws, and glue if you wish, make them rigid. Make the joints as neat as possible, as this will improve strength in the construction and will save tidying up work later on.

6 If the trellis is to be coloured then some painting of the inside faces prior to assembly is essential, as these will be inaccessible later on. Once made up, the exterior faces, and any exposed ends, can be coated.

1 Working out what the 'footprint' of your structure will be is the key starting point to this project. Some composite boards laid out on a flat surface will enable you to get a full-size perspective.

2 To understand the angles involved in the construction, draw out a section of the panels full size.

3 Although this is a six-sided gazebo, there are only five frames. Three will have solid panelling from top to bottom and the other two half panelling. The sixth side is simply left open, to enable access to the gazebo.

Cutting list

Component:	Qty:	LENGTH nominal:	WIDTH finished:	THICKNESS finished:
Solid panels:	9	2.1m/7in	50mm/2in	50mm/2in
	6	1.1m/3ft6in	50mm/2in	50mm/2in
Enough feather-edged boarding to fully cover frames.				
Side panels:	4	2.1m/7ft	50mm/2in	50mm/2in
	8	1.1m/3ft6in	50mm/2in	50mm/2in
Enough feather-edged boarding to cover lower frames.				
Trellis panels:	8	1.1m/3ft6in	50mm/2in	25mm/1in
Enough thinner material to make a trellis panel pattern.				
Plywood webs:	6	380mm/15in	200mm/8in	12mm/½in
Rafters:	6	1.8m/6ft	75mm/3in	75mm/3in
	6	1.8m/6ft	38mm/1½in	25mm/1in
Roof:		Enough feather-edged boarding to cover the six sections.		

7 The trellis panels should fit if they have been carefully prepared in line with the cutting list on page 125. However, they can be planed along their edges if they are too big when they are attached to the frame. A couple of screws through the outer frame into the trellis frame will secure them in place.

8 To help with the overall, larger construction process some plywood 'webs' need to be shaped for the jointing corners. These have a number of functions. They help provide a strong joint in each corner, they ensure the sides are set at the right-angles required and, finally, they provide a flat surface onto which the rafters will sit.

9 The first two solid panels are fixed together with the web at the top and a light metal bracket supporting them at the bottom. The latter can be discarded later on if the gazebo is to be fixed down onto the surface it will stand upon (for example, decking or a solid concrete base).

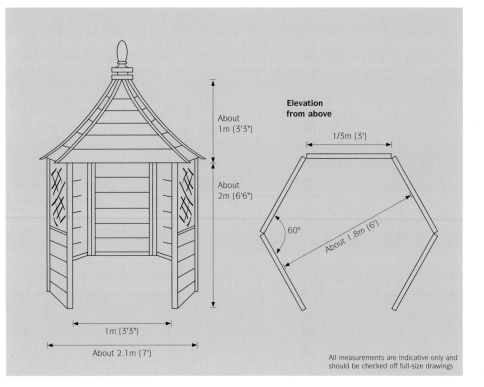

About 1m (3'3")

About 2m (6'6")

Elevation from above

1/3m (3')

60°

About 1.8m (6')

1m (3'3")

About 2.1m (7')

All measurements are indicative only and should be checked off full-size drawings

10 All the other panels of the gazebo are joined up in a similar fashion. The top rail for the open section is also fitted in place using the plywood webs. The dimensions and angles of this rail can be taken directly off the full-size drawings. As with all other aspects of the construction, the tighter the fit of this piece, the better the completed structure will look.

11 Next, fit the facing strips around the opening of the gazebo and adjacent to the trellis panels. Some vertical panel end stops are also fitted full height in the four back gaps.

12 Measure across the width of the assembled structure and draw out, full size, the base of the roof. The pitch should be anything from twenty-five to forty-five degrees. Make up a core six-sided centre boss.

LEFT: *This larger variation on the gazebo in preparation on these pages has open sides and a trellis, as opposed to a solid, roof.*

13 Once the rafters have been shaped, fitted with the roofing end stops and coloured as necessary, they can be fixed in place. Attaching two to the boss before mounting will assist this process. A large disc on the top of the boss will accommodate the finial and will also help to direct rainwater off the roof of the gazebo.

14 Cut and fit one section of the roof. If the rafters have been fixed evenly, five more sets can be cut to exactly the same dimensions, using the first section as a template. Once cut to size, all the roofing sections should be coloured before they are fixed in place.

15 Turn or cut a decorative finial to sit at the apex of the roof. This can be designed however you see fit and can add a personal touch to this design. It should be coloured and fixed in place before the roof is finally finished off.

OPPOSITE: *The finished gazebo, blending into its surroundings.*

Alternative materials for garden gazebos

A garden gazebo or summerhouse can be constructed from just about any material you like – the choices are really only limited by your budget and imagination. For a rustic look, why not construct a gazebo from country-style posts and rails (see pages 100–103), or you could use bamboo for an oriental, jungle-like effect (see the top image below). Alternatively – for example, if you have a large garden with a formal design and other grandiose features – you could build a more ornate structure with a multi-tiered roof clad with expensive slate, like the gazebo pictured in the image at the bottom of this box.

Making a multi-section wooden compost container

Tips, tools and materials

SKILL LEVEL
- This is a relatively straightforward project but some DIY skills would be useful.

BEST TIME TO DO
- Whenever the weather is reasonably fine and the ground is not too wet or muddy.

TOOLS REQUIRED
- Saw (ideally powered); powered hand drill; screwdriver; spirit level; rule; tape measure; pencil.

MATERIALS REQUIRED
- Preservative-treated softwood and plywood. (See the cutting list on the opposite page for a detailed breakdown of the dimensions of the pieces.)

TIME REQUIRED
- 1–2 days or a weekend will normally be required to construct these wooden compost bins.

Making up a pair or more of compost bins is a great way to recycle any household and garden waste. In most cases you will effectively build up a 'wormery' that breaks down the rubbish into useable material. Occasionally enough heat is generated to accelerate the composting process. Whatever the outcome, you should get some top-quality material out of the bins over a period of time. Ideally you will need two or more compost bins. One will be filled first, maybe over a year or so, and this is then capped off and left whilst the second is in use. An old section of carpet laid on top of the full bin will help the process. At the end of the first cycle the good stuff is removed and this bin is filled again as the other works. This project is made up from pressure preservative-treated softwood and exterior grade plywood. Site your compost bins where the smell will not be noticed.

1 Having worked out the basic size of your project, cut the plywood sections to size. This can be done with a hand saw but will be greatly assisted with a hand-held power saw. Set a straight edge up on the sheet being cut to provide a good edge.

2 Start the assembly process with the back. Two long framing pieces are screwed on from what will be the inside of the bin. Countersink all holes.

5

6

7

3 Cut the three vertical framing pieces to length. They need to be marked out to overlap the two pieces already fixed in place.

4 Cut the notches out on a bench. Try to keep the joints good so that they are a tight fit when made.

5 Position these pieces one by one on the back section. You can glue these on in addition if you wish. Use G cramps to hold them steady.

6 Now make up the two side panels for the bins and then the centre one. The process is as before. If the pieces overlap, cut notches.

7 The guides for the sliding front section can now be made up. Screw the pieces on, setting them slightly wider apart than the thickness of the front material. Remember that in damp conditions the front pieces are likely to swell up and increase somewhat in size.

8

8 With the three panels now made up, attach each of them to the back of the compost bin. Drill some pilot holes through the adjoining frame pieces and use long, strong screws to joint them up. Check with a spirit level and make any necessary adjustments. It is important to ensure that everything is level and square so that the other components will fit.

Cutting list

Component:	Qty:	LENGTH nominal:	WIDTH finished:	THICKNESS finished:
Exterior grade plywood.				
Back:	1	2.4m/8ft	1m/3ft 3in	12mm/½in
Sides:	3	1.2m/4ft	1m/3ft 3in	12mm/½in
Top:	1	1.2m/4ft	1.2m/4ft	12mm/½in
Treated softwood.				
Back frame:	3	1m/3ft 3in	75mm/3in	50mm/2in
	2	2.4m/8ft	75mm/3in	50mm/2in
Side frames:	2	1m/3ft 3in	50mm/2in	50mm/2in
	2	1m/3ft 3in	75mm/3in	50mm/2in
	4	1.2m/4ft	75mm/3in	25mm/1in
Centre frame:	2	1.2m/4ft	75mm/3in	18mm/¾in
	2	1m/3ft 3in	75mm/3in	25mm/1in
	2	1m/3ft 3in	38mm/1½in	32mm/1¼in
Front slide guides:	8	1m/3ft 3in	25mm/1in	21mm/7/8in
Fronts:	16	1.2m/4ft	100mm/4in	25mm/1in

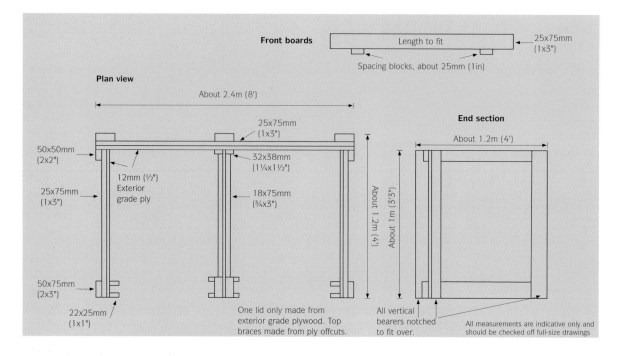

Front boards

Length to fit

25x75mm
(1x3")

Spacing blocks, about 25mm (1in)

Plan view

About 2.4m (8')

50x50mm
(2x2")

25x75mm
(1x3")

12mm (½")
Exterior
grade ply

25x75mm
(1x3")

32x38mm
(1¼x1½")

18x75mm
(¾x3")

About 1.2m (4')

50x75mm
(2x3")

22x25mm
(1x1")

One lid only made from
exterior grade plywood. Top
braces made from ply offcuts.

End section

About 1.2m (4')

About 1m (3'3")

All vertical
bearers notched
to fit over.

All measurements are indicative only and
should be checked off full-size drawings

9 Work on level ground, as otherwise you will have trouble making straight joints. A sash cramp will help hold the sections together as you make the joints. Try not to move this structure about too much at this stage unless you are building where it will finally be located.

10 To strengthen the joints you should make some plywood braces/webs to go across each top corner. Any offcuts from the previous sizing process will provide the raw material. Size is not too critical, as this is a fairly rough build.

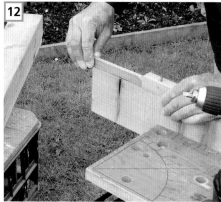

Summerhouses, sheds and storage

11 The braces/webs are screwed down onto the framework for the compost bins from the top. Make sure the structure is squared out before you start. Use more rather than fewer screws to secure each brace/web in place.

12 Each sliding front piece has a pair of spacing blocks fitted. For the sake of continuity and consistency, use a simple gauge to set the distance from the ends before screwing on. This will ensure the fronts slide easily.

13 Once made up the fronts should simply drop into place in the runners. When the compost bins are in use, start with a couple of front boards at the bottom and build them up as the bin being worked gradually fills up with material.

14 Finally, slip the single top piece of plywood into place. This is used as a cover over the filled bin and also serves as a handy work surface in the garden. Paint or stain the compost bins in a colour of your choice.

ABOVE AND BELOW: *Compost bins can smell and often attract flies and other insects, particularly in hot weather. For this reason, it is a good idea to locate them in a secluded part of the garden which also has good wheelbarrow access.*

Making a simple wood and glass cold frame

Tips, tools and materials

SKILL LEVEL
- This is a relatively straightforward project but some DIY skills would be useful.

BEST TIME TO DO
- Whenever the weather is reasonably fine and the ground is not too wet or muddy.

TOOLS REQUIRED
- Saw (ideally powered); powered hand drill; screwdriver; spirit level; rule; tape measure; pencil.

MATERIALS REQUIRED
- Preservative-treated softwood. Plus a sheet of exterior grade polystyrene cut to fit the lid. You will also need some hinges and offcuts to make the stays and polystyrene retention strips.

TIME REQUIRED
- 1–2 days or a weekend will normally be required to construct this wooden cold frame.

A cold frame in the garden will give you an early start to the growing season and, later on, will allow you to produce some of the more tender fruits such as peppers and cucumbers. This project shows you how to construct a cold frame that is suitable for a smaller garden, patio or balcony. It uses some very basic materials and can be scaled up or extended to make a whole series of units if required. If you make a full-size drawing of one end section you will find it easier to mark out and cut the joints. The framing is standard 50 x 50mm (2 x 2in) pressure preservative-treated softwood. Retreat any cut ends to preserve the integrity of the treatment. Once the basic carcase frame is assembled, it is simply clad with feather-edged boarding. For lightness and convenience the lid is made up with a wooden frame and a polystyrene sheet.

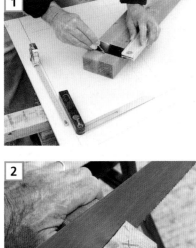

1 Begin by making a full-size drawing of the end section. Mark each piece from the drawing.

2 Once marked out, cut the shoulders of each joint to start.

3 The waste is discarded when the saw cuts down the 'cheeks' of the joints.

4 To lift the interior shelf further off the ground each bottom rail is set into the legs about 50mm (2in) up.

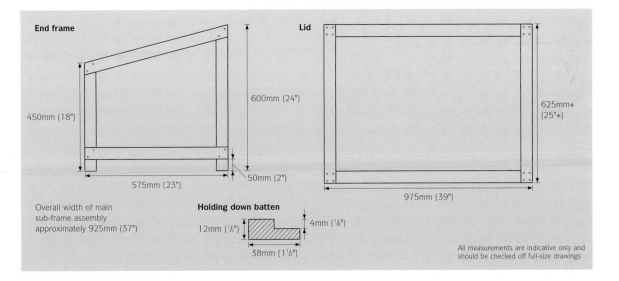

End frame

450mm (18")

575mm (23")

600mm (24")

50mm (2")

Overall width of main
sub-frame assembly
approximately 925mm (37")

Lid

625mm+
(25"+)

975mm (39")

Holding down batten

12mm (½")

4mm (⅛")

38mm (1½")

All measurements are indicative only and
should be checked off full-size drawings

5 Assemble each of
the end frames first,
followed by the four
back and front rails.

6 A single screw
into each end of
the feather-edged
boarding holds it all
in place.

7 Finish the main
container off by fitting
a mitred capping
frame around the top.
Inside the shelf, slats
can be fixed across
the lower, front and
back rails.

8 The lid is made
up from 25 x 75mm
(1 x 3in) wood with
halving joints in the
corners. Join it with a
couple of screws and
a dollop of glue to
make sure it is rigid.
Check for square,
paint and finish.

PROJECT: Making a simple wood and glass cold frame

133

Making a rabbit/ chicken hutch and run

Tips, tools and materials

SKILL LEVEL
- This is a relatively straightforward project but some DIY skills would be useful.

BEST TIME TO DO
- If building outdoors in situ, whenever the weather is reasonably fine and the ground is not too wet or muddy.

TOOLS REQUIRED
- Saw (ideally a powered bandsaw); hand drill; screwdriver; spirit level; marking gauge; rule; tape measure; pencil.

MATERIALS REQUIRED
- Preservative treated softwood; some plywood; galvanized mesh. (A small-hole, galvanized mesh is fitted to the top, two sides and one end of the run.)

TIME REQUIRED
- 1–2 days or a weekend will normally be required to construct this animal coop/ hutch and run.

This rabbit hutch and run is equally as useful for other pets such as chickens and guinea pigs. It is light and portable, relatively easy to make and can be scaled up or down to suit your specific requirements. On the front end of the hutch is a small ramp that can be raised and fixed in place to shut off the inner chamber. On the back end of the structure a full-width door opens to reveal a flush floor that enables the hutch to be easily cleaned out. Start with the lower frame construction of the hutch. Before forming the completed chamber, cut the floor so that it fits round the corner posts and onto the rails front and back. Put this in place before the roof goes on. Once the run has been made, you will need a couple of catches to hold it in place against the hutch. A pair of cabin hooks, one each side, will do the job nicely. Make sure everything is fox-proof before introducing any animals.

1 Draw out the detailed end section of your hutch on a flat board. This will help you with the proportions and scale of the project.

2 Once the drawing has been made, use it to take measurements and mark these directly onto the components.

3 Mark one of each series of pieces and then transfer these measurements to the others for the sake of consistency.

4 The interior floor of the hutch is set up off the ground; therefore, the lower rails are cut in further up rather than on the ends.

5 A marking gauge sets the depth of the halving joint on each component.

6 Some of the joints can be simply cut with a saw.

7 The joints on the bottoms of the legs have their shoulders cut first. The waste is then chiselled out level with the depth marked on the sides.

8 The main hutch structure can be made up in sections before final assembly. A spacer should be used to position the cladding. Drill a pilot hole for each screw to avoid splitting.

9 One screw only will hold each piece of cladding firmly to each piece of sub-framing. With the two sides clad, join them together with rails to form the front and back. Put the floor in as you go along.

10 The roof rafters hang over the side of the main lower

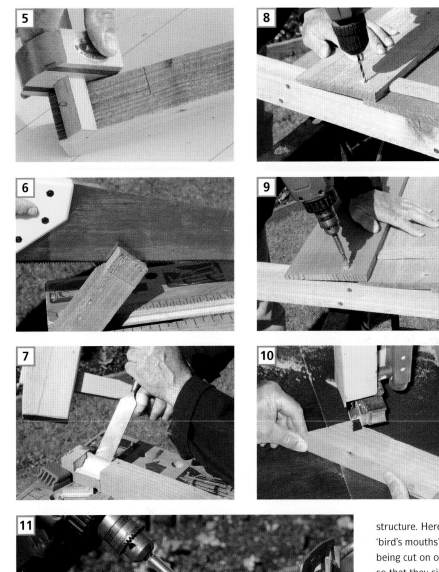

structure. Here some 'bird's mouths' are being cut on one end so that they sit firmly in place.

11 The roof pitch is set at forty five degrees so a simple mitre is all that is needed for the top of the rafters. A cramp helps to hold each one in place as the screws are driven home.

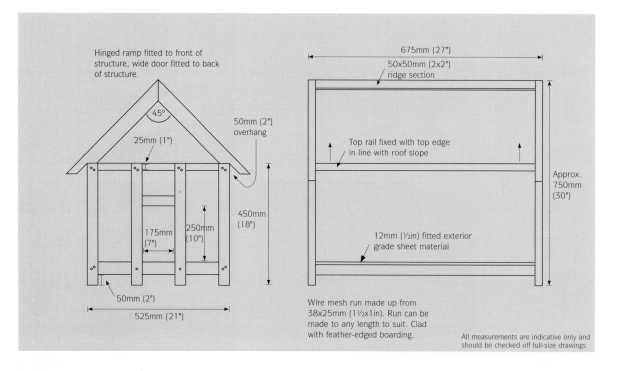

Hinged ramp fitted to front of structure, wide door fitted to back of structure.

45°

25mm (1")

50mm (2") overhang

175mm (7")

250mm (10")

450mm (18")

50mm (2")

525mm (21")

675mm (27")

50x50mm (2x2") ridge section

Top rail fixed with top edge in line with roof slope

Approx. 750mm (30")

12mm (½in) fitted exterior grade sheet material

Wire mesh run made up from 38x25mm (1½x1in). Run can be made to any length to suit. Clad with feather-edged boarding.

All measurements are indicative only and should be checked off full-size drawings

12

14

13

15

12 Cut the cladding to fit the front hutch ramp and also the pitch of the roof. These pieces are fixed in place with an end stop to ensure a tidy finish.

13 The ramp can be made up from a piece of plywood with some small slats fixed on to help the animals' feet grip as they walk up the ramp. Use a spacer to ensure that the slats are set equally apart all the way up.

14 The run should be made to fit the ramp end of the hutch and can be constructed to any length you like. The framing is made up from 38 x 50mm (1 ½in x 2in) pieces with some diagonal braces to provide strength and rigidity to the structure.

15 Before fixing on the metal mesh consider colouring the frame of the run. Some cabin hooks attached to the run and hutch will make sure everything stays correctly in place.

Adapting the design for other animals and multiple occupants

This design is based on the same construction principles used for much larger animal habitations. For example, if you wanted to keep chickens for producing eggs, you could scale up the coop to accommodate up to a dozen birds or so. The same applies to other creatures.

LEFT AND ABOVE: *This fox-proof structure is perfect for housing egg-laying chickens and cockerels.*

ABOVE: *This design will accommodate any reasonably small domestic animal and can be easily scaled up or down.*

PROJECT

Constructing a basic tool/ storage shed

Buying and erecting a pre-manufactured shed kit is an easy way to create covered and secure space quickly and inexpensively. There are a large number of options available. Some, like the example featured on these pages, will be simple four-sided structures. Others will come in several sections and will form a substantial building. Consider carefully the use to which you want to put the building and then make your choice accordingly. Hopefully the kit you purchase will have all the components required to build the shed you desire. There will be a packing list. Check this out to make sure that everything is included. Each of the pieces of wood or sheet materials will be cut to size ready for assembly. If the building has a felt roof there may be some cutting to do here but, in the main, a simple set of hand tools will be all you need to put it together. Please do read the instructions! The manufacturer will have built numerous structures before and the assembly sequences are carefully thought through. Try to avoid over-engineering the build process, so that the shed can be easily dismantled if necessary.

Tips, tools and materials

SKILL LEVEL
- This is a straightforward project but some DIY skills would be useful.

BEST TIME TO DO
- Whenever the weather is reasonably fine and the ground is not too wet or muddy.

TOOLS REQUIRED
- Saw; powered hand drill; screwdriver; spirit level; rule; protractor; tape measure; pencil.

MATERIALS REQUIRED
- Preservative-treated softwood. (This project is based upon a ready-made kit. These are widely available, but you could construct a shed to your own design by adapting the instructions on these pages.)

TIME REQUIRED
- 1–2 days or a weekend will normally be required to construct a shed of this type.

1 When your kit has been collected or delivered lay everything out on a flat surface adjacent to where the shed is to be erected and check through the contents list. Any missing pieces should be identified and the supplier contacted for replacements. Do not be tempted to make a start without absent components.

2 Having chosen the location of your building, lay out the base. Sometimes these come with bearers already attached. Level the base up in both planes using a medium or long length spirit level.

3 Read the instructions! Some will advise part assembly of the door into the end, for example. Only vary the sequence of construction if you are confident you can complete the project correctly at the end.

4 If the door is to be fitted lay the end section down on a flat surface to start. Position the hinges so that the bearers on the back of the door will take the screws as they go through the facing.

5 Start the building assembly by positioning one side on the base. Help to hold it at this point would be useful but not essential. Brace off any adjacent structure or, in this case the tree! If nothing is handy, drive a short post in nearby and brace from that.

6 Attach the back piece of the shed to the first side next. Don't make this a permanent job yet; just loosely fix a couple of screws to hold the panels in place. The other side should then be attached loosely in the same manner. Ideally the jointing sections on the pieces should have pilot holes drilled into them to take the screws easily and to make the overall assembly less fraught.

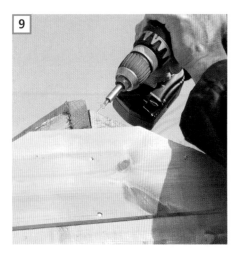

7 Once all four sides are connected and the building has been checked for square, make the job permanent. Fix extra screws in the corners and down into the base of the shed.

8 You may have already fitted the door furniture when the door was originally hung. If not, do so now.

9 To complete this part of the building fit and fix the ridge into place. Larger buildings may have additional rafters and braces to be fitted at this stage, as well.

10 Roofs are usually made up from one or more pieces of sheet material. As per the instructions, fit any battens to these sheets before mounting them on the building.

11 Some help in holding the roof panels in place at this stage would be useful. Tack the first into place, as near as you can. Position the second one, tacking and adjusting it until it is in the correct place, then finish off by bringing the first panel up to it.

12 A felt roof cover is likely to come in a roll. Pick a warm, but not hot, day to handle this. If it's too hot the felt can have a tendency to tear and the asphalt will be sticky and difficult to handle. If the roll of roofing felt is too cold it will crack. Measure the lengths you need and cut them to size with a sharp knife. When measuring out, allow plenty of overlap at this stage.

13 Most felting operations will firstly involve placing the material on one side with the overlap going over the top. A few of the supplied wide-headed tacks will hold this in place. The second is then positioned and overlaps the first. Use no more than the recommended amount of nails to fix the felt down. Too many will provide more potential for leaks.

14 Now most of the exterior of the building is completed. There will be a number of pieces of trim to affix which are designed to tidy up the edges. Fix these in place now.

Alternative materials for garden sheds

Although a pre-manufactured, ready to assemble shed kit offers a practical storage solution, it is not the most stylish or individualistic of items. As an alternative, you could consider going to your local reclamation yard and buying old timber to construct something more characterful (see right).

ABOVE: *Some gardeners favour sheds made of metal, because they do not rot, are inexpensive and impressively weatherproof. A bright colour adds a touch of individualism.*

RIGHT: *Rustic materials for sheds and outbuildings work well in informal gardens.*

15 At the roof ends there will be some pre-shaped 'barge boards' to go on. Take care that the fixing nails go into solid wood behind.

16 The last job before occupancy will be to fix in place any windows. On most models, the weather bar at the bottom is designed to help the water run off, not in. Make sure you get it the right way round.

The shed interior

Once you have erected your ready-to-assemble shed or constructed one to your own design, it is time to turn your attention to the interior. Think about what you intend the main purpose of the shed to be. Will you be spending much time in the shed? In this case, it might be worth insulating the interior, perhaps laying a carpet or vinyl flooring and installing sources of heat and light. Do you need to maximize your storage space? Now might be the time to build in some additional shelving to your own specification and put up some racks and tool hooks. If you plan to work in the shed as well as using it for storage, it might be worth installing a free-standing or permanent workbench and maybe a stool.

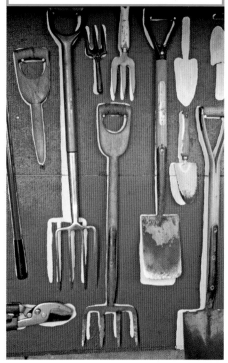

LEFT AND OPPOSITE: *The completed structure. If you follow the instructions to the letter and do not over-complicate the construction, the shed will be easy to dismantle and relocate in the future.*

Garden furniture

Garden furniture can be expensive to buy and is often mass-produced. How many times have you seen the same bench or table and chair set in friends' or neighbours' gardens? Many self-assembly items are also often poorly manufactured or constructed from inferior materials. For these reasons, if you have some basic DIY skills it is often a better idea to create your own purpose-built, individualistic items.

This section of the book offers a broad selection of wood- and canvas-based projects for the handy gardener who wants to create something different. There is both practical furniture for day-to-day use and a swing and tree hammock for relaxation after a hard day's gardening. As always, these projects can all be easily modified or adapted.

General design tips for

garden furniture

Coming home at the end of a day at work, school or college and taking a seat in a quiet corner of the garden helps recharge the batteries. Relax in a swing seat and let the gentle rocking dispel stress or sit beneath a bower of fragrant flowers listening to the sound of a trickling fountain!

Take time to position seats carefully, creating a landscape around them that is conducive to relaxation, which invites use or which emphasizes their importance in the overall design.

ABOVE: *This tranquil bower and seat positioned beside a decorated patio is a perfect place to relax.*

Year round seating

A permanent seat beckons you out into the garden and helps to create a relaxed and carefree atmosphere. You are much more likely to sit out for a few moments if the furniture is already available, not locked away in the shed! The weather can be so changeable and you sometimes have unexpectedly bright warm days in winter and early spring when being out in the garden would be a real treat. Anticipate using the garden out of season, so to speak, by positioning a bench in the most sheltered and sunny part of the garden, perhaps against a warm wall. If the garden is quite exposed, consider erecting some trellis panels to create a little more shelter. Surround the seat with pots of winter and spring bedding and bulbs, especially fragrant varieties, so that you are sitting in an oasis of colour, even when the rest of the garden is quiet.

BELOW: *This highly unusual covered seat is a permanent fixture made from all-natural materials. It blends seamlessly into the surrounding landscape.*

BELOW RIGHT: *Al fresco dining is one of the great pleasures of outdoor living and a good reason to build your own bespoke garden furniture!*

Outdoor living

On the terrace, deck or patio, a table and chairs set or picnic table arrangement with bench seats encourages dining al fresco, especially when the furniture is conveniently close to a barbeque or outdoor kitchen. Food and drink seem to taste better outdoors and you can make the most of any fine weather by eating breakfast or sipping coffee facing the morning sun (you will need a sheltered, east-facing spot); relaxing at lunchtime in the dappled shade of a pergola or sipping a glass of wine with friends at sunset (west-facing) surrounded by the soft mood lighting of candles and lanterns so that you can carry on chatting long after sundown. Raised beds, retaining walls and shallow steps can double as impromptu seating for when guests arrive unexpectedly. Keep some outdoor cushions and throws to hand for extra comfort and warmth.

LEFT: *Not all garden furniture need be fancy and brand new looking. A homemade rustic bench will complement a potting shed or vegetable patch far better than a slick-looking metal table and chairs from the local garden centre or DIY store.*

Functional seating

Don't forget that you also need seats in more workaday parts of your plot such as overlooking a vegetable garden or next to the potting shed. When you have been hard at work it feels good to sit for a while, rest your back and survey your progress. A few moments calm contemplation halfway through a gardening job can sometimes make all the difference to the success of the final outcome. A seat next to the back door, perhaps surrounded by potted herbs and salads, would be a useful spot for taking time out from cooking or household chores. This kind of seating doesn't need to be particularly stylish or ornate. A simple bench made from reclaimed timber supported on brick or breeze block 'legs' would suffice. Rustic furniture works particularly well in the productive garden. If you have a formal potager (vegetable garden), consider placing an arbour at the end of a straight pathway to draw the eye towards it and make it more of a feature.

Contemplative mood

Being out in the garden, either tending plants or simply relaxing, helps us to feel closer to nature. A well-placed seat or hammock could become a spot in which to contemplate wildlife. If you have an old tree in the garden, a seat built around its base encourages you to sit under the shelter of its branches, leaning back against the trunk listening to the melodious strains of bird song. Try putting a simple bench seat next to

a pond – you will be mesmerized by the toings and froings of the wildlife it will attract! Water is such a magnet for creatures of all shapes and sizes, including dazzling dragonflies, frogs and, at dusk, bats. Birds will soon become used to you sitting in the same spot, so to get a really good view, position feeders and a water bath near to a bench that is part-camouflaged with climbers and shrubs. Or why not rig up a hammock in the flower garden and lie in it with your eyes closed focusing on the steady hum of bees? As with all the projects in this book, the choice is yours as to how you interpret them. Think about your preferences and then follow or adapt one of the ideas in these pages as you see fit.

ABOVE: *A garden hammock is a timeless luxury that any busy gardener should have the right to enjoy! See the hammock construction project on pages 168–171.*

garden furniture

ABOVE: You can use banks and screens of plants to create a sense of seclusion in even the smallest plot. The plants will insulate the garden from external noise and reduce the likelihood of being overlooked by neighbours.

RIGHT: Create secret corners in your garden and locate seats and other furniture in them. A canopy will enhance the feeling of privacy and will help protect any furniture placed beneath.

Urban seclusion

To emphasize the sensation of getting away from it all for a while, especially in a town or city location, set at least one seat in a place hidden from overlooking windows, preferably in a spot where you can't see the house or those of any of your neighbours. In small urban plots this can be particularly difficult. Try creating overhead cover with a climber-clad pergola or for a lighter effect, use heavy gauge galvanized wires strung between walls using vine eyes. Cover with a tracery of climbers and hang a wind chime to counter any man-made noise. You could also use a sail-like awning that is wound out across the space as required, or put up a large canvas sunshade or gazebo for the summer. Plants have significant sound dampening qualities, so clothe walls and fences with climbers and wall shrubs and plant a deep mixed border between the road or noise source and the garden. Include some small trees to filter the wind and therefore sound. This arrangement might make the sitting area smaller but cocooned by foliage and flower, unable to

see the garden's boundaries, you will feel protected from the outside world and more able to enjoy the experience of being outside.

Seat locations

A seat can become a strong focal point in the garden and there are a number of classic positions you can use to create impact or appeal with a bench or arbour. When a seat is situated in a formal hedge or border alcove, you come across it unexpectedly. In relaxed rural or cottage-style gardens you might even have an arc of stepping stones leading to a bench set deep within a border. Sitting there, half-hidden by foliage and sheltered from the wind, creates a feeling of seclusion and child-like amusement as you view the garden unseen by others. Similarly, try putting a seat in a secret corner – an offshoot from the main garden or lawn area, for example, that is accessed by a narrow opening cut in a hedge, say. Create a special atmosphere for this type of garden by setting up a modest fountain, planting a circular scented lawn or laying a mosaic floor.

A bench or arbour at the end of a pathway draws attention immediately and encourages you forward. Sitting at the head of a major garden axis, whether a paved path, long lawn, canal or rill, gives you prime position. A place to survey your domain! A seat at the highest point of a garden also has a similar appeal. If you want to make a short garden appear longer, place the bench in one corner to draw the eye across the longer diagonal line and curve the lawn or border towards it.

General pointers

Furniture can work as an ornamental feature if it has pleasing sculptural or architectural lines. You can also make it more eye-catching by painting or staining it in an attractive shade. Pick a product designed for exterior woodwork. Newly pressure-treated wood tends to repel stains and paints and might have to be left to weather for a few months.

Set the legs of wooden tables and chairs on paving or gravel if possible to lessen the chances of rotting. Do this even if the bench is set within a border or on a lawn. Simple benches set on brick or breeze block legs take much longer to rot provided they can dry off between rain showers.

Consider using reclaimed hardwood timbers to make your own simple furniture pieces, which are more durable than untreated softwoods like pine. Reclaimed wood and rustic timber already look weathered and fit in well with the garden. Otherwise choose pressure-treated, tanalized timber for outdoor work rather than wood that has merely been dipped. Ask your local timber or builder's merchant or salvage yard to advise on the different qualities of the various woods.

ABOVE: *Sometimes a single piece of garden furniture can act as an eye-catching feature in its own right, provided it is sufficiently ornate or painted in a bright colour. Much also depends on how the piece is positioned.*

LEFT: *Reclaimed timber is generally quite inexpensive and can be used to create garden furniture with an ancient, weathered quality and feel. Pieces like this look best when they are located in the wildest, most informal parts of the garden.*

Making wooden seating around a tree trunk

Tips, tools and materials

SKILL LEVEL
- This is a fairly advanced project requiring strong DIY skills.

BEST TIME TO DO
- Whenever the weather is reasonably fine and the ground is not too wet or muddy.

TOOLS REQUIRED
- Saw (ideally a powered bandsaw); router (not essential but useful); hand drill; chisel; screwdriver; spirit level; marking gauge; rule; tape measure; pencil.

MATERIALS REQUIRED
- Preservative-treated softwood framing with applied hardwood seat slats. The latter will require about 70m (225ft) of 25mm (1in) nominal seat slat/batten material 32mm (1¼in) or more wide.

TIME REQUIRED
- 4–5 days or at least two weekends will normally be required to construct this tree seating.

A tree seat is a great way to smarten up your garden. This one uses basic materials but is shapely, stylish and very comfortable with its curved seat and sloping back. It is made in two halves so that it can easily be fitted around a tree. It might seem obvious, but you should always check that the centre hole in the tree seat is big enough for the intended tree and that there is plenty of room for growth. The seat may look silly with a small sapling in place when you first construct it, but once that sapling grows into a full-size tree the seat may be too small! Do bear this in mind as you build – it can be an easy thing to overlook at the outset. This tree seat can be scaled up or down in size, but anything much larger will require extra sections. The curve in the seat is a stylish design feature which also makes it particularly comfortable to sit on.

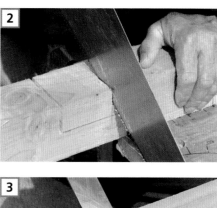

1 Mark out the joints on the sub-frame sections. This is a fairly straightforward job but would be greatly helped by the production of full-size drawings in advance of commencing the project.

2 All joints in this project are simple butt or halving types. Cut the shoulders first and follow on with the cheeks, making the cuts as neatly and precisely as you can.

3 If it is a 'T' halving joint the waste is cut away with a chisel. Ensure that the chisel is very sharp before you start and that you can make the cuts neatly and accurately. The tightness of the joints will ultimately make all the difference to the comfort and stability of the finished tree seat.

4 Once all the joints have been made for the leg assemblies, fix them together. Use a G-clamp to secure the pieces to the workbench as you fix them up together. Check that each of the legs is properly square off the seat rail. Make any adjustments as necessary. When fixing the pieces together, a couple of screws and a dollop of glue per joint will do nicely. Clean away any excess glue as you work.

5 The seat is curved for comfort. Make a pattern with a pencil and a piece of paper, cut out one piece as a template and then mark out each of the assembled leg frames in turn.

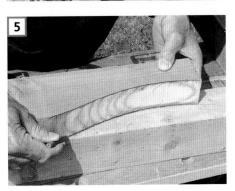

Cutting list

Component:	Qty:	LENGTH nominal:	WIDTH finished:	THICKNESS finished:
Back legs:	4	1m/39in	75mm/3in	75mm/3in
	4	1m/39in	75mm/3in	38mm/1½in
Front legs:	4	450mm/18in	75mm/3in	75mm/3in
	4	450mm/18in	75mm/3in	38mm/1½in
Seat rails:	4	750mm/30in	75mm/3in	75mm/3in
	4	750mm/30in	75mm/3in	38mm/1½in
Back rails:	4	450mm/18in	75mm/3in	50mm/2in
	4	450mm18in	38mm/1½in	50mm/2in
Sub-frame braces:	6	900mm/36in	75mm/3in	25mm/1in
Top frame capping:	6	450mm/18in	100mm/4in	25mm/1in

6 The shaping process is made a lot easier through the use of a bandsaw, if you have one. If not, cut the pieces by hand as accurately as possible and then finish them off neatly with a spokeshave or belt sander.

7 The back rails need to have the appropriate angles cut on each end for a tight fit. Again, mark one piece up, cut it out and then use it to apply the same angles to the other back rails. Once this is done, fix the pieces in place with screws and glue.

8 For added strength, although this is not absolutely necessary, some diagonal braces can also be fitted into the lower part of the leg corner joints..

9 Working off a flat surface, and ideally with a helping hand, cut and fix on the top frame capping. This should overhang the front of the back rails by the thickness of the seat slats or thereabouts. It will then sit about flush with the slats when they have been fixed on to the seat frame.

10 Cut and fix on the sub-frame braces. A couple of small, wedge-shaped supports secured in each corner will give these a bit of extra strength.

11 Starting at the lower, front of each section, cut the seat slats/battens to fit onto each of the six sections. If you start with the longer ones at the front first, any errors you make can be cut back, with little waste, for a following slat.

OPPOSITE: *The finished item, sitting neatly around a cherry tree.*

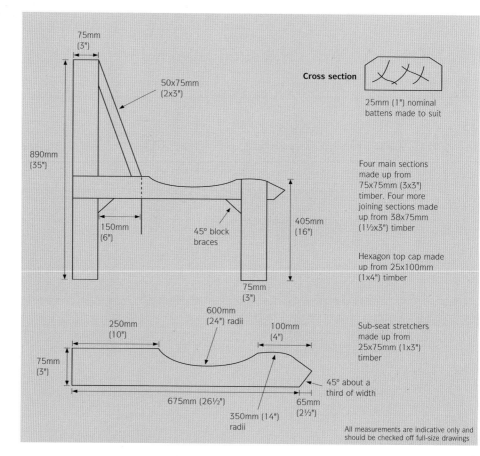

75mm (3")

50x75mm (2x3")

Cross section

25mm (1") nominal battens made to suit

890mm (35")

150mm (6")

45° block braces

405mm (16")

Four main sections made up from 75x75mm (3x3") timber. Four more joining sections made up from 38x75mm (1½x3") timber

Hexagon top cap made up from 25x100mm (1x4") timber

75mm (3")

600mm (24") radii

250mm (10")

100mm (4")

Sub-seat stretchers made up from 25x75mm (1x3") timber

75mm (3")

675mm (26½")

350mm (14") radii

65mm (2½")

45° about a third of width

All measurements are indicative only and should be checked off full-size drawings

8

10

9

11

Making a rustic table and benches

Tips, tools and materials

SKILL LEVEL
- This is an intermediate level project requiring some DIY skills.

BEST TIME TO DO
- Whenever the weather is reasonably fine and the ground is not too wet or muddy.

TOOLS REQUIRED
- Saw (ideally a powered bandsaw); router (not essential but useful); hand drill; chisel; screwdriver; spirit level; straight edge; marking gauge; rule; tape measure; pencil.

MATERIALS REQUIRED
- Preservative-treated softwood. (See the cutting list on the opposite page for quantities required.).

TIME REQUIRED
- 2–3 days or maybe two weekends will normally be required to construct this table and benches.

When the weather is suitable, outdoor eating is becoming more and more popular. With global warming increasing temperatures the further north we go, it is likely that this will be an ever-increasing trend. This project provides you with an opportunity to make and build a table and benches set for just that purpose – al fresco dining with style. The design of this table and benches set is simple and attractive. It offers you the potential to increase or decrease the dimensions to suit the space available. The basic sub-frame structure remains the same, but the top of the table and seats can be lengthened or shortened as desired. Any outdoor furniture, if left in the garden all year, will eventually weather down to a light grey colour. Using coloured shades can be an attractive alternative and there are many different types on the market.

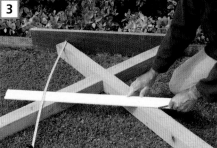

1 Start out by laying a pair of legs on a flat surface. Use some short pieces to pack up the top leg and a straight length to mimic the ground level. The cross-over position should be at right-angles. Adjust until the legs suit your requirements.

2 The legs are simply joined using cross-halving joints. Once you have marked them out cut the shoulders and then chop out the waste with a chisel.

3 Having made the joint, with the correct lower leg length, place the bottom of the legs against a straight edge. Now measure up the desired amount to the underside of the top and, making sure it is parallel, mark across the top edges of the legs.

4 Each set of legs are sawn off to length and halving joints cut into the tops to accept the cross rails. Once this is done, the joints should then be fixed with glue and screws.

5 Each end of the top rails has an angle cut on it. The width of these rails should be enough to accommodate the top planks. The halving joints should be slightly shallower in depth so that the rails protrude slightly above and beyond the ends of the legs.

6 To hold the top portion of the sub-frame together there are two link rails set into the top rails. Trenches are cut to accommodate these. Once in place these long, link rails should not protrude above the top rails.

Cutting list

Component:	Qty:	LENGTH nominal:	WIDTH finished:	THICKNESS finished:
THE TABLE:				
Top:	6	2m/6ft6in	150mm/6in	50mm/2in
Legs:	4	1m/3ft3in	75mm/3in	75mm/3in
Centre rail:	1	2m/6ft6in	75mm/3in	75mm/3in
Top rails:	2	1m/3ft3in	75mm/3in	50mm/2in
Top, link rails:	2	2m/6ft6in	75mm/3in	25mm/1in
TWO BENCHES:				
Seats:	6	2m/6ft6in	100mm/4in	50mm/2in
Legs:	8	600mm/24in	50mm/2in	50mm/2in
Top rails:	4	400mm/15in	75mm/3in	50mm/2in
Centre rails:	2	2m/6ft6in	50mm/2in	50mm/2in

7 Once they have been made each top rail is attached to the leg assembly with plenty of glue and screws at each end.

8 To avoid the top width of each bench being too wide, the legs are trimmed off.

9 The construction of the bench legs is similar to that for the table.

10 If the sub-frames of the tables and benches are to be coloured now is a good time to do it.

11 Assemble the table sub-frame by fixing, with glue and long screws, the lower, centre rail. Then fix the two link rails, making sure that everything is square.

12 Place the table top boards onto the sub-assembly. When you have positioned the two outside pieces, use a straight edge to line up their ends. The centre rails for the benches are screwed and glued on through the bottom faces. Just as with the top of the table, the bench seat slats are fixed on with a couple of screws each at even intervals.

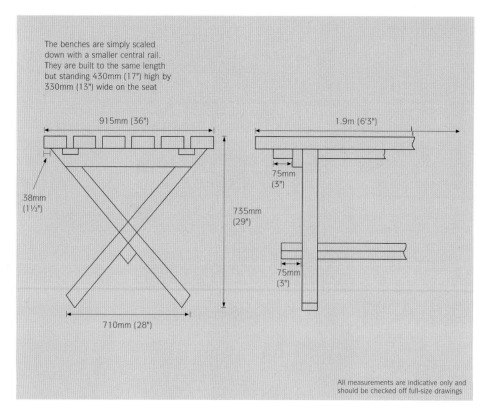

The benches are simply scaled down with a smaller central rail. They are built to the same length but standing 430mm (17") high by 330mm (13") wide on the seat

915mm (36")

1.9m (6'3")

75mm (3")

38mm (1½")

735mm (29")

75mm (3")

710mm (28")

All measurements are indicative only and should be checked off full-size drawings

OPPOSITE: *The finished table and benches. Provided you use preservative-treated wood in the construction, these can be left outdoors all year round. However, they will weather and might benefit from being covered.*

Making an arbour with a seat

Tips, tools and materials

SKILL LEVEL
- This is a fairly advanced project requiring strong DIY skills.

BEST TIME TO DO
- Whenever the weather is reasonably fine and the ground is not too wet or muddy.

TOOLS REQUIRED
- Saw (ideally a powered bandsaw); router (not essential but useful); over and under planer; hand drill; chisel; screwdriver; spirit level; marking gauge; rule; tape measure; pencil.

MATERIALS REQUIRED
- Preservative-treated softwood framing with applied hard- or softwood seat slats. (See the cutting list on the opposite page for quantities required.)

TIME REQUIRED
- 2–3 days or perhaps two weekends will normally be required to construct this arbour and seat.

Sitting on a comfortable bench with a scented rose or climber close at hand is a nice way to relax in your garden. This integrated seat and trellis – traditionally known as an arbour – can achieve that for you. It could be free-standing or incorporated into a grander scheme of things. The shaped seat and sloped back, along with the wide arms, make it an ideal place to sit and have your 'sun-downer'. The seat slats can be made from a hardwood and left natural, or softwood and coloured. Don't use anything much over 50mm (2in) wide, unless it is intended for the back. Narrower slats will follow the contour of the seat much better and will make it more comfortable to sit on. Even if you are planning on colouring this project in only one shade, as opposed to the two shown here, try to plan ahead and cover any awkward spots before final assembly.

1 All the joints are simple halving, butt or bridle joints. Here the two bridle joints for the tops of the back legs are carefully marked out.

2 Cutting on the waste side of the lines the cheeks of the joints are sawn firstly from one side and then from the other.

3 The waste is trimmed out with a chisel and left for final fitting once the tenon part of the bridle joint is made.

4 With the second part made, the joint should be tested for fit and any adjustments made as necessary. The tighter the joints, the better the final assembly.

5 Some of the halving joints are part way up the legs. The shoulders should be cut first and then a series of further cuts should be made to help with waste removal.

6 A chisel and mallet will soon clean out the waste wood. Trim the recess back level with the lines marked on the faces.

7 If you have a hard, flat surface available it is often better to work off this than, say, a lawn, when assembling larger structures. Each joint should have pilot holes drilled into it before gluing and screwing up takes place.

8 The front rail is attached to the legs with a halving joint and plenty of screws. Once it is set square, fix on a piece of gash stock, across the legs, to keep them in place until assembly.

Cutting list

Component:	Qty:	LENGTH nominal:	WIDTH finished:	THICKNESS finished:
Back posts/legs:	2	2280mm/90in	75mm/3in	75mm/3in
Front legs:	2	900mm/36in	75mm/3in	75mm/3in
Top rail:	1	1675mm/66in	100mm/4in	50mm/2in
Seat, back frames:	3	600mm/24in	100mm/4in	50mm/2in
Seat bases:	3	750mm/30in	100mm/4in	50mm/2in
Back middle and lower rails:	2	1675mm/66in	100mm/4in	25mm/1in
Front rail:	1	1675mm/66in	100mm/4in	25mm/1in
Arms:	2	750mm/30in	100mm/4in	25mm/1in
Trellis frame:	4	1675mm/66in	50mm/2in	25mm/1in
Trellis laths, about:	16	1800mm/72in	50mm/2in	12mm/½in
Seat slats, about:	18	1500mm/60in	38mm/1½in	22mm/7/8in

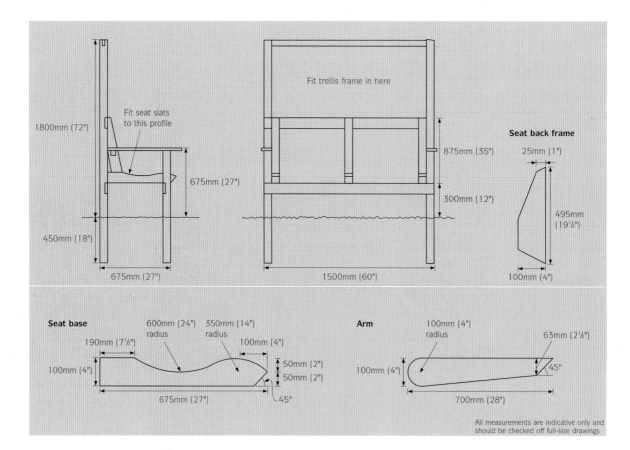

1800mm (72")

Fit seat slats to this profile

675mm (27")

450mm (18")

675mm (27")

Fit trellis frame in here

875mm (35")

300mm (12")

1500mm (60")

Seat back frame

25mm (1")

495mm (19½")

100mm (4")

Seat base

190mm (7½")

600mm (24") radius

350mm (14") radius

100mm (4")

100mm (4")

50mm (2")

50mm (2")

675mm (27")

45°

Arm

100mm (4") radius

63mm (2½")

100mm (4")

45°

700mm (28")

All measurements are indicative only and should be checked off full-size drawings

9 The curved seat bases make it comfortable. They can be cut by hand or on a bandsaw.

10 Once the seat bases and back frames have been fitted, a small bracket needs to be fixed on to support the arms at the back. The other ends are fixed to the top of the front legs.

11 Shaping the arms can be done with anything that comes to hand!

12 The trellis and frame is made up in two sessions. Use halving joints in the corners of the frame and then fit one lot of trellis only.

13 Paint the trellis as you wish, let the paint dry thoroughly, and then begin final assembly. Use the same spacer bar to ensure the trellis 'diamonds' are balanced across the entire design.

14 The seat slats should be fairly narrow to help follow the contour of the curved seat base. Once they have been prepared, cut the slats to length and

Plants for growing on arbours

For centuries arbours have been used to grow climbing plants, both for decorative effects and for produce. A well-established vine like the one shown in the picture above both provides shelter for the seat and a rich supply of fruit, come the season. A sturdy structure is required for a plant of this weight and volume, but if you are looking for lighter alternatives there are many, from the countless varieties of clematis to hop plants (*Humulus lupulus*), bougainvillea, honeysuckle and periwinkle.

TOP AND ABOVE: *The vine draped over the arbour in the picture at the top of this box is* Vitis coignetiae – *a vigorous climbing plant. The clematis shown above is the flower of* Clematis *'H.F. Young'.*

pre-drill them ready
for fixing on to the
seat frame.

15 Paint the seat
slats, and anything
else that still requires
decorating, at this
stage, prior to final
assembly. Use an
external paint or
wood preservative
if the structure is to
remain uncovered.

16 Attach the
trellis panel to the
seat frame using half
a dozen or so evenly
spaced screws along
each side.

17 Some of the
slats may need to be
trimmed to go round
the front legs. If this
was not done earlier,
some touching up
on the ends might
be necessary at this
point.

18 Each slat
should be fixed in
place using one screw
per rail. Start at
the front and work
backwards, using
spacers to make sure
they are even.

OPPOSITE: *The finished
item. This one has
been painted in a
slightly different
colour scheme. It can
be left free-standing
or attached to a
structure, as you see fit.*

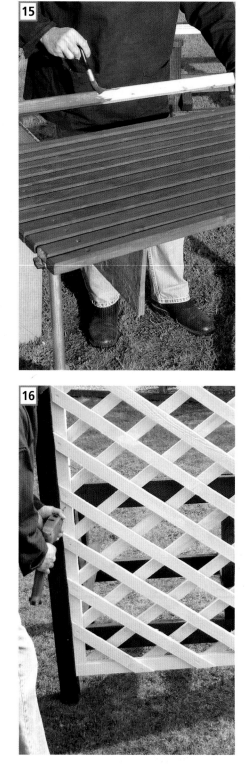

15

17

16

18

Garden furniture

Making a wooden and canvas swing seat

Tips, tools and materials

SKILL LEVEL
- This is an intermediate level project for which some basic DIY skills would prove very useful.

BEST TIME TO DO
- Whenever the weather is reasonably fine and the ground is not too wet or muddy.

TOOLS REQUIRED
- Saw; chainsaw (not essential but useful); hacksaw; hand drill; chisel; rasp; screwdriver; spirit level; marking gauge; rule; tape measure; pencil.

MATERIALS REQUIRED
- Preservative-treated fencing rails and poles; canopy sheet; two metal seat brackets; some chain; connectors.

TIME REQUIRED
- 2–3 days or perhaps two weekends will normally be required to construct this wooden and canvas swing seat.

This is a distinctly 'rustic' project that uses a core of basic fencing rails and poles as its basis. However, the result is just as useful and comfortable as a seat made with much more expensive material. Made as a 'two seater', the project could easily be extended to sit three, but probably no more. There are no fancy joints involved and the project can be made in fairly short order. However, there is a requirement for a couple of simple metal frames to be made up. These have a dual purpose; they provide the seat with strength and enable the hanging chains to be attached. Any blacksmith can make the pieces up for you and they should not be too expensive. As each seat will vary slightly in size, make yours up first before ordering the metal sub-structures. A fabric screen or a full-blown canopy can be fitted to the top of the seat to provide shade and shelter.

1 Start by laying out two of the side rails. They should be crossed over with the flat faces together. Remember to 'hand' each frame when it is made up so that the front and back legs match evenly. This will make for a more stable finished seat.

2 When the centre point of the cross over has been found, drill a single 10mm (3/8in) or 12mm (½in) hole through both pieces.

3 Connect the two sections together with coach bolts that are long enough to go right through both pieces. Alternatively, use a threaded bar, with nuts and washers on both sides, and cut it off dead to length, as shown. If a bar is used, file off any rough ends.

4 Cut the side braces to length and fix them onto the lower part of the legs on each side. Two large screws at each end should be enough to secure them. Now drive in two more screws adjacent to the centre bolt to give that joint more strength.

5 The higher part of the side frame assembly protrudes above the top pole to take the screen or canopy. Mark the required lengths out with a slightly longer one in front to give the structure a backwards tilt.

6 Saw off the top pieces so that they are even and keep the offcuts. They will be used for braces and small support blocks later on. The beauty of using rustic fencing posts and rails for this project is that there is very little wastage of materials.

7 The top pole needs to be slightly notched to fit over each side frame. It is quickest to use a chainsaw for this purpose, but the cuts can be made by hand if you do not own one. Use a rasp to clear out any excess wood and to make the notch smooth.

8 To fit the top pole you will need some help to hold the side frame assemblies. The alternative is to use a couple of saw horses and clamp the frames to them. Either way, ensure the structure is steady.

9 Once the top pole is in place, square up the whole lot and fit the one long, back rail. Make sure it is level, then fix it to the frame with screws at both ends.

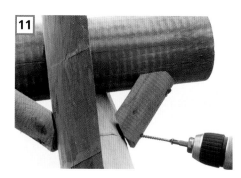

10 From the offcuts previously saved, cut the braces. Use some longer ones across the back rail and legs.

11 A short brace each side of the top rail will not impede the chains for the swinging seat.

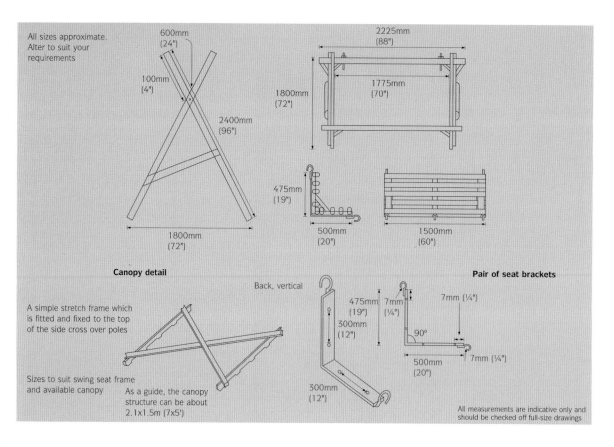

All sizes approximate. Alter to suit your requirements

600mm (24")

100mm (4")

2400mm (96")

1800mm (72")

2225mm (88")

1800mm (72")

1775mm (70")

475mm (19")

500mm (20")

1500mm (60")

Canopy detail

A simple stretch frame which is fitted and fixed to the top of the side cross over poles

Sizes to suit swing seat frame and available canopy

As a guide, the canopy structure can be about 2.1x1.5m (7x5')

Back, vertical

475mm (19")

300mm (12")

300mm (12")

7mm (¼")

Pair of seat brackets

7mm (¼")

90°

500mm (20")

7mm (¼")

All measurements are indicative only and should be checked off full-size drawings

12 The top pole needs to be drilled to take the two eyes from which the seat will be suspended. Make sure that the centres are an exact match to the seat frame.

13 The seat is simply constructed from some of the smaller sections of half round poles. The three back rails are notched to take the three seat rails.

14 Fix each half round pole to the rails with two screws each. This time the flat faces are not put together.

15 A couple of long screws through the back joint will connect the two parts of the seat together. Cut some short braces to fit in between the gaps. Paint the structure to your preference.

16 Fit and fix on the two metal straps and hanging hooks to the underside of the seat. This holds everything in place and provides the points from which to hang the seat. The canopy/screen frame is fairly lightweight and should be made to suit the cover.

ABOVE: *The finished swing seat. Painted in a stylish two-tone scheme, as here, the seat looks remarkably sophisticated, considering it is made from such inexpensive, rustic-style materials. Dress the seat with cushions for maximum comfort.*

PROJECT: Making a wooden and canvas swing seat

167

Making a tree hammock

Tips, tools and materials

SKILL LEVEL
- This is an intermediate level project for which some basic DIY skills would prove very useful.

BEST TIME TO DO
- Whenever the weather is reasonably fine and the ground is not too wet or muddy.

TOOLS REQUIRED
- Saw; hacksaw; hand drill; chisel; plane; screwdriver; spirit level; marking gauge; rule; tape measure; pencil.

MATERIALS REQUIRED
- Rope; canvas; wood. Plus some good quality string, for finishing off, and some cable ties to secure the rings.

TIME REQUIRED
- 1–2 days or perhaps a weekend will normally be required to construct this wooden and canvas hammock.

Although there are a huge number of hammocks available on the market it is often fun to make up your own unique version. The most common type of hammock is made up from knotted ropes. However, a more comfortable and secure solution is to use a sheet of canvas as the key component. Any good marquee, tent or sail maker should be able to supply and make up the canvas base to your specification. If you find it difficult to source the canvas, try a ship's chandler. Once you have the canvas to hand, make up a solid wood bar for each end. This should be something substantial with no knots or other defects in it. The rope needs to be load-bearing, so check with your supplier that it will stand the weight of a fairly heavy person. Use one single shade of rope or mix coloured ropes to add a bit of life and visual flair to the project.

1 With the basic canvas hammock made up, lay it out on a flat surface to calculate the other material requirements.

2 A strong, defect-free piece of hardwood is required for each end. Having planed it up and removed the edges, mark out and drill the holes centrally.

3 The ends also need to be chamfered and the holes countersunk.

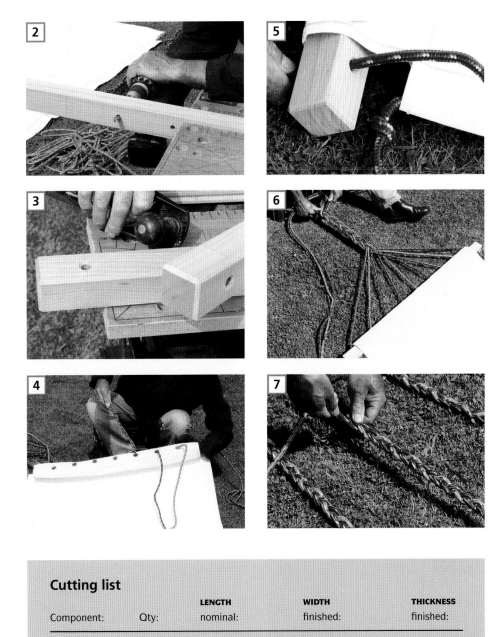

4 Each shorter length of rope is knotted and threaded through the seven middle holes of each of the two end bars. Feed the tail ends of these ropes through the eyelets before inserting the bars in the end sleeves on the canvas.

5 The two outside ropes are threaded through the long sleeves and knotted on the inside face of the bar before being passed through. This ensures that all nine lengths of rope emerging each end are of a similar length.

6 Securely fix one end of the hammock and start work on the other. A group of three sets of three ropes are firmly grasped and plaited to form the central suspending cord. Start the plaiting process about 300mm (12in) out from the end.

7 An alternative plaiting method for the ropes is to use three individual plaits. Start the plaiting process the same distance out from the end as above (see Step 6).

Cutting list

Component:	Qty:	LENGTH nominal:	WIDTH finished:	THICKNESS finished:
The canvas:	1	2.1m/7ft	1m/3ft3in	
The bars:	2	1m/3ft3in	45mm/1¾in	45mm/1¾in
The rope:	1 or more	45m/150ft or more	12mm/½in or bigger	
The metalwork:	2	50mm/2in strong, galvanized rings		

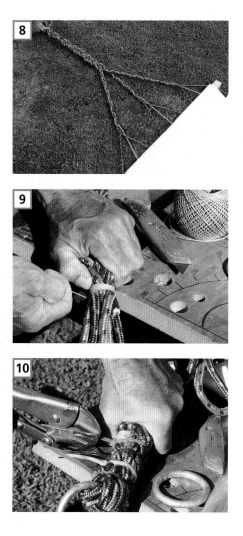

8 The three plaited sections are then plaited together into one combined tail rope at a further point.

9 Each end of the main, central cord is then tied off. Use a good quality string to bind and sow the ends together. Trim off the excess when finished.

10 You will need a strong metal ring as a connector. Fold the main cord through this so that the end is on the underside. Use some quality cable ties to joint this bulk together. Trim the tails off.

OPPOSITE AND BELOW:
The finished hammock and another example made from rope mesh.

The history of the hammock

The hammock was developed in Pre-Columbian Latin America and continues to be produced widely throughout the region. Though it is unknown exactly who invented the hammock, many maintain that it was a device created out of tradition and need. The English language derivation of hammock and various European equivalents was borrowed from the Spanish word *hamaca* or *hamac* around 1700, which in turn was taken from a Taíno culture Arawakan word (a society living on the island of Haiti) meaning 'fish net'.

Hammocks were first introduced in Europe by Christopher Columbus when he brought many hammocks back to Spain from the group of islands that is now known as the Bahamas.

One of the reasons that hammocks grew in popularity in the New World was because of their ability to provide safety. By being suspended, hammock users were better protected from snakes and other harmful creatures when they were sleeping out in the wild. Hammocks also allowed people to avoid water, dirt, and other unsanitary conditions on the ground beneath them. They were also entirely portable – a huge advantage for travellers.

Children's garden toys and furniture

It is easy to buy children's garden toys and furniture from any number of dedicated outlets, but they are nearly always made of plastic in garish colours and can actually be real eyesores once situated in a garden context. Children often appreciate something a little different – and always like the idea of a gift made especially for them – so why not invest a little time and energy in creating some personalized, purpose-built garden kit for them instead?

The possibilities are endless. There are any number of permutations that could be made to the basic play sandbox featured here, and the same applies to the children's swing, the climbing frame and even a bespoke treehouse and playhouse. By attempting the projects in this chapter, you can have some fun while giving your kids a treat they will never forget.

toys and furniture

Anything parents can do these days to encourage children to have more exercise and fresh air is a bonus and in this respect, the garden is a very valuable resource. Not only can you introduce little ones to the natural world and gardening in the relative safety of your plot, but you can also create a fun place in which to run around and have adventures. There are no limits to children's imaginations – you just need to start them off with some simple games and props. This chapter looks at creating play equipment for children of different ages. You will almost certainly save money compared with buying off the peg and these projects should blend into the garden more easily than most shop-bought items.

ABOVE: *Most children will be held rapt by the delights of a sandpit. We show you how to build one in a neat box on pages 178–181.*

RIGHT: *Kids love treehouses, which give them a place of their own with a unique style and vista. A simple one like this is inexpensive and not too difficult to build.*

RIGHT: *Children love helping out their parents in the garden, and if you provide them with the toys and kit to do that, they will spend many happy hours alongside you as you work your plot.*

Sandpit

A sandpit situated next to a deck or patio by the house is ideal for young children who still need supervision. Mum or Dad can observe from the kitchen window or whilst sitting out in the garden. A large sandpit filled with soft clean play sand offers hours of entertainment for toddlers and for slightly older children provide seaside style buckets and spades, trowels and scoops as well as less conventional items such as jelly moulds and cookie cutters. Sand can be contoured into a mini dirt track course for toy cars and other vehicles or a farm for toy sheep, cows, pigs and horses. Your children will find myriad ways to keep themselves occupied – all you need to do is to supply the sand and the space!

A close-fitting cover will ensure that the sandpit does not fill with rainwater, leaves or litter and it will discourage the local cats from using it as their own personal toilet. Periodically sift through the sand to retrieve lost toys and top up levels, as some sand will inevitably be lost in the course of everyday play. At some point children will tire of the sandpit, but you could convert it to a shallow pebble pool or maybe a herb planter.

RIGHT: *A children's swing is a great addition to any family garden, and the more unusual the better.*

BELOW: *Your children are bound to get stung by a wasp or a bee at some point – it's one of the unavoidable hazards of the garden. However, for most a sting will not be a serious problem.*

Swing

Children love to swing on dangling ropes and old tyres hung from tree branches and so will love the project featured on pages 182–185. Position the swing away from delicate border plants, anything prickly that could scratch them or with branches they could get caught on. Since children may also fall or jump off a swing whilst flying high, you should also avoid putting it near a wall or hard flooring surface that they could fall onto.

Lawn grass makes a good play surface but with regular use, you may find that the turf becomes worn and compacted under the swing. Aerate the ground in autumn and spring using a garden fork or hollow-tined lawn aerater and feed in early autumn with a low nitrogen fertilizer designed to encourage root growth.

You can attach different seats to a swing depending on the age of your child. Ones with bars like a high chair allow toddlers to have supervised fun as well. Check the swing regularly to make sure the construction is still sound.

Safety in the garden

Whilst it is essential to think about potential accidents or mishaps that children might have, there is no need to view the garden as a no-go zone for kids or to become overly protective. Have a properly kitted out first aid kit to hand and see to scrapes and scratches straight away to prevent infection. There will inevitably be splinters and thorns and nettle rashes and the occasional bee or wasp sting. Here is a safety checklist to consider.

■ Put gates and fencing up to contain small children in safe areas and check and secure boundaries to ensure that children or pets cannot wander out onto roads.

■ Fence-off ponds, cover them with a secure metal grille or fill them in until children are old enough to be around open water. Use paddling pools only under adult supervision and empty immediately afterwards.

■ Don't leave gardening and power tools out around the garden and lock up garden chemicals, paints, preservatives and barbeque fuel, etc. Encourage children to put away toys when they have finished playing. A large waterproof garden locker can be very useful if you are short of storage space.

■ With little ones around, avoid spiny or prickly plants, those with sharp-edged leaves like some tough ornamental grasses and any that are poisonous or potentially irritant. Teach children from a young age about the dangers of poisonous plants and berries – they may come across them in other people's gardens!

■ Periodically have an expert arboriculturist check the health of any big old trees in the garden, especially any that might look tempting to climb! If the tree has a preservation order on it you may still need to contact your local council for permission to carry out pruning or felling.

■ Prepare for hot sunny days outdoors with high factor children's suncream and a sun hat and encourage children to drink water and diluted fruit juices regularly to maintain hydration.

■ Sand down wooden play equipment periodically to smooth the grain and lessen the risk of splinters. Use only child-friendly wood paints and preservatives.

■ Get children to wash hands thoroughly after playing in the garden or helping with gardening.

toys and furniture

Climbing frame

Wooden climbing frames like the one described later in this chapter can be scaled up or down depending on the age and size of your children, but try to build in some features that will keep the same child challenged and excited by the frame over a number of years. Help children to adapt and customize the frame using old sheets or a tarpaulin to create a den or tent, for example, or turn it into a fort with flags, toy shields and look-out posts.

There is always a risk of children falling whilst climbing or hanging from the frame, so make sure the surface below is soft. Dry, compacted turf is not very forgiving, especially overlaying clay which can bake like concrete. Play bark (which doesn't contain sharp fragments of wood) makes a much safer surface and can be laid deep and contained by an edging of logs. Consider building a fence around the play area if you have dogs running free in the garden as they may foul the area. You can also buy specialist play surface materials for making outdoor flooring under frames and slides, some of which needs professional installation, and can be expensive.

ABOVE: *Leave areas of your garden relatively unkempt and informal, so that your children can play to their hearts' content without damaging plants.*

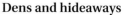

BELOW: *A giant chessboard is worth considering for your garden if you have the space and the time to construct such an ambitious project.*

Dens and hideaways

Having your own secret place or den free from adult intervention is something that most children dream about. Hidden from view up in the canopy, a treehouse offers a perspective on the house and garden that would not normally be possible. Some treehouses are entirely supported by the branches of the trees into which they are built, but more adaptable and almost certainly safer designs have extra support from the ground and can be built around a much smaller tree.

In larger gardens you could make a trail for children that links structures such as a climbing frame, a Wendy house or a treehouse, using turf-covered earth mounds, timber ramps, see-saws, raised boardwalks, rope bridges and sturdy ladders. Do bear in mind, though, that there is a lot of work and expense involved in creating such an idyll for children, who will grow up surprisingly quickly and might stop using your carefully constructed projects long before you expect them to!

A pirate motif for a Wendy house or another structure in the garden is sure to inspire fun

LEFT: *The beauty of a structure like this climbing frame is that it can be continually customized and added to as your children grow bigger and become more demanding in their tastes and requirements.*

and games. On a wet, indoor play day invite the children to paint their own Jolly Roger using fabric paints and canvas, as well as signs on old pieces of wood designed to ward off intruders or to point to buried treasure! Why not make a treasure map with clues for the crew to follow round the garden and a pot of gold chocolate coins hidden in the greenery? And don't forget to collect clothes, big buckled belts, hats, headscarves and 'jewels' for a piratical dressing-up box.

Children's furniture

If you are daunted by the prospect of constructing something as large and challenging as a climbing frame or treehouse, you could always consider some more modest creations for your children instead. Like adults, children love to eat out in the garden on a warm, sunny day, so why not construct their own tailor-made table and benches or chairs so they can do just that? You could easily scale down and adapt the rustic table and benches project featured on pages 154–157 in the chapter on adult garden furniture, or you could

come up with your own individual designs for kids' furniture, based on the construction principles used in the wooden structures in this chapter and elsewhere in this book. Another good idea is to create scale furniture for the larger structures like the playhouse and treehouse. Your children will be delighted by such thoughtful personalization of their own special den or house.

BELOW: *This children's playhouse has been thoughtfully constructed to match the materials and colours used in the house behind it. It looks just like a miniature version!*

Constructing a children's sandbox

Tips, tools and materials

SKILL LEVEL
■ This is an intermediate level project requiring some DIY skills.

BEST TIME TO DO
■ Whenever the weather is reasonably fine and the ground is not too wet or muddy.

TOOLS REQUIRED
■ Saw; hand drill; chisel; screwdriver; spirit level; tape measure; pencil.

MATERIALS REQUIRED
■ Plywood and treated softwood. Enough 12mm (½in) exterior grade plywood to cover the pit area and make the two lid sections. (See the cutting list on the opposite page for quantities required.) The lid is fixed using three 300mm (12in) 'T' hinges and three 225mm (9in) strap hinges.

TIME REQUIRED
■ 2–3 days or maybe two weekends will normally be required.

One of the key features of this project is the concertina lid that folds back to form a seat. It is always important to cover a sandbox, when it is not in use; there are many small creatures which would like to use it for their deposits, given the chance! This sandbox is simply made from sawn softwood sections and plywood. The ply needs to be, at the very minimum, exterior grade to ensure it is long-lasting. This sandbox design enables the sizes to be altered to suit the space or materials available. Just scale it up or down to suit your personal requirements. Make sure that any finishes applied to the sandbox are child friendly. If you use colours, check out what each of the colouring agents contains before you begin applying them. Most acrylic paints for exterior use should be safe enough for coming into contact with children, but do read what it says on the can.

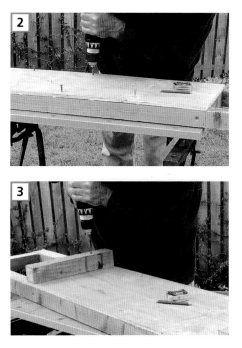

1 Start by making the two side frames. These are simple butt joints that are glued and screwed together.

2 Cut the two strips of plywood to fit on the inside, side faces of the box. Countersink the screw holes. Use zinc coated or stainless steel screws to avoid corrosion.

3 Onto the plywood side panels now fix the short, vertical end frame pieces.

4

6

5

7

4 Measure and cut the two pieces of plywood for the end panels.

5 Fix the two pieces of plywood across the width of the box.

6 Glue, cramp and fix in place the longer end frame pieces.

7 Around the inner bottom section fix a batten all round and one or two bearers across the middle. With these in place, cut the plywood to fit the base and secure it in place with evenly spaced screws.

Variations on the theme

As is the case with most of the projects in this book, the item demonstrated can be adapted in a number of different ways with a little imagination and innovation. For example, instead of constructing a lid for your sandbox, you might prefer to incorporate a decorative canopy like that pictured above.

Cutting list

Component:	Qty:	LENGTH nominal:	WIDTH finished:	THICKNESS finished:
Side frames:	4	1.5m/5ft	50mm/2in	50mm/2in
	6	300mm/12in	50mm/2in	50mm/2in
End frames:	4	1'/300mm	50mm/2in	50mm/2in
	4	1.2m/4ft	50mm/2in	50mm/2in
Floor bearers:	2	1.2m/4ft	50mm/2in	50mm/2in
	3	1.0m/3ft	50mm/2in	50mm/2in
Lid & lower seat	1	1.2m/4ft	75mm/3in	50mm/2in
cross members	2	1.2m/4ft	75mm/3in	1"/25mm
Pit, top framing:	1	1.2m/4ft	63mm/2½in	12mm/½in
	2	1.0m/3ft	63mm/2½in	12mm/½in
Lid framing:	4	1.2m/4ft	63mm/2½in	12mm/½in
	6	450mm/18in	63mm/2½in	12mm/½in

8 There are three pieces to run across under the folded back seat. The one at the extremity of the frame is notched to fit over the framing. The others are just glued and screwed on.

9 Fit some framing around the three outer, top faces of the box. This should be mitred in the corners and finishes off the box area, covering any rough edges.

10 The sandbox lid is made up of two

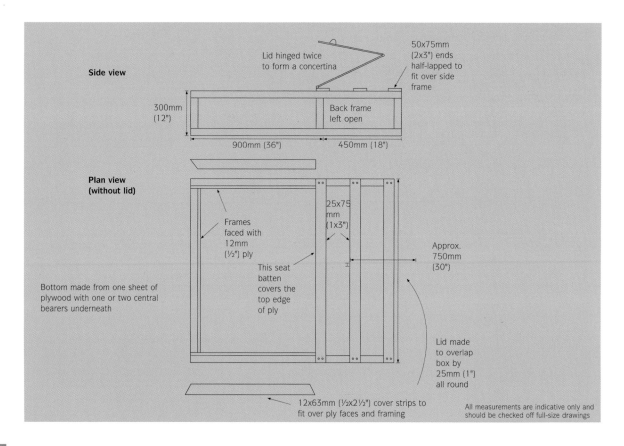

Side view

Lid hinged twice to form a concertina

50x75mm (2x3") ends half-lapped to fit over side frame

300mm (12")

Back frame left open

900mm (36")   450mm (18")

Plan view (without lid)

Frames faced with 12mm (½") ply

This seat batten covers the top edge of ply

25x75 mm (1x3")

Approx. 750mm (30")

Bottom made from one sheet of plywood with one or two central bearers underneath

Lid made to overlap box by 25mm (1") all round

12x63mm (½x2½") cover strips to fit over ply faces and framing

All measurements are indicative only and should be checked off full-size drawings

sections of plywood. This is strengthened with some framing that is glued and screwed on.

11 The strap hinges are fitted to the underside of the lid sections.

12 Three 'T' hinges secure the lid in place.

BELOW: *The finished sandbox. Keep the lid firmly closed when the box is not in use so that the sand remains dry and clean.*

Making a children's swing

Tips, tools and materials

SKILL LEVEL
- This is an intermediate level project requiring some DIY skills.

BEST TIME TO DO
- Whenever the weather is reasonably fine and the ground is not too wet or muddy.

TOOLS REQUIRED
- Saw; hand drill; chisel; screwdriver; spirit level; tape measure; pencil.

MATERIALS REQUIRED
- Preservative-treated softwood. (See the cutting list on the opposite page for quantities required.) Plus rope and hanging gear.

TIME REQUIRED
- 1–2 days or maybe a weekend will normally be required.

Swings are an ever-popular item for the kids' play area. Although there are plenty of ready-made versions on the market, it is a lot of fun to make up your own unique take on this perennial children's favourite. This project shows you how to make a single-seater (even allowing room for growth!). Alternatively, you can expand the width and strengthen the timber sections of the swing if you need to accommodate more than one child at a time. It is important that the swing structure is solid and secure. The joints are simple but should be bolted together carefully and checked over regularly. Timber expands and contracts during the changing seasons. This leads to a loosening of the nuts and bolts; hence the need to check them regularly. Use big, flat washers to help reduce some of this movement. A dollop of glue on each permanent joint will also help.

1 Lay out a pair of legs to make the first 'A' frame on a flat surface. Use a bit of gash stock to line up the transom position at the top of the apex.

2 Mark the top of each leg and cut the angle to fit the transom. Then, using the short length of the dummy transom, establish the angles for the 'A' frame braces.

3 Once marked out cut the two short and two long side braces.

4 Cramp up a frame and drill right through both pieces. The holes need to be 10mm (3/8in) or 12mm (½in) wide in order to match your bolts.

5 Fix the braces to the legs with a couple of coach bolts or alternatively a threaded bar with nuts and washers.

6 Trim off the bottom of each leg parallel with the ground surface.

7 Trim the transom to length and cut a 45-degree piece off each end. Now cut some short, wedge-shaped pieces and fix those at each end of the transom with glue and screws.

8 Prop the two 'A' frames up, or get some help to hold them in place. Slip the transom over the top and into place. Once the transom is positioned, drill a centre hole through each 'A' frame top right through the transom as well.

9 Use a threaded bar to fix on the transom. The short, wedge-shaped braces are also secured with long screws.

Cutting list

Component:	Qty:	LENGTH nominal:	WIDTH finished:	THICKNESS finished:
'A' frames:	4	3.2m/8ft	100mm/4in	50mm/2in
	2	600mm/24in	100mm/4in	50mm/2in
	2	1.2m/4ft	100mm/4in	50mm/2in
Main transom:	1	2m/6ft6in	100mm/4in	50mm/2in
Braces:	4	600mm/24in	50mm/2in	50mm/2in
Seat, in hardwood:	1	750mm/2ft6in	150mm + /6in	+ 25mm/1in

10 To make the structure firm four short braces are cut to fit from the side of the 'A' frames up to the transom.

11 Once cut the braces are fitted and then fixed in place.

12 The hanging gear for the swing seat ropes is easier to fit if the transom is removed.

13 The seat is prepared and drilled to take the rope, which must be strong.

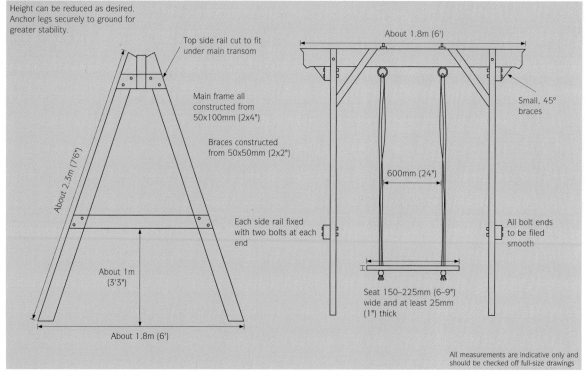

Height can be reduced as desired. Anchor legs securely to ground for greater stability.

Top side rail cut to fit under main transom

Main frame all constructed from 50x100mm (2x4")

Braces constructed from 50x50mm (2x2")

Each side rail fixed with two bolts at each end

About 2.3m (7'6")

About 1m (3'3")

About 1.8m (6')

About 1.8m (6')

Small, 45° braces

600mm (24")

All bolt ends to be filed smooth

Seat 150–225mm (6–9") wide and at least 25mm (1") thick

All measurements are indicative only and should be checked off full-size drawings

OPPOSITE: *The finished article. You can paint the structure easily enough once it has been completed. It can then be secured to the ground with stakes or left portable so that it can be moved around the garden as necessary.*

Making a wooden climbing frame

Tips, tools and materials

SKILL LEVEL
- This is an advanced level project requiring strong DIY skills. Some assistance would also be useful.

BEST TIME TO DO
- Whenever the weather is reasonably fine and the ground is not too wet or muddy.

TOOLS REQUIRED
- Spade; pickaxe; sledgehammer; saw; hand drill; claw hammer; chisel; screwdriver; spirit level; large square; straight edge; tape measure; pencil.

MATERIALS REQUIRED
- Preservative-treated softwood. Plus whatever else you choose to add to the basic climbing frame, such as a scramble net, knotted rope and climbing blocks and such like. Ready-mixed concrete.

TIME REQUIRED
- A project of this scale will normally take at least a week to complete.

Climbing frames are always an instant hit with kids. Children have a natural sense of adventure and need to test themselves. A climbing frame offers the perfect structure on which to do this. You must start by making detailed drawings. They don't need to be anything too sophisticated, but without working through and laying out each of the features to be included in the climbing frame, the project will be a mess before you start! Let your imagination roll. What would have excited you as a child? Using preservative-treated softwood as the core material for your climbing frame offers endless options. Although this project incorporates a number of features, there are still many more you could add. Check out what is on the market and design your own unique climbing frame that will be the envy of all your children's friends.

1 Having drawn out your plans in detail, and identified the site, mark out the pole positions carefully. A long tape measure, some string and a big square will help you to do this accurately. Depending upon the size and shape of the climbing frame, and the supporting legs, each pole hole should be dug deep and wide enough to accommodate at least one barrow full of concrete. Put a short peg in the centre of each hole and level the tops of these across the whole site, using a long straight edge and a spirit level.

2 The next stage of the hole preparation is to fill up the bottoms with concrete to the top of each peg. This levels each hole across the site and enables you to cut the poles to length before final fixing.

3 The poles are now inserted into their appropriate hole. Each one is braced, from adjacent stakes, and from each other. They should all be vertical, unless designed otherwise, and should match your plan as closely as possible.

4 Once the poles have been positioned the rest of the concrete is back-filled around each of them to secure them firmly in place. Finish the top level of the concrete a little below ground level so that an extra layer of impact material can be laid on top of the hardened concrete. This will prevent children from falling off the

structure and directly onto a hard surface. This is an important consideration with all features that you decide to incorporate in your own version of the climbing frame.

5 If you are incorporating some 'monkey bars' into the frame these can be made up before erection. Centre and drill out the bar retention holes in the side joists. The bars should be a good fit and not be able to be pulled out when the feature is installed.

6 Paint the monkey bars in a variety of bright colours to make the whole thing

a bit more fun. This part of the frame also supports a level of platform above and leads to the knotted rope. For this reason it must be braced and sturdy.

7 Leave the concrete around the poles to harden for at least three days. Then install the first stage of floor joists. Bolt all the way through each joist and secure it with a further pair of long nails or screws.

8 Intermediate joists can be made from slightly narrower materials, to build extra strength into the structure. Once their positions are established joist hangers are a quick and easy way to install them.

9 With all the main frame and joists in place the platforms can be built. Using grooved decking provides some extra grip. Cut each piece to length and screw down in place.

10 Like the monkey bars, the climbing blocks can be home-made. An off-cut from the poles is sliced through to create a thick disc. This is then

cut to create a curved, rough surface to climb upon.

11 The blocks can be painted before fixing to the wall.

12 Access to the platforms is via various routes. Here a simple bar ladder is made up and

then attached to the designated access point on the frame.

13 The fireman's pole needs to be securely fixed through a large beam set across the top of two uprights. Some screws and a galvanized strap should ensure it is stable.

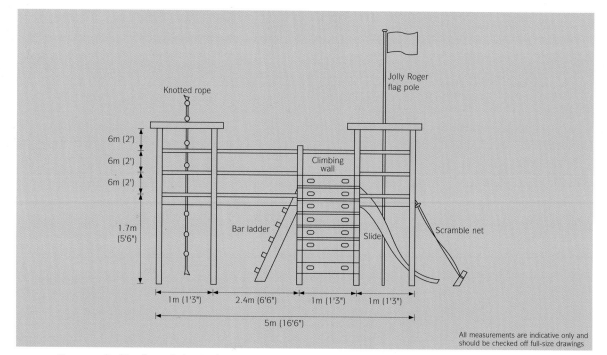

Knotted rope

Jolly Roger flag pole

.6m (2')
.6m (2')
.6m (2')

Climbing wall

1.7m (5'6")

Bar ladder

Slide

Scramble net

1m (1'3")   2.4m (6'6")   1m (1'3")   1m (1'3")

5m (16'6")

All measurements are indicative only and should be checked off full-size drawings

OPPOSITE: *Your own climbing frame design can incorporate as many or as few elements as you like.*

Constructing a treehouse

Tips, tools and materials

SKILL LEVEL
- This is an advanced level project requiring strong DIY skills. Some assistance would also be useful.

BEST TIME TO DO
- Whenever the weather is reasonably fine and the ground is not too wet or muddy.

TOOLS REQUIRED
- Saw (ideally powered); plane; hand drill; claw hammer; chisel; screwdriver; spirit level; large square; straight edge; tape measure; paintbrush; pencil.

MATERIALS REQUIRED
- Preservative-treated softwood. Standard material available from any DIY outlet or builders/timber merchants. (See the cutting list opposite for amounts required.)

TIME REQUIRED
- A project of this scale will normally take about five days to a week to complete.

Treehouses are great fun for kids, offering a world of wonder for a youthful imagination. They can be themed as pirate ships, castles or simple log cabins and, in truth, you don't strictly need a tree in order to build one! If you do have a suitable tree, so much the better, but, as is the case with this project, you may not actually want to attach the structure to the tree itself. An alternative is simply to build the house alongside a tree – rather than in it – for a similar effect When designing your own treehouse, consider all aspects of safety. Take advice from the specialists. The structure should not be too high. Make sure you build in something soft to land on if anyone is unfortunate enough to fall off the structure by accident. A good, thick cushion of tree bark, recycled rubber waste or special matting should do the job, depending on the height of the treehouse.

1 Digging out the post holes can be quite arduous but it is critical that they are as near to their required positions as possible. Make a sketch plan and work from that. In most cases the poles should be set in concrete about 450mm (18in) deep or more.

2 Once the poles are in place, and the concrete has been left to cure, the serious building can start. Establish the first level and attach

Cutting list

Component:	Qty:	LENGTH nominal:	WIDTH finished:	THICKNESS finished:

A guide only, basic materials.
THE PLATFORMS

Component:	Qty:	LENGTH nominal:	WIDTH finished:	THICKNESS finished:
Poles:	10	3.6m/12ft	100mm/4in diameter.	
Main joists:	2	4m/13ft	150mm/6in	50mm/2in
	2	3m/10ft	150mm/6in	50mm/2in
	4	2m/6ft6in	150mm/6in	50mm/2in
Intermediate joists:	8	2m/6ft6in	100mm/4in	50mm/2in

Plus 16 joist hangers, some 150mm/6in coach screws and washers plus 100mm/4in nails. Enough decking material to cover two areas 2m/6ft6in long by 3m/10ft wide when spaced out.

Component:	Qty:	LENGTH nominal:	WIDTH finished:	THICKNESS finished:
Half round poles:	8	3.6m/12ft	100mm/4in half diameter	
Ladder step stringers:	4	1.5m/5ft	75mm/3in	50mm/2in
Ladder bars:	9	1m/3ft3in	50mm/2in	50mm/2in
THE HOUSE				
The framing, about:		60m/200ft	50mm/2in	50mm/2in
Door and window linings, about:		9m/30ft	75mm/3in	25mm/1in
Door and window stops, about:		18m/60ft	25mm/1in	12mm/½in
End stops for 4 corners:		1.8m/6ft	75mm/3in	32mm/1¼in
Feather-edged boarding:		Enough to cover 12 plus m²/130 sq ft		

Enough odds and ends to make the stable doors to fit the spaces left for them. Plus 4 'T' hinges, 2 cabin hooks, exterior grade plastic window material plus a length of felt.

two of the main joists in place with coach screws and, for added strength, a couple of long nails.

3 The intermediate joists can be slightly smaller. These are held in place with 'joist hangers' set no more than 600mm (24in) apart. Pack the hangers with strips of off-cuts to level up the joists if necessary.

4 To make life easier start laying the first series of decking boards onto the lower level. You will be able to work off this when fixing some of the second level timber in place. One centre screw per joist per board should be sufficient. Use stainless steel screws to avoid corrosion or marking.

5 The second level joists can be installed in a similar fashion. Take care when working off ladders. You will probably need some help at this stage to hold the other ends of the joists.

6 Simple bar ladder steps are made to gain access to the first and second levels. A couple of boards on the back will help hold them square. Use glue and screws to fix the bars in place.

7 Fix the bottom end of the ladder steps by driving a stake into the ground on each lower side and secure with screws. From the first to second levels the steps can be screwed directly into the decking at the lower end and the joists at the upper end.

8 If you have any decking overhanging the joists, make up some simple brackets and fix these in place to provide support.

9 The joist hangers will most probably be bent over and around the main joists. If you wish to mask them, cut some thin material, cover them and nail in place.

10 The house itself can be made before, during or after the platforms have been built. You will need four simple, studded framing structures as your base.

11 Each end frame has an additional ridge section to create the roof frame. Work out the angles and fix them onto the basic frames. Leave a gap at the top for the ridge board to drop into.

12 Clad the frames with feather-edged boarding or something similar. Use a simple spacing bar to ensure that each board overlaps and is placed correctly before fixing to the studding.

13 Overlap and fix the outside boards working from the bottom up. One screw, or nail, through each into the frame studding behind is sufficient.

Length of house is about 1.7m/5'7".
Roof boards overhang front and back by about 150mm/6".
Side and back windows made square to fit into centre section of studding.

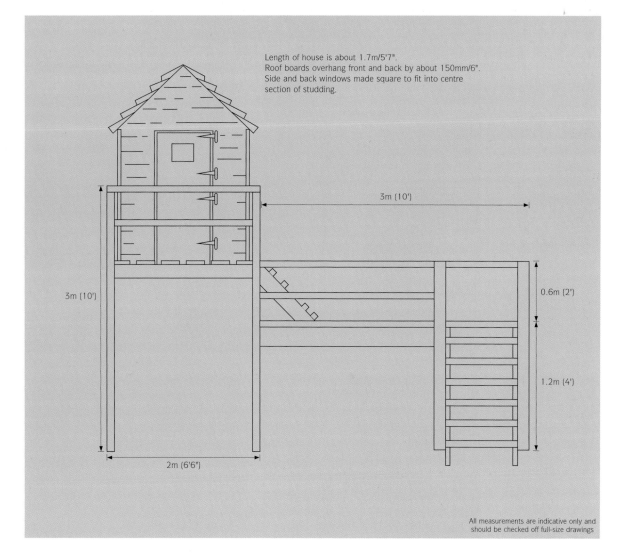

3m (10')

3m (10')

2m (6'6")

0.6m (2')

1.2m (4')

All measurements are indicative only and should be checked off full-size drawings

14 If the main house structures are to be painted, do this before final assembly takes place. You will find it much easier to do this than to paint the treehouse when it is in situ, especially if it is to be located quite high up in, or against, a tree.

15 Once the house sections are on site some of the trims can be fitted before the house is mounted on its platform. The end stops for the boarding are pictured here. They provide a clean finish and cover the overlapping board ends.

16 As soon as the house sections are on their allocated platform lock them together by driving some long screws through in the adjacent studs. Don't yet fix down to the decking until all four sections have been joined, the building squared and set in its final position.

17 With the house fully erected, finish off by fixing on the handrails. Short, off-cuts from the poles

can be cut to size and fixed in place to provide intermediate supports.

18 To help avoid any adventurous pets hurting themselves on the open steps up to the levels of the treehouse, a sheet of ply can be fitted behind the ladder bars.

OPPOSITE: *The finished treehouse, in the lea of a big old tree.*

Constructing a children's playhouse

If you want to make yourself popular with your children, build them a playhouse! The ideal age range for such an item is three or four to about ten years old; after that age, other interests generally take over. However, the playhouse need not fall into disuse once the children grow up; their parents could take it over and turn it into a storage shed, or maybe even somewhere for them to hide! By using a basic framing and studding construction technique, all manner of playhouse shapes and sizes can be built. You are really only limited by the space, time and money available. You might decide upon a simple, four-sided structure or construct a whole range of interconnecting buildings. Let your imagination match those of your children and go for it! Construct the playhouse where you can see your kids playing and then sit back and enjoy....

1 The playhouse is simply constructed from pre-treated softwood studding. 50 x 50mm/2 x 2in timber is sufficient. Pre-drill all screw holes to avoid splitting.

2 Each joint within the frame needs a couple of screws. Make the outer frame up first, with four pieces, and then fill in the width with the intermediate studs and any short horizontal lengths for windows and doors.

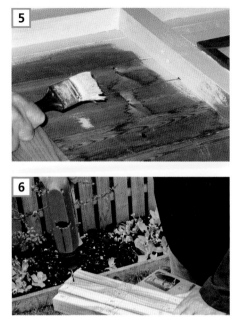

5

6

Cutting list

Component:	Qty:	LENGTH nominal:	WIDTH finished:	THICKNESS finished:
Base, (exterior boarding):	1	2.4m/8ft	1.2m/4ft	12mm/½in
Base bearers:	4	2.4m/8ft	50mm/2in	50mm/2in
Sidewall framing:	4	1.8m6ft	50mm/2in	50mm/2in
	20	1.5m/5ft	50mm/2in	50mm/2in
	2	1.2m/4ft	50mm/2in	50mm/2in
	4	750mm/2ft6in	50mm/2in	50mm/2in
	5	600mm/2ft	50mm/2in	50mm/2in
Door and window lining:	2	1.5m/5ft	70mm/2¾in	18mm/¾in
	1	600mm/2ft	70mm/2¾in	18mm/¾in
	4	375mm/1ft3in	70mm/2¾in	18mm/¾in
Door and window stop:	2	1.5m/5ft	21mm/7/8in	12mm/½in
	1	600mm/2ft	21mm/7/8in	12mm/½in
	8	375mm/1ft3in	21mm/7/8in	12mm/½in
Corner posts:	4	1.5m/5ft	63mm/2½in	63mm/2½in

Enough sidewall cladding to cover around 10m²/110 sq.ft. Plus some exterior grade polystyrene for the windows and 12mm/½in ply for the doors.

The roof panels, (chipboard/ply):	2	2.4m/8ft	900mm/3ft	12mm/½in
Roof rails and holding pieces:	2	1.8m/6ft	70mm/2¾in	18mm/¾in
	2	2.4m/8ft	45mm/1¾in	18mm/¾in
	2	1.8m/6ft	45mm/1¾in	18mm/¾in
	10	900mm/3ft	45mm/1¾in	18mm/¾in
	2	600mm/2ft	45mm/1¾in	18mm/¾in
Ridge piece:	1	1.8m/6ft	70mm/2¾in	18mm/¾in
Barge boards:	4	900mm/3ft	100mm/4in	21mm/7/8in
Centre moulding:	2	225mm/9in	125mm/5in	21mm/7/8in

Enough sanded roofing felt and 12mm/½in galvanized felt nails to cover and fix on roof.

3 Once the frames have been constructed, calculate how much cladding you will require. Try to base all dimensions on easily available materials. Therefore, the side wall height should equal a specific number of boards that will cover it. Position windows and the tops of doors to coincide with a horizontal joint in the cladding to avoid cutting.

4 The cladding of choice is laid and fixed from the bottom of the frame up. Two nails, or screws, per stud for the first length/ lengths and one thereafter.

5 Once they have been covered with cladding the four main sections of the building should be painted at this point, prior to assembly. To make the playhouse as bright as possible inside, use a light shade of paint for the interior. Two coats of paint all round should normally be sufficient.

6 Prepare the doors, windows and balcony prior to final assembly. The latter is simply made from some small, square sections in pieces. Top and bottom rails should be pre-drilled to avoid splitting when the pieces are screwed together.

7  Use a good dollop of exterior grade glue and a single screw to attach the individual balusters to the top and bottom rails.

8 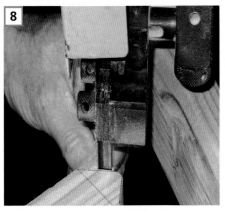 The corner posts are made up from some slightly larger, square section stuff. Cut to length and then point one end of each.

9 The balcony is formed by joining each of the longer, side sections of balusters to the shorter, front one using a corner post. Each set is 'handed' and another post is fitted to each side set to form the opening. To create a seat, and add strength, a short, diagonal piece can be fixed across the corners.

10 Position the base piece where the finished playhouse is to stand. The ground should be carefully levelled before starting to fit the side walls. If not, it may affect the clearance on the lower door opening. You will need help to erect the big panels; or some long sash cramps to hold everything in place as you screw it all together.

11 Fix all four sides down, but not permanently at this stage, getting their alignment as close to perfect as you can. Next, slide the roof panels into place. To make sure everything fits snugly you may need to release some of the side panels and slightly adjust their positions. Once you are satisfied, secure everything properly in place.

13

13

Cutting list (continued)

Component:	Qty:	LENGTH nominal:	WIDTH finished:	THICKNESS finished:
Balcony:	4	600mm/2ft	38mm/1 ½ in	38mm/1 ½ in
	4	300mm/1ft	38mm/1 ½ in	38mm/1 ½ in
	16	450mm/1ft6in	38mm/1 ½ in	38mm/1 ½ in
Balcony corner posts:	4	600mm/2ft	50mm/2in	50mm/2in

Plus door furniture to suit and exterior, colourful paints to finish.

12 With the two roof panels in place, and correctly located, fix them onto the main structure at both ends and along the sides. The ridge points can also be screwed together at this stage.

13 Cut the roofing felt to length, leaving some overhang at each end; this can be trimmed off later if need be. Lay the first strip of felt so that it overlaps the ridge of the playhouse. Where it laps over, underneath the second sheet, fix with a limited number of large headed felt or 'clout' nails. The second sheet of felt should lap over the top again to provide a double thickness protection. Smooth out any creases and kinks in the roofing felt as you work.

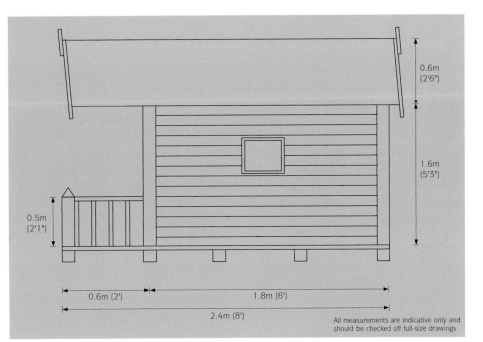

0.6m (2'6")

1.6m (5'3")

0.5m (2'1")

0.6m (2')

1.8m (6')

2.4m (8')

All measurements are indicative only and should be checked off full-size drawings

Alternative styles of playhouse

The construction technique demonstrated in this project can be adapted in any number of different ways. If you want to be a little more adventurous with your own design, you could incorporate stylish gables like the two featured in the ambitious playhouse pictured here. Detail makes all the difference, so maybe add a couple of windowboxes and even some decorative window pelmets.

14 Once the roofing felt is fixed and neatly trimmed to length, fold and nail down the lower corners as tidily as possible. A similar, double fold, is made at the top by the ridge. Longer nails will be required for these thicker, fold-over sections.

15 Once the roof has been made thoroughly weatherproof, set about fitting on the playhouse doors and accessories. Some adjustment to the position of the lower door or base board may be necessary to allow clearance for opening.

16 The barge boards and ridge detail can be cut with a coping saw, shaped and painted in their finished colours at this stage.

17 Each set of barge boards will cover and tidy up the ends of the overlapping felt. To complete the roof design, shape a detail to go over the top joint and fix this in place with a couple of screws. Paint it in a different colour so that it stands out.

18 The last job is to attach the pre-constructed balcony sections to the short verandah at the front of the playhouse.

RIGHT AND OPPOSITE:
The finished playhouse. Regularly check to ensure that all components are securely screwed together to avoid any unfortunate accidents.

Water features

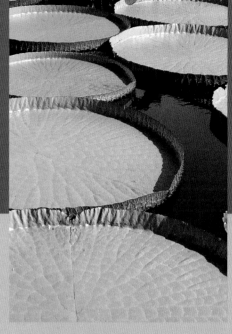

If you want to create an instant focal point in your garden, consider building or installing a water feature. The gleam of water in a pool or pond, the sparkle of a fountain and the shapes and colours of lush water plants are irresistible. Most water features are not especially difficult to install and they offer the benefit of attracting a wide range of wildlife to the garden as well as being a source of visual and aural delight.

In a small plot, a conventional pond is rarely practical. However, there are many smaller variations on the theme that serve much the same purpose, from a miniature water lily pond to a child-safe ornamental barrel. Alternatively, you could convert an area of your garden into a small-scale bog garden. Whatever you decide to construct, if you have children, ensure it is child-friendly.

water features

The appeal of water

The sight and sound of water bring a magical quality to a garden and there are many ways of introducing it from simply filling a birdbath or an Eastern-style glazed water jar to installing a fountain or digging out a pond. Droplets sparkle in sunshine but even in a shady spot, water catches the light in an enchanting way. A water feature is a refreshing and cooling sight in summer and can become the focal point of a garden room such as an outdoor dining area. And children find water fascinating, so setting up a child-safe feature in a family garden is bound to be popular. Different kinds of water features attract wildlife to a greater or lesser degree. A natural pond with a shallow access point is the most effective.

ABOVE RIGHT: *With a little thought and imagination – as well as introducing unusual materials or making the most of what is already there – you can create unique water features to decorate your garden.*

Water courses and cascades

Cascades and mini-waterfalls work best on sloping sites or running down a bank where the source or header pool can be camouflaged to maintain the illusion. However, all kinds of stylish effects can be achieved using the wall of a building or boundary or taking advantage of a retaining wall around a terrace. Specialist aquatic firms make a range of DIY items for building everything from a rocky stream course to a sleek fibreglass or metal-lined canal. They can also supply a perspex, stone-effect or stainless steel letterbox outlet for creating a contemporary water curtain. These need to have a pool or hidden water reservoir set directly behind the outlet to provide sufficient volume and flow.

RIGHT: *If you have the space, there is no limit to what you can achieve. Specialist aquatic feature companies can create self-renewing waterfalls and pools like this one for less than you might think.*

Wild streams

You can make your own streambed by digging out the course (including changes in level for the cascades and waterfalls), removing stones, lining with sand and underlay and covering with black butyl pond liner – that is, following similar steps used to make a pond (see pages 224–227). The margins are camouflaged with rocks, stones and planting and the course itself can be hidden with pebbles. Given dimensions, companies will cut liner to fit your feature without the need to piece together or overlap sections. This is a good idea given water's capacity to travel via capillary action, find gaps and leak, eventually emptying the reservoir. Seek specialist advice on the size and type of pump required. You will need to know the height the water is being pumped to, the length of the watercourse, the diameter of the feed pipe and the desired flow rate in litres or gallons.

ABOVE: *This stream looks entirely natural but in fact has been created artificially using a butyl liner and lots of natural camouflage.*

Small powered water features

A moving water feature can energize a small courtyard, patio or garden room and really bring it to life. Additionally, in urban areas, the sound provides a 'white noise' effect that helps block out traffic and other unwanted noise. You will need an electricity point relatively close to where you plan your feature and an indoor or waterproof outdoor switch to turn it on and off, easily saving power. Garden centres and aquatic outlets as well as internet stores now offer a wide range of water sculptures for any style of garden. However, whether you choose one of these or simply use a fountain head attachment fixed directly to the pump, the set up is very similar (see pages 216–219).

Position fountains in a spot where the wind won't distort their symmetry (especially the smooth dome of a bell fountain) or blow water outside the reservoir, as this can empty the tank surprisingly quickly. You can extend the catchment area of an underground reservoir by lining with an overlapping piece of pond liner that diverts droplets back down into the main tank. Cover with pebbles or rocks. A simple geyser-style fountain looks well set amongst a swathe of pebbles, cobbles and rounded boulders and could be combined with a millstone for a rustic or cottage garden look.

water features

ABOVE: *Even the most modest barrel can be easily converted into an eye-catching feature with a few additions or adjustments.*

RIGHT: *One of the most delightful aspects of water gardens is the way that they instantly attract wildlife, like this Common Blue Damselfly.*

Mini ponds

You can create a pint-sized pool on the patio without digging a hole simply by using a large container like a barrel; there are mini-aquatics and marginals that won't outgrow their allotted space and which will help to keep the water fresh and well oxygenated. On a more formal note, a miniature water lily pond could become an oasis at the heart of a Mediterranean-style gravel garden planted with sun-loving succulents and herbs. And even with this relatively small volume of water, you will still attract a range of creatures. A small pool like this would also enliven a paved courtyard and could be set at the centre of a modular paving circle, for example. The leaves of water lilies shade the water and help to prevent algal build-up and the plants flower more reliably in a well-lit spot. Ensure that formal pools are perfectly level and overlap edges with stones or decking to camouflage exposed liner.

For a fun and simple project for children and to attract wildlife such as birds and frogs, sink a large black plastic planter into the border so that the rim is level with the soil. Put gravel in the base, a brick or stone for birds to perch on and a wooden ramp for frogs and fill with water. A few submerged aquatic plants will help keep the pool healthy.

Ponds and bog gardens

Open water in the form of a pond or pool instantly attracts insects and in turn these provide food for dragonflies, birds and even bats, so it won't be long before your pond is a hive of activity. Still water reflects the sky and surrounding vegetation and so offers a constantly changing scene. In addition, ponds offer habitat and drinking stations for gardener's friends such as frogs, toads, hedgehogs and songbirds. However, if you have little ones, it is best to build only child-safe features, especially those with hidden reservoirs, or alternatively, create a bog garden. You can reap many of the same benefits of a wildlife pond by planting a bog. The dampness and lush vegetation

will appeal just as much to amphibians in search of shelter and the plants will create the illusion of open water and some of the ambience of a pool.

Black pond liner looks most natural for garden pools and provides the best reflections. It is worth using more expensive UV-resistant butyl rubber, which comes in different grades depending on the type of project and how long you want the feature to last for. You can often buy cheaper off-cuts of the same material for lining relatively small projects.

Position ponds in a well-lit spot well away from trees and deciduous shrubs as autumn leaf litter can foul the water. Consider providing a shallow, beach-like access point camouflaged with pebbles as well as deeper areas that are suitable for creatures to overwinter and escape predators. Plant marginals on the various shelves or contoured levels of the pond and allow floating plant foliage to cover part of the water surface in order to shade and discourage algae. However, it is important to keep a good proportion of the water surface clear for reflections and for the general aesthetics of the pond.

ABOVE: *A pond need not be large in size in order to be effective. The addition of some floating water lilies and attractive surrounding wooden decking brings this modest pool to life.*

BELOW: *A decorative surround will contain the pond and adds a touch of formality.*

Wall fountains

When setting up a cascade or wall mask fountain on a house wall, ensure that the water doesn't splash back against the building above the level of the damp proof course. Otherwise, fit some kind of waterproof backing board or paint with a suitable brick sealant. The water reservoir could be in the form of a raised pool of brick or stone, rendered breeze blocks or railway sleepers (ties) lined with butyl rubber, or a large container such as a stone trough. If you have young children or if there isn't room for a wall pool, use a hidden underground tank camouflaged with pebbles. Small wall fountains come complete with a built-in reservoir and simply hang on the wall or fence and connect to an electricity supply, but the tank needs regular refilling to prevent the tiny submersible pump from burning out.

Making a child-safe barrel pool

Tips, tools and materials

SKILL LEVEL
- This is a beginner level project which is easy to complete so long as the pump can be easily plugged into a mains electricity supply.

BEST TIME TO DO
- Mid- to late spring, when you will have the best choice of pond plants.

TOOLS REQUIRED
- Scissors; hosepipe; watering can; screwdriver.

MATERIALS REQUIRED
- Wooden half barrel, at least 60cm (24in) in diameter; pond liner; bricks and decorative pebbles, cobbles and boulders; small mains-powered submersible pump with bubble/bell fountain adaptor; RCD or circuit breaker; marginal pond plants.

TIME REQUIRED
- Half a day to set up.

One of the problems with water features is that they are often not safe for children. However, this bubble fountain in a wooden half barrel is totally safe for young children because there is no depth of water in it to speak of. It will fascinate children and adults alike and is easy to set up. Using cobbles and pebbles spread around a rubber liner at the bottom of the barrel you can hide the submersible pump and at the same time create a feature that is just like a miniature pond, complete with a variety of marginal plants. Most plants don't like to have their foliage constantly splashed by water, but here the water is contained within the shape of the bubble. Barrels have quite a rustic feel and work well in country and cottage-style gardens, but for a more modern or oriental feel you could also use a glazed ceramic jar with the drainage hole blocked.

1 The wooden barrel is unlikely to be completely waterproof, so it will need lining with a piece of pond liner. Various types of liner are available. The best ones are those made from butyl rubber, which will last longer than other liners. Push the liner firmly down inside the barrel.

2 Cut the liner to fit using a pair of scissors. Leave some excess around the edge of the barrel.

3 Stand the pump on a piece of brick to give it stability and to raise it up to the right level in the barrel. Place other bricks around the pump for extra weight and stability. This small mains-powered model of pump is ideally suited to such a water feature.

4 Add some cobbles to fill in the spaces between the bricks at the base of the barrel. These will help to stabilize the bricks and will also stop the pump moving around once the feature is operating.

5 Add the plants, potted into plastic mesh pond baskets. Plan the planting in advance. A low-growing water forget-me-not towards the front will work well.

6 Add the larger stones that will sit at the top of the feature and will be the most visible. Place them carefully around the plants.

7 Add smaller pebbles and cobbles around the larger stones and plants for visual variety.

Pumps and electricity

For fountains or any powered water feature, check on the required pump type and capacity with an expert. It is better to have spare capacity, and adjust the flow with the tap on the outlet, than to just have enough power, as pumps work less effectively over time. For most projects a small submersible pump running off a transformer, rather than mains power, will suffice. Large projects and filtration systems, for example for fish ponds, may need a mains-powered pump housed in a dry external chamber. Consult a qualified electrician for advice on power points and any electrical installations. Where mains cables run across the garden, pass them through armoured ducting.

8 Using a hosepipe, add water to the barrel until it reaches the base of the larger stones. This will leave enough expansion room to add extra plants and any final stones.

9 Turn on the pump at the mains and adjust the rate of flow as necessary, depending on the size of bubble you want.

OPPOSITE: *The finished barrel, filled with plants and stones.*

Suitable plants for a half barrel water feature

There are many different marginal pond plants that are suitable for planting in a half barrel like the one featured. Any good garden centre should have a decent selection. The plants shown here all grow naturally in the wild and can be found beside most ponds and lakes. *Myosotis palustris* (top left) has delicate white flowers with yellow centres and is good for underplanting taller plants, while the spearwort *Ranunculus flammula* (bottom left) has robust, spreading, bright yellow blooms. For a splash of brilliant colour, try the bright blue *Iris versicolor* 'Quebec' pictured below.

Making a miniature water lily pond

Tips, tools and materials

SKILL LEVEL

- This is a beginner level project which is easy to complete for any gardener.

BEST TIME TO DO

- In early summer, when you will have the best choice of suitable plants.

TOOLS REQUIRED

- Scissors; hosepipe; watering can; paintbrush.

MATERIALS REQUIRED

- An ornamental pot or wooden barrel, preferably around 60cm (24in) in diameter. Paint to seal or line with butyl rubber or heavy duty polythene if not watertight; a miniature water lily and two other plants; a sprig of Canadian pondweed; gravel and pebbles for the base and to cover the soil in the planting baskets; aquatic compost.

TIME REQUIRED

- Half a day to set up.

If your garden is small and you do not have room for a conventional pond, then a potted pond might be just the answer. Planted with a miniature water lily as the centrepiece, this can make an attractive and eye-catching feature that will grace the corner of a patio or terrace or would look good in a conservatory. Be sure to put the container in position first, as it will be difficult to move once it has been filled with water and plants. You can use normal tap water, but if possible fill the tub and allow it to stand for 48 hours before introducing plants. This allows much of the chlorine in the water to disperse. When choosing plants, opt for those with a long season of interest. A single miniature water lily could be used alone; it will quickly fill a 45cm-(18in)-diameter barrel with foliage, and flowers all summer. Alternatively, add up to two other plants.

1

2

1 Select a suitable pot for your miniature pond. A wooden half barrel will suffice, but there are any number of decorative pots that might be suitable. Colour code your selection to tie in with surrounding plantings or decor.

2 Paint waterproof sealant on the inside of the pot to ensure that it is watertight. A couple of coats of any proprietary brand sealant will normally do the job.

3

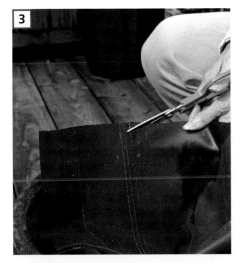

3 If you do not want to paint the inside of your pot or are concerned that sealant will not waterproof it sufficiently well, you can line the pot with a piece of plastic pond liner. Cut the liner to size using scissors.

4 Use either a hosepipe or a watering can to half-fill the pot with water. Ideally, use rainwater from a water butt, as the plants will acclimatize to this right away. If you use tap water, let it stand for 48 hours before introducing plants.

4

5 Add a tall leafy plant, such as a type of grass, to the pot. This will give the arrangement some height.

6 Add gravel to the top of the pot to prevent the compost from leaching away.

7 Add a second plant to complement the first – submerge the planting baskets.

8 Add oxygenating plants and secure them to the bottom of the container using pebbles to weight them down.

5

6

7

8

9 Carefully lower the water lily into the container. It does not matter if the lily is not actually in flower when you introduce it to the miniature pond, as in this case. In fact, the flowers could easily be damaged when you are setting up, so this might be preferable. The oxygenating plants make the water suitable for fish, so when the pond is finished, with everything in place, you might choose to add some.

Designer pots and plants

A miniature pond can be made as simple or as complicated as you like. Any container will do – so long as it is watertight – and there are many stylish choices now available. Try furniture stores as well as garden centres for the broadest selection.

Like anything else, plants come and go in terms of fashion. Your local garden centre will advise you as to what is currently in vogue, or you can go for stalwarts like these pictured below, *Cyperus alternifolius* (top) and *Lysimachia thyrsiflora* (bottom).

ABOVE: *A very simple, rustic pot like this one makes for an interesting alternative approach.*

OPPOSITE: *The finished miniature water lily pond. The lily will only flower at certain times of year, but the overall planting is attractive nevertheless.*

Installing a water feature with a hidden reservoir

Tips, tools and materials

SKILL LEVEL
- This is a beginner level project which is easy to complete so long as the pump can be easily plugged into a mains electricity supply.

BEST TIME TO DO
- This feature can be prepared at anytime.

TOOLS REQUIRED
- Electric drill; watering can.

MATERIALS REQUIRED
- Plastic terracotta or stone-effect patio planter; terracotta or stone-effect urn; small submersible pump; piece of wire to secure outlet tube; length of plastic tubing that fits snugly over pump outlet; gravel, pebbles or cobbles, depending on the size of the feature.

TIME REQUIRED
- Once all the necessary materials have been assembled, half a day to set up.

Moving water always makes for the most captivating water features in gardens, but not everyone has the space for a fountain or waterfall. However, a small and simple feature involving water bubbling up out of the ground like a spring can make an intriguing effect. To make a feature like this, first excavate a hole big enough to take an underground reservoir. A plastic cold-water tank from a plumber's merchants is ideal but you can also use a large sheet of butyl liner over a base of soft sand. Place the submersible pump in the reservoir; connect plastic tubing to the outlet so that it passes through the hole in your drilled pebble or millstone. Alternatively, fit a geyser attachment to give the effect of a bubbling spring emerging from a bed of pebbles. To support this kind of surface camouflage, use a sheet of rigid wire mesh that overlaps the edge of the reservoir.

1 Select a suitable pot. This feature does not require a lot of water in order to work effectively, so the pot need not be very deep. However, it should be big enough to accommodate the pump and any other vessel you use.

2 Use a tiny pump that will work in a small quantity of water. Ensure that the pump will sit comfortably in the base of the pot before proceeding.

3 Drill a hole in the side of the terracotta urn that is big enough to take the nozzle of the pump.

4 Insert the length of plastic tubing into the hole. The other end of this should fit snugly over the end of the pump nozzle.

5 Connect the nozzle of the pump to the end of the length of plastic tubing. Push the tubing as far into the urn as it will go without being obviously visible.

Variations on the theme

There are plenty of variations on this theme that would work well as an alternative to the project described above. For a grand statement, place a large boulder-like feature in a bowl and let the water bubble down the sides (left). Otherwise, a bird bath-type affair featuring a pagoda-style fountain will create a neat cascade effect using only a small amount of water.

ABOVE AND LEFT: *There is a wide range of pumps available to power water features of any size and description.*

6 Position the urn so that it is lying with its mouth towards the centre of the pot. Fill the pot with gravel, so that the pump and attachment are completely buried.

7 Use a watering can to fill the pot with water. Do not allow the level to rise above the gravel. When the pot is full, switch the pump on at the mains and enjoy the simple fountain effect as water trickles gently over the gravel.

ABOVE: *All manner of different fountains can be installed with a hidden reservoir.*
OPPOSITE: *The finished project, with water flowing over the gravel in the bowl.*

Planting water features

In order to integrate your water features successfully in the garden, consider how you want to plant them up before you begin any installations. Most larger features lend themselves easily to planting – for example, a bog garden is really nothing more than the plants themselves and any number of marginals can be easily situated beside a pond or small pool. However, for smaller features, a little more thought may be required.

A small bowl like the one featured in the project on these pages is not big enough to accommodate plants as well as gravel, a pump and a vessel. In a case like this, either position the bowl in the middle of a border where it is surrounded by plants that are already in situ or surround it with brightly coloured potted plants on a patio or terrace. Flowers that complement the colours of the materials used in the feature will always work well, as will plants that trail down and over the item in question.

Making a bog garden

Tips, tools and materials

SKILL LEVEL
- This is a beginner level project which is easy to complete so long as the ground to be dug out is not too hard.

BEST TIME TO DO
- A bog garden can be installed whenever the ground is not frozen or too hard.

TOOLS REQUIRED
- Spade; garden fork; trowel; scissors; hosepipe.

MATERIALS REQUIRED
- Sheet of butyl pond liner or heavy-duty polythene; gravel; bricks or boulders to hold liner in place temporarily; length of perforated hose; aquatic planting mix; selection of moisture-loving plants; decorative boulders and cobbles.

TIME REQUIRED
- Depending on the size of the bog garden to be created, 1–2 days or perhaps a whole weekend.

A bog garden is probably the most natural-looking water feature that it is possible to create in the garden. It offers you the chance to grow a wide range of exciting marginal plants in many different colours, textures, heights and styles. Another good reason to make one is that this is a rewarding water feature that does not require expensive excavation work. Ideally, the site should be sheltered from prevailing winds with a little, but not too much, shade. The most natural position is adjoining the banks of an informal pond or pool, but if you are planning an individual bog garden, then any slight depression or poorly-drained area will be ideal. It is important to keep the area poorly drained and to make allowances for fluctuations in the water level according to the differing levels of rainfall throughout the year. Avoid positioning the bog garden too near any tree.

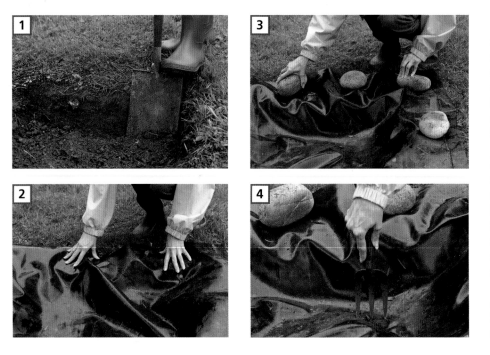

1 Using a garden fork to get started, and then a spade, excavate the area designated for the bog garden to a depth of about 35cm (14in).

2 Level the base of the excavated area and spread out a large sheet of pond lining material. Butyl or polyethylene are the best choices of material.

3 Anchor the pond liner with a few large, smooth stones.

4 Puncture the bottom of the liner a couple of times with a garden hand fork, so that some water can escape from the liner later on.

5 Add a layer of washed gravel to the bottom of the pond liner. This will both help disguise and weigh down the liner and will assist with drainage if the bog garden becomes too waterlogged.

6 Lay a section of pipe, perforated at 30cm (12in) intervals, on the gravel. Allow the end of the pipe to extend beyond the bog garden area and conceal it in the undergrowth.

7 In dry spells, trickle water into the pipe as needed. Fill the area to the original ground level with rich, moisture-retaining, aquatic planting mixture.

8 Soak the ground thoroughly, so that a layer of water about 7.5cm (3in) deep remains standing on the top of the soil before you start putting in any plants. Everything needs to be very wet indeed!

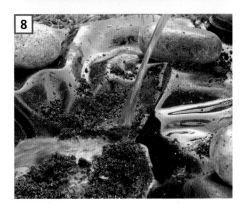

Plants for bog gardens

Ajuga reptans (bugle)
Alchemilla (lady's mantle)
Aruncus dioicus (goat's beard)
Astilbe
Eupatorium (hemp agrimony)
Filipendula (meadowsweet)
Gentiana (gentian)
Geum rivale (water avens)
Gunnera
Hemerocallis (day lily)
Hosta (plantain lily)
Iris (bog garden iris)
Phormium tenax (New Zealand flax)
Primula

ABOVE: *Filipendula* (top);
Gunnera (middle);
Primula denticulata *'Rubin'* (bottom).

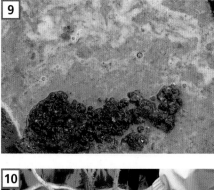

9 Once the area is throughly saturated, it is time to begin planting the bog garden. Although moisture is the key, do ensure that plenty of soil remains.

10 Position the plants so that they are at the same depth as they were in their pots. Firm them in. Arrange more delicate plants, such as primulas, in clumps. Aim for a variety of shape, size and colour for year-round plant interest.

ABOVE: *One of the great benefits of a bog garden is that over time, as things become more established, it will attract a variety of wildlife.*

OPPOSITE: *A lush, fully established bog garden.*

A well-established bog garden

Depending on the amount of space you have available, your bog garden could become a vast natural feature within a matter of years. True bog gardens should not be carefully tended – they should be allowed to flourish and spread, so that the magnificence of their bog and marginal plants can be fully appreciated.

ABOVE AND RIGHT: *Bog garden plants are among the most natural-looking and eye-catching of all.*

PROJECT

Installing a pond with a rigid liner

Installing a pond with a rigid, moulded liner is a relatively quick and easy procedure which can be undertaken by any gardener and particularly those who are pressed for time. Many people like rigid pond liners because their shapes are predetermined, so it is easy to see what the pond will ultimately look like before it has actually been installed. The other great advantage of rigid pond liners is that they usually come with built-in shelves, which means that it is easy to place and position plants without them disappearing to the bottom of the pond. Rigid pond liners are inexpensive and widely available from garden centres and DIY stores. The cheapest are made from vacuum-formed plastic but longer-lasting PVC-based and rubberized compounds are also available, as is moulded fibreglass. These are not so easy to find and more expensive.

Tips, tools and materials

SKILL LEVEL
- This is a beginner level project which is easy to complete so long as the ground to be dug out is not too hard.

BEST TIME TO DO
- A pond can be installed whenever the ground is not frozen, too hard, wet or muddy.

TOOLS REQUIRED
- Spade; trowel; spirit level; straight edge; hosepipe.

MATERIALS REQUIRED
- Rigid, moulded pond liner made from plastic, PVC-based or rubberized compounds or moulded fibreglass; builder's sand.

TIME REQUIRED
- Depending on the size of the liner to be installed, 1–2 days or perhaps a whole weekend.

ABOVE: *A large variety of rigid and moulded plastic pond liners is available.*

1 Set the liner on the ground and mark out around its edge with a spade, a stick or handfuls of sand. Dig the hole out to the depth and shape of the liner, keeping it as tight as possible.

2 As you dig the hole, periodically place the liner in it to check for fit. Use a spirit level and straight edge to check for level as you work. When you are satisfied that the hole is the right depth, remove any large or sharp stones and spread a 5cm (2in) layer of builder's sand in the bottom of the hole.

3 Place the liner in the hole and carefully check for level in six or seven different directions. Add or remove sand from the bottom of the hole until you are satisfied the liner is set completely level.

4 Using a hosepipe, fill the pond liner with water. Leave room for the plants to be added.

5 Place your plants carefully onto the ledges or shelves in the pond liner. Re-position as necessary.

ABOVE: *Rigid pond liners now come in an extraordinary array of sizes. This very large one has been given a cobble surround for a great effect.*

Plants for your pond

There are any number of marginal, bog and water plants that are suitable for planting in and around a garden pond. As with most planting, the key is to include a mixture of different species that will provide year-round interest allied with plenty of colour and strong form. Combine hostas with irises, astilbes with mimulus and tall, ornamental grasses like *Phormium tenax*. If in doubt, consult your local garden centre or a specialist aquatic plant centre.

LEFT: Astilbe *x* arendsii.
RIGHT: Mimulus lewisii.

Installing a pond with a flexible liner

Tips, tools and materials

SKILL LEVEL
- This is a beginner level project which is easy to complete so long as the ground to be dug out is not too hard.

BEST TIME TO DO
- A pond can be installed whenever the ground is not frozen, too hard, wet or muddy.

TOOLS REQUIRED
- Spade; trowel; spirit level; straight edge; scissors; hosepipe.

MATERIALS REQUIRED
- Flexible pond liner made from butyl rubber sheeting, PVC or low-density polyethylene (LDPE); builder's sand; sand and cement/ready-made mortar; bricks for edging.

TIME REQUIRED
- Depending on the size of the liner to be installed, 1–2 days or perhaps a whole weekend.

If you choose to construct your pond using a flexible liner, this will enable you to create whatever size or shape of pool you desire. More planning is required for this type of pond than is necessary for one made from a rigid liner, and calculating the amount of liner you will need is not always easy. Flexible pond-lining material is ideal for informal schemes, since the sheeting will fit most shapes and contours, albeit with varying amounts of creasing. Many raised ponds, which at first sight appear to be constructed entirely of bricks or concrete, are actually lined inside. The best liner to use for a pond is rubber sheeting known as butyl. This is the most durable and the most expensive flexible material available. PVC and LDPE (low-density polyethylene) are also recommended, but inexpensive polythene should be avoided, as it lacks pliability.

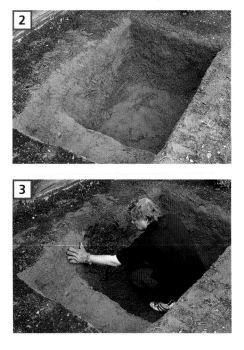

1 Having calculated how much liner you need – with the help of your dealer, if necessary – select your material and have it cut to length and width.

2 Dig the hole for the pond out to the required width and depth. It is a good idea to hire a digger for a very large pond.

3 Shape the sides of the hole with your hands or a trowel, creating ledges and nooks for plants.

4 Clear the hole of any large or sharp stones that could puncture the liner. Then, ideally, lay some old carpet or sacking as an underlay for the pond liner. Next, place the liner in the hole, fill it with water and weigh down the edges with bricks.

5 Use a pair of sharp scissors to cut away excess liner at the edge of the pond. Leave sufficient width all round to form a decent overlap.

6 Select your materials for the pond edging – in this case, house bricks – and secure them in place. Be careful not to puncture the liner as you do so.

LEFT: *This raised pond uses flexible liner and is an ideal solution where a very deep pond is required, as less excavation is required.*

Flexible liner: calculating how much you will need

When digging a hole for your pond, you can make it any shape you like, but accurately calculating the amount of liner required can be a nightmare. Use this simple formula for the best way to calculate the amount of liner required:

Length of sheet required = pond length plus 2 x pond depth, plus an extra 60cm (2ft)

Width of sheet required = pond width plus 2 x pond depth, plus an extra 60cm (2ft)

Decorative garden extras

O ne of the greatest pleasures in gardening is creating an individual look or feel to your plot. This is most commonly achieved through plant combinations of every description. However, there are many other things that you can introduce to the garden by way of stylish pots and containers and other decorative extras that will brighten up the space and give it a truly unique feel.

This chapter offers a selection of ideas to complete the transformation of your plot. The decorative effects with containers, ornamental bird bath, dovecote and other features described in the following pages are all very different, but they share a singularity of design that will help set your garden apart.

patio pots and containers

Gardening in pots

Containers enable plants to be grown in the most inhospitable of situations. Use them to cover bare walls and fences, to frame windows and brighten up decks and patios. You can even create colourful potted oases on balconies, rooftops, concrete courtyards and tarmac drives. If part of your garden has soil that is too dry and impoverished, badly drained or of the wrong pH for growing acid-loving camellias, for example, you can still grow your favourite varieties by picking an appropriate soil or compost mix.

Almost any plant, including trees and shrubs, can be grown in a pot provided it is big enough. As well as ornamentals there are scores of salads, herbs, fruits and vegetables that tolerate and even thrive in containers. So there is nothing to stop you creating a kitchen garden by the back door.

ABOVE: *Many fruits and vegetables will thrive in pots and containers and there is a lot of satisfaction to be had in growing your own.*

BELOW: *Vary your displays by making seasonal changes to plants and mix up your containers so that you have lots of different types on show.*

Practical pointers

Changing displays Some long-lived varieties can stay in the same pot from year to year but seasonal containers, including mini vegetable and salad gardens, need replanting once or twice a year. Temporarily take plants like summer lilies and spring daffodils, crocus and such like off display after flowering so that they can die down unobtrusively. A platform on castors makes moving heavier pots and troughs easier and you can also use plastic liners that lift out when the show is over, allowing instant replacement.

Feeding Keep plants well supplied with nutrients in the growing season. Feed twice a year via slow-release fertilizer granules mixed into the compost at planting time or sprinkled on the surface or apply liquid feeds when watering. Pick one relatively high in potassium (potash, chemical symbol K) for flowering and fruiting plants and one with more nitrogen (N) for ornamental foliage plants and leafy vegetables. Use a specialist acidic plant fertilizer for ericaceous or lime-hating specimens like rhododendron and camellia.

Soils and composts For longer-term pot growing – for example, for flowering shrubs such as hydrangeas and patio roses or for herbaceous and evergreen perennials, use a potting compost that contains a good proportion of loam (John Innes and some crushed bark or Perlite) to help maintain the soil structure and drainage. These are available ready mixed.

Drainage Cover the drainage holes in the base of pots with broken clay pot shards (crocks) and/or several centimetres of gravel to help prevent them from clogging with soil. The bigger the pot, the deeper the layer of drainage required. Drought-tolerant succulents, Mediterranean herbs and shrubs and most alpines hate being waterlogged so need added grit or gravel adding to a soil-based potting mix to create sharp drainage.

Pests and diseases Grow plants such as hostas in pots to reduce damage by slugs and snails. But watch out for vine weevil grubs especially with vulnerable plants like heuchera, strawberry, ivy and primula, especially when using soil-free compost. Organic gardeners can control this pest using a microscopic parasitic nematode worm which is watered onto the soil. Remove yellowing leaves and fading flowers to lessen the risk of fungal diseases and keep plants like verbena well fed and watered to reduce the risk of powdery mildew.

Insulation and frost protection Line metallic pots with bubble wrap or greenhouse insulation to protect rootballs against extremes of heat or cold. Alternatively use sheets of polystyrene (Styrofoam) or slot a plastic pot inside. Before winter, wrap marginally hardy plants in situ or move to the shelter of greenhouse or conservatory. Use bubble plastic or Hessian sacking filled with straw to wrap and insulate the pot and roots and horticultural fleece for the foliage or branches.

Watering and moisture conservation

■ Place a plant pot saucer or dish-shaped piece of black plastic in the base of a wire hanging basket to act as a reservoir.
■ Use a clip-on pulley device to raise and lower baskets easily for watering and maintenance.
■ A long lance attachment fixed to a hosepipe helps reach high wall planters and baskets.
■ Soak dried out hanging baskets in a sink or bowl of water overnight adding a couple of drops of washing up liquid to the water to help rewet the compost. After recovery, trim away permanently wilted foliage.
■ Line terracotta pots with polythene (keep the drainage hole clear), to prevent moisture loss through the sides OR use plastic 'terracotta' or glazed ceramic pots.
■ Leave several centimetres space between the compost surface and the rim of the pot to allow water to soak in efficiently.
■ Mulch the soil surface with fine bark chippings, recycled glass chips, gravel or pebbles to retain moisture.
■ Consider installing an irrigation system for groups of pots. A timer fitted to the tap controls watering even when you are away.
■ Use drought-tolerant succulents, herbs, etc., to reduce the need to water.
■ Place saucers under patio pots in summer but remove for winter to prevent overwatering.

ABOVE LEFT: *Always ensure that the container you select is large enough for the plant you intend to put it in, allowing plenty of room for growth and making provision for good drainage.*

LEFT: *Line terracotta pots with polythene and mulch the top of the soil with gravel or similar to retain moisture and keep the plants fresh.*

General design and planting tips for
patio pots and containers

RIGHT: *A hanging basket in the form of a woven brushwood cone is a very fashionable design statement in the garden. It makes a refreshing change from a standard plastic or metal version with a conventional round shape.*

BELOW, CLOCKWISE FROM TOP LEFT: *Geranium; artemisia, sea pink; a crate of mixed house leek.*

Hanging gardens

Windowboxes can be either positioned free-standing on stone ledges or are supported by metal windowbox brackets. The brackets can be screwed into the wood for greater safety and security, especially on upper floor windows. This is a particularly good idea if you live in an urban environment and people regularly walk beneath your windows. You can also fix chains at either end of the box to the wall and suspend it for an even more visually pleasing effect. Line wooden boxes with inexpensive plastic troughs or polythene to help preserve the wood and to make replanting easier. If you have room, grow substitute troughs in the background ready to replace flagging displays. Paint windowboxes to match or contrast with the colour of doors and windows using a microporous exterior quality paint or stain. Simple motifs and stencilled designs can also add an individual touch. Treat the interiors of all windowboxes with timber preservative.

Drought-resistant container plants

- *Aeonium* 'Zwartkop'
- *Armeria* (thrift, sea pink)
- *Artemisia*
- *Convolvulus sabatius*
- *Dorotheanthus* (mesembyranthemum, ice plant)
- *Echeveria secunda* var. *glauca*
- *Erigeron karvinskianus* (fleabane)
- *Felicia amelloides* (kingfisher daisy)
- *Festuca glauca* (blue fescue)
- *Gazania* (treasure flower)
- *Hedera helix* cultivars (English ivy)
- *Helichrysum petiolare*
- *Iberis sempervirens* (perennial candytuft)
- *Lavandula* (lavender)
- *Lotus berthelotii* (parrot's beak)
- *Osteospermum*
- *Pelargonium* (geranium)
- *Plechostachys serpyllifolia*
- *Plectranthus madagascariensis* 'Variegated Mintleaf'
- *Portulaca* (sun plant)
- *Rhodanthemum hosmariense*
- *Rosmarinus* (rosemary)
- *Sedum* (stonecrop)
- *Sempervivum* (house leek)
- *Senecio cineraria* (cineraria)
- *Thymus* (thyme)

RIGHT: *A wire manger or hayrack provides a simple yet effective hanging container that will hold a lot of plants and can be used to disguise a large, bare or ugly expanse of wall or fencing. Ensure that compost is well compacted and does not drop out.*

Manger- or hayrack-style metal wall planters look well on old stone buildings or period houses and cottages with rendered walls. As well as fixing to walls, some can be fitted underneath windows as an alternative to a windowbox. This style of wall planter often contains a greater volume of compost than a similarly styled wire hanging basket, so they don't tend to dry out as quickly.

Terracotta wall pots, including classical head planters, are ideal for Mediterranean-style courtyard gardens but as they tend to be on the small side and dry out quickly, always use drought-tolerant plants (see box).

Traditional wire hanging baskets lined with moss and crammed with an assortment of annual bedding and tender perennials are a cheerful sight round a doorway. Small baskets dry out too quickly and a 35cm (14in) diameter is best. Remember to use the appropriate size of bracket – too small and it could buckle under the weight and might not hold the basket far enough away from the wall. Alternatively, suspend from a pergola using a solid, screw-in hook.

Modern baskets are available in various finishes and shapes including woven brushwood cones and these are invariably lined with plastic. Cut some small drainage holes (about a third of the way up from the base) before planting. You can also buy plastic baskets with a self-watering system that require far less maintenance.

BELOW LEFT, CLOCKWISE FROM TOP LEFT: *Mexican orange blossom; viola; fuchsia; bamboo.*

Shade-tolerant plants for pots

- *Aucuba japonica* (spotted laurel)
- Begonia
- *Buxus sempervirens* (boxwood)
- Camellia
- *Choisya ternata* (Mexican orange blossom)
- Dryopteris (fern)
- *Euonymus fortunei* 'Emerald Gaiety'
- *Fargesia murielae* 'Simba'
- *Fatsia japonica* (false castor oil plant)
- Fuchsia
- *Hedera helix* (English ivy)
- *Heuchera* 'Pewter Moon'
- Hosta
- *Hydrangea macrophylla* (mophead and lacecap hydrangeas)
- *Hydrangea paniculata*
- *Impatiens* (busy Lizzie)
- *Narcissus* (daffodil)
- *Nicotiana* (tobacco plant)
- *Ophiopogon planiscapus*
- *Phyllostachys* (bamboo)
- *Pieris* – compact forms (lily of the valley bush)
- *Polystichum* (shield fern)
- *Skimmia japonica* 'Rubella'
- *Vinca minor* (lesser periwinkle)
- *Viola* (viola, pansy)

accessorize your garden

Decorating your garden

There is tremendous scope within a garden to create decorative detail without introducing any conventional sculptures or ornaments at all. The overall design and fabric of the garden including garden buildings and structures as well as boundary and flooring details – mosaics, steps and so on, can be very pleasing to the eye. Adding colour in the form of painted woodwork and walls as well as lighting further enhances the look and mood of the garden. Water features, even simple fountain jets bubbling over cobbles, draw admiring looks just as effectively as a classical stone sculpture. Depending on the style of your garden, you may also find that functional pieces such as well-designed garden furniture, pots and planters, trellis obelisks, wall lights, sundials and dovecotes sit far more comfortably in an outdoor setting than purely ornamental additions.

ABOVE: *You can use mirrors, baubles and ornaments of all descriptions to decorate the tops or sides of garden containers and features.*

Easy embellishments

It's not hard to bring some designer style to the garden. Try topping patio pots with a zingy coloured mulch of acrylic chips or pour a few bags of shiny black pebbles around planters on a deck or modern terrace for textural contrast. String white, or for a more contemporary look, neon-blue, LED fairy lights through climbers on a wall or pergola.

In a formal or traditional setting you might fix wooden ball-shaped finials onto the tops of fence or trellis posts. Or try your hand at a trompe l'oeil, or trick of the eye. An old mirror, the back sealed with bituminastic paint, could be fixed to a wall or fence and a piece of trellis, a wrought ironwork panel or gate, added to the front. Train some climbers and wall shrubs to camouflage the edges and you have an imaginary door or window through to another part of the garden.

Traditional topiary can be expensive to buy ready-trimmed but you could make your own

BELOW: *Gardens don't always need extra adornment. This is an attractive garden without any ornaments to speak of – just lots of great plants.*

spirals and cones quite easily using topiary frames and ivy (see pages 248–249) or clip some spheres or domes using a quick growing hedging shrub like *Lonicera nitida*. Roughly trim young plants to shape using secateurs. Water and feed to encourage regrowth and then during the rest of spring and summer, use small hand shears to clip more precisely until the form becomes a solid ball (see page 248 for more topiary tips).

DIY sculpture

Weatherproof items such as a collection of shells, coloured glass bottles or teapots could be showcased in a corner of the patio, ranged along the top of a retaining wall or set into wall niches. Make a cairn by piling flat pieces of stone on top of one another or fill stacked mini gabion cages with logs, tiles, bricks and slates to create a habitat wall for mini beasts that also doubles as a piece of modern art. And continuing the theme of recycling, why not give a new lease of life to an old kitchen chair by painting it with eye-catching colours or patterns? Disused machinery parts or tools and equipment can also act as sculptural elements. Find a spot for metal wheels and cogs, an old hand pump, a mangle or antique lawn roller. And on a more surreal and fun note, a salvaged fireplace could become a focal point for a courtyard garden, the grate filled with hot coloured flowers.

ABOVE: *This old water wheel may not be in use any longer but it still makes an absolutely stand-out feature when set up against white weatherboarding.*

BELOW: *This old wooden step ladder has been put to imaginative use as an alternative multiple plant stand.*

Placing ornaments

■ Raise small pieces up on a plinth, steps, retaining wall or table or set in a wall niche. Alternatively 'anchor' them with a large object such as a big plant pot, topiary spiral or garden bench.

■ Set sculptures, figurines and decorative containers half-hidden amongst border plantings, just peeping out from among them.

■ Frame tall elements, for example an urn on a plinth, using a climber-covered archway, a pair of columnar conifers or view through a gap in a border or hedge.

■ Use pathways, lawns, and rectangular shaped pools to direct the eye to the ornament in the distance.

■ Highlight within shaped paving features, for example, place at the centre of a stone paved or gravel circle.

■ Create niches and alcoves in hedges and borders or along the edge of a pathway to showcase decorative elements including garden furniture.

■ Repeat objects at regular intervals to create a rhythm along a path, border or terrace, for example potted topiary spheres, wooden obelisks, lanterns.

ABOVE: *These stone goblin figurines have been deliberately placed amongst these ferns, where they look real and draw the viewer's eye towards themselves.*

accessorize your garden

RIGHT: *These candle holders, tea lights and placemats have all been carefully colour coordinated, together with the floral decorations on the table.*

BELOW RIGHT: *This bright purple painted wall becomes a feature in its own right, such is the strength of the colour that has been used.*

Colour coordination

Just as with interior design, you can use colour to create a distinctive look and feel for certain areas of the garden. For example in an outdoor dining and barbeque space, use colour coordinated tableware, candles, chair cushions and so on as well as toning pots and containers, foliage and flowers. For a party or special occasion, you could even drape a pergola with matching voile or muslin.

Create a visual link through the whole garden by selectively painting or staining elements such as wooden garden furniture; a summerhouse, gazebo or shed; fence and trellis panels and window shutters. Take care that you don't annoy neighbours by using fence colour that bleeds through to the other side or by painting a garden building or wall such a vibrant shade that it spoils their view – colour choice is very personal!

In cooler, cloudier parts of the world, the quality of light means that blues, greens and blue-biased reds, purples, browns and rusts work better outdoors than clear bright yellows, oranges, orange-reds and pinks. As well as exterior quality wood paints and stains you can have masonry paint mixed to whatever shade you please and so it is possible to paint a brick, stone or rendered wall to make a bold statement or to give a sitting or entertaining area more character.

BELOW: *This garden has been colour coded with a green and blue theme right across it – the fence, wall, furniture, slate and so on all correspond to the theme.*

ABOVE: *This unusual 'silk bag' container brings a touch of style and works beautifully in association with the colours in the flowers and wall behind.*

Potted style

A well-chosen and carefully positioned container has the potential to act as a sculptural element or focal point and the type and colour of pot you choose can help to strengthen the overall design theme. For example, in a contemporary garden a line of sleek metallic containers filled with a single subject like agapanthus might be used to line a rill-like water feature, or you could place a pair of white terrazzo bowls planted with blue grasses on either side of steps. Meanwhile a more traditional garden, perhaps one inspired by the Italian renaissance, could feature an ornate terracotta pot with a lush, subtropical arrangement, a topiary bay tree perhaps or a vibrant planting of geraniums. Glazed ginger jars in jade, lacquer red or black look distinctly oriental but choose wide-necked pots for planting using compact bamboos like *Fargesia murielae* 'Simba' as well as Japanese maples, variegated sedges and hostas. Wooden barrels, old milk churns, wicker baskets and chimney pots have cottage garden charm and in this type of garden you can turn all kinds of once functional containers into pots and feature a jumble of herbs, vegetables and flowers. And for Greek island simplicity, choose dusty white tinged terracotta pots, large unplanted olive jars (pithoi) and amphora.

Surface treatments

Weathered pots and other objects often look more at home in a garden than those that are brand new, especially in more rustic settings. Try the following techniques:

Terracotta pots are often dark orange-brown at first and need time for the white salts to work to the surface and for a bloom of green algae to appear. To speed up this process:
■ Stand new clay items in a damp, shady spot having soaked them in a bowl of water first.
■ OR paint dry terracotta with a dilute solution of white artist's acrylic paint or the remains of a paint tester pot diluted down with water. The water soaks in quickly and leaves the paint on the surface as a dusty patina.
■ Work round embellishments and under the pot rim with a piece of natural sponge, pre-soaked in water and dipped in a diluted mix of green and yellow acrylics to simulate algae and lichen.

Plastic terracotta can be a very convincing alternative and weighs far less. Use the paint techniques described above – you may need to apply several layers, allowing each coat to dry first. Dab off excess paint with kitchen towel.

New reconstituted stone and concrete ornaments and pots:
■ Apply a proprietary stone ageing solution.
■ OR paint on a dilute solution of manure or natural yogurt to encourage algal growth.
■ OR use artist's acrylic paints to build up layers of colour to simulate weathered stone.

Painted wood can be distressed as follows:
■ Roughly paint on a base coat of white universal primer.
■ Paint parts to be distressed with an exterior quality wood paint. Choose a colour a few shades darker or lighter than the top coat.
■ Apply one or two top coats of your main shade.
■ Once dry, selectively sand down to expose some of the previous layer with fine or medium-grade sandpaper. Choose areas that would naturally wear first such as the middle of a bench. Seal with exterior quality matt varnish.

PROJECT

Making a decorative wooden trug

This is a fun and useful way to convert some of your waste wood and offcuts into a useful item. The beauty of this project is that you are not restricted to any one size. In fact, the more rustic and aged the trug looks, the better! Some of the offcuts from the other wooden projects featured in this book would form ideal sides for the trug. Use something thicker for the ends, so that there is something substantial to nail into. The slopes on the sides and ends can be as much as 25mm (1in) or so, but watch out not to make them too great so that you can bend the handle around them. The bottom can be made from an old piece of plywood. You may not be able to bend the handle into shape, as shown. Use a length of thick rope, plaited string or twisted withies as alternatives. If you have them to hand, use brass or copper pins and some exterior grade glue to make the joints.

Tips, tools and materials

SKILL LEVEL
- This is a beginner level project that anyone can undertake. Some DIY skills would be useful.

BEST TIME TO DO
- Anytime, if you plan to construct the trug indoors.

TOOLS REQUIRED
- Hammer; drill; screwdriver; saw; spanner; spirit level; tape measure; pencil.

MATERIALS REQUIRED
- This project can normally be constructed from offcuts and waste materials. You will also need a couple of small bolts and some fine nails or pins and glue.

TIME REQUIRED
- It will take a day or possibly a weekend to make up this wooden trug. Allow more time if you plan to make up several different trugs at once.

1 It's a good idea to plan ahead with this little project. Cut and progressively curve your handles by soaking them in a water butt. Alternatively steam bend them round a former.

2 The trugs can be made up from any old bits of waste or offcut wood that you might have lying around. Decide on the size of trug you want to make and mark out and cut the end angles.

3 Pre-drill the ends of each side with a small pilot hole to avoid splitting. Put some glue under the joint and nail the sides to the ends.

4 The bottom should be bevelled to fit the slope of the sides and ends. Make it slightly bigger so that it sits up from the lower edges slightly. Pin and glue in place.

5 Having used up some of the odds and ends, colour the inside of the trug with some left-over paint.

6 Once your handle has reached its final shape, trim it to the desired length and drill the bolt holes in each end.

7 Ideally, use brass or stainless steel bolts to attach the handle to the body of the trug. This will help avoid corrosion and staining.

8 A small, copper pin driven right through the handle and side, and bent over on the inside, will help to hold the handle steady. Varnish the exterior of the trug to give it some protection.

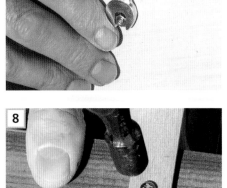

PROJECT: **Making a decorative wooden trug**

239

PROJECT

Planting a metal container

Tips, tools and materials

SKILL LEVEL
- This is a beginner level project that anyone can undertake. Some knowledge of plants might be useful.

BEST TIME TO DO
- Mid- to late spring or whenever potted bulbs are available.

TOOLS REQUIRED
- Scissors; trowel.

MATERIALS REQUIRED
- Metal container; greenhouse insulation or bubble-wrap; sticky tape; gravel; potting mix (with added loam); *Anemone coronaria* (single or double); Viola (bedding variety); *Senecio cineraria* 'Silver Dust'; *Lysimachia nummularia* 'Aurea'; *Hedera helix* 'Little Diamond' (or similar).

TIME REQUIRED
- Allow half a day to assemble materials and make up this container.

Spring patio displays often have a cottage garden feel with a bright jumble of old-fashioned bedding varieties like double daisies, wallflowers and forget-me-nots as well as traditional bulbs. This scheme shows that you can update your displays by choosing contemporary containers and simple colour schemes. Select pots with a streamlined or perhaps angular shape, made from rustproof metals like zinc and aluminium. Metal pots have poor thermal insulation qualities so must be lined to prevent plant roots from getting too hot or too cold. To make re-planting easier, add an inner plastic pot after the insulation, to neatly contain the compost. Black, white and grey terrazzo pots as well as plain ceramic planters with metallic glazes, also look good in an urban setting. Another technique for adding a contemporary feel is to use just one plant or flower to fill the pot.

1 Line the container with plastic bubble-wrap or greenhouse insulation. Tuck under the rim and hold it in place as you work with sticky tape. Do not cover the drainage hole.

2 Add around 8cm (3in) of gravel to provide drainage at the base of the pot.

3 Fill two-thirds of the container with a potting mix that contains a proportion of loam or John Innes.

240 | Decorative garden extras

4 Using either three pots of a single De Caen anemone or a double-flowered Saint Brigid type, plant at the centre of the container.

5 For sparkle and textural contrast, form a backdrop to the deep blue anemone with several plants of *Senecio* 'Silver Dust'.

6 Create a surround of a bedding viola like the long-flowered Sorbet Series, and fill the spaces in between all the plants as you go with more potting mix.

7 To soften the front of the container, plant trails of golden creeping Jenny (*Lysimachia nummularia* 'Aurea'). Trim overlong stems with scissors.

8 Use a compact English ivy cultivar such as the white-variegated *Hedera* 'Little Diamond' used here or a gold splashed form. Dig your fingers into the pot of cuttings to open it out into a strip. Fill any remaining gaps in the planting with more compost and water the container thoroughly. Stand it in a sunny or lightly shaded spot.

Spring bulb alternatives for the anemone

Choose varieties that are compact, early flowering and weather resistant and which have a relatively long flowering period. Try the following:-

- *Muscari* (grape hyacinth) deep blue
- *Narcissus* (cyclamineus types) – daffodil
- 'Dove Wings' (white)
- 'February Gold' (yellow)
- 'Jack Snipe' (yellow and white)
- 'Jenny' (cream)
- 'Jetfire' (yellow and orange)

- *Narcissus* 'Tête àTête' (multi-headed daffodil) (yellow)
- *Tulipa* 'Red Riding Hood' (Greigii tulip) (scarlet)
- *Tulipa* 'Toronto' (multi-headed Greigii tulip) (pink)
- *Tulipa* 'Fusilier' (multi-headed tulip) (scarlet)

PROJECT

Planting a tub of shade-loving plants

Most patio plants prefer a bright location to perform well but not all sitting areas are bathed in sunlight. To add colour to a shady patio, it's best to rely mainly on a combination of attractive foliage plants, which will tolerate fewer sunshine hours, and just a scattering of blooming specimens. Flowers for containers in shade include fuchsias (bush and trailing varieties); begonias of which there are now many forms; busy Lizzie (bedding impatiens); lobelia, pansies and violas. Vary the leaf shape, texture and overall habit of the plants, combining big solid shapes with lighter, filigree forms such as ferns. Shade-tolerant grasses and sedges (Carex) also work well with broad-leaved plants like hostas and bergenia (elephant's ears). A half-barrel is wide enough to accommodate a range of plants and is ideal for informal and country and cottage garden settings.

Tips, tools and materials

SKILL LEVEL
- This is a beginner level project that anyone can undertake. Some knowledge of plants might be useful.

BEST TIME TO DO
- Any time from late spring (after the last frosts) to mid-summer, when a good range of plants is available.

TOOLS REQUIRED
- Trowel.

MATERIALS REQUIRED
- Wooden half barrel; crock; trowel; gravel; potting mix containing loam (John Innes) – you can buy these ready mixed; slow-release granular fertilizer; *Hosta* 'Golden Tiara'; *Dryopteris erythrosora* (copper shield fern); *Brunnera macrophylla* 'Jack Frost'; *Hakonechloa macra* 'Alboaurea'; *Begonia* 'Peardrop'.

TIME REQUIRED
- Less than an hour.

1 Particularly with large containers, it is important to create efficient drainage. Cover the hole with a piece of broken pot, tile or slate to prevent potting mix washing down and blocking it.

2 Next add several centimetres (inches) of gravel or stone chippings. Excess water will run down into this layer and away from the plant roots. This will prevent the roots from rotting.

3 Cover the gravel with potting compost. This should be a fibrous mix containing ground composted bark and loam to mimic woodland soil.

4 For convenience and to provide a steady supply of nutrients through a large part of the growing season, mix in an appropriate amount of slow-release fertilizer granules into the potting compost.

5 Check that the potting mix is at the right height and then after removing the pot, add the hosta. 'Golden Tiara' is one of a range of petite, small-leaved hostas that are ideal for pots and tubs.

6 For more texture and colour, next add the copper shield fern. This has reddish new growth that lasts well into summer.

7 The beautiful heart-shaped, white-marbled leaves of *Brunnera* 'Jack Frost' really stand out in shade and this woodlander enjoys the same conditions as the fern and hosta.

8 Add the Japanese variegated grass, *Hakonechloa*

macra 'Alboaurea', arranging the soft, ribbon-like leaves so that they cascade over the rim of the barrel.

9 For a splash of colour that fits in well with the fresh palette already established by the foliage plants, introduce the apricot-flowered begonia.

This arching variety has double, as well as less showy single blooms. The single female flowers, either side of the double males, have a winged seed case behind the petals, and can be nipped out with thumb and forefinger early on in their development in order to stimulate continued flowering.

Conserving moisture

It's a good idea to plunge all plants in a bucket of water before adding them to a container arrangement to ensure that moisture has reached right to the centre of the rootball. It is difficult to do this once they have been planted. Water the finished container well after planting to settle the soil around the roots and then consider mulching (topping) with a layer of fine chipped bark around 2–3cm deep. This will help to seal in the moisture and also prevent the potting mix wearing away and exposing the plant roots during subsequent waterings. Other mulching options for containers include coloured glass or acrylic chips, gravel and slate.

Planting a hanging basket

SKILL LEVEL
- This is a beginner level project that anyone can undertake.

BEST TIME TO DO
- Any time from mid-spring (if frost protection is available) to mid-summer.

TOOLS REQUIRED
- Trowel; watering can; bucket.

MATERIALS REQUIRED
- 36cm/14in traditional wire hanging basket; coir pre-formed liner; heavy/stable pot; water gel crystals; potting mix designed for container plantings; *Nemesia* 'Claudette'; Zonal Pelargonium (geranium); Impatiens – New Guinea hybrid (busy Lizzie); Verbena Tapien Pink; *Hedera helix* (English ivy); *Salvia officinalis* 'Tricolor'.

TIME REQUIRED
- Up to an hour to plant the basket, but up to three hours in total if using water gel crystals.

A bare wall can be considerably enlivened by the addition of a hanging basket. Traditional baskets have upright, arching and trailing ingredients to create a balanced and elegant shape and with regular attention including watering and feeding they can grow to be an impressive summer spectacle. Keep an eye open for pests such as aphids on shoot tips and deal with them promptly. The appropriately named powdery mildew sometimes appears when plants are in too hot and dry a position. Trim back affected growth, feed and water well and move to a cooler spot if possible. The plants in this arrangement were chosen for the way their colours blended and complemented one another and for the way the different shapes, textures and overall forms contrasted. You can follow the same approach no matter what colour scheme you prefer.

1 Place the basket in the top of a heavy clay pot and to assist planting, unhook one of the chains and move them to one side.

2 Add the liner. Here, a coir or coconut fibre liner has been chosen. This retains the compost and helps to keep the roots moist.

3 Put in some of the pre-mixed, water-retentive compost. At this stage you can also add slow-release fertilizer granules to keep the plants well fed for a few months.

4 Place the semi-trailing nemesia towards the back of the basket. This plant can flower all summer long without being dead-headed and will survive mild winters given a sheltered spot

5 Add the vibrantly coloured zonal pelargonium.

6 Next set the large-flowered New Guinea hybrid impatiens (better known as busy Lizzie) in position. Keep filling the spaces between the plants with compost as you go. It is easier than doing this at the end.

7 For foliage colour and to brighten the centre of the display, add the drought-tolerant culinary sage (*Salvia officinalis* 'Tricolor'). The leaves are splashed pink and cream and tie the colours together well.

8 Ease a couple of pots of the ferny-leaved trailing verbena Tapien Pink. This series comes in a range of colours to suit any arrangement.

9 Finally, continue the bright creamy-white variegation theme with falls of English ivy. Finish filling in any gaps between the rootballs and water well. If planting a basket before the end of the spring frosts, hang it in a protected space to settle. Keep the hanging basket well watered at all times.

ABOVE: *Just about any lightweight container can be suspended on chains or wires to serve as a hanging basket.*

PROJECT: Planting a hanging basket   245

PROJECT

Planting a hay rack

Tips, tools and materials

SKILL LEVEL
- This is a beginner level project that anyone can undertake.

BEST TIME TO DO
- Late spring to mid-summer.

TOOLS REQUIRED
- Trowel, drill with masonry bit, spirit level.

MATERIALS REQUIRED
- Wrought iron or plastic-coated wire hay rack; wall plugs and screws for mounting the hay rack; a coir pre-formed liner; potting mix suitable for pots and containers containing loam (John Innes); *Hebe* 'Silver Queen'; *Euonymus fortunei* 'Golden Harlequin'; *Angelonia* 'Deep Plum'; *Hedera helix* (yellow variegated cultivar) English ivy.

TIME REQUIRED
- Between one and two hours to plant the hay rack as well as to fix the screws in to the wall to hang it on.

Black wrought iron manger and hayrack wall planters work well in period settings and in places where you want to achieve a country or cottage garden feel. They have an advantage over terracotta wall pots in that they are generally larger and more practically shaped, allowing for more varied and impressive planting displays. Consequently, they will require more space, however. Try adding small shrubs, long-flowering herbaceous perennials, tender perennials or patio plants, and flowering annual climbers used as trailers as well as dwarf bulbs. Most importantly, do ensure that the fixings are properly secured as these baskets can weigh a lot once watered. Follow the manufacturer's instructions. Mark the position of the screws on the wall using the empty hayrack as a guide and check with a spirit level before drilling.

1 Prop the hay rack up on a couple of bricks ready for planting and add the preformed inner liner. This is made from coir, a by-product of the coconut industry. Press the liner firmly into the hay rack until it sits snugly in the bottom.

2 Part fill the liner with potting mixture and check that it is at the correct level to begin planting by trying the largest plants while they are still in their pots.

3 Water plants beforehand by plunging them in a bucket of water. Wait for the air bubbles to finish escaping – which tells you that the rootball is soaked – and then put the plants to one side to drain. Next, add the variegated hebe to the hay rack. At this stage it doesn't matter if it is not quite upright. You can adjust as more plants and compost are added.

4 Balance the weight of the hebe by adding the variegated euonymus on the other side. This should stabilize the hayrack.

5 Place one of the angelonia plants towards the front of the basket. The flowering colour can be spread through the arrangement to produce a more informal look.

6 Select an ivy with long trails but plenty of leaf coverage at the base. Take it out of its pot and, using your thumbs, prise the rooted cuttings apart to turn them from a circular arrangement into a row. This will take up less space, allowing for planting behind, and will form

ABOVE: *The completed hay rack. A secure mounting is essential for this heavy item.*

a curtain of ivy trails to cover the front of the basket.

7 Plant the ivy, arranging the trails to hang over the middle front of the hay rack. Once the hay rack is hung on the wall, you may need to trim the ivy from time to time to keep it in proportion.

8 Add the final two angelonias and correct the angle of any of the other plants in the hay rack, at the same time as feeding more potting mix in between them. Firm in all the plants and water thoroughly.

Decorative effects with woven and sculpted ivy

Tips, tools and materials

SKILL LEVEL
- This is a beginner level project that anyone can undertake. Some experience in growing and training plants would be useful.

BEST TIME TO DO
- Any time from mid-spring through to early autumn.

TOOLS REQUIRED
- Trowel; watering can.

MATERIALS REQUIRED
- Three pots of rooted ivy cuttings (6–8 in a pot) with long trails.; topiary frame – galvanized metal or plastic-coated wire (to prevent rust); terracotta pot; crock for drainage hole; potting mix containing loam (John Innes).

TIME REQUIRED
- Up to an hour for initial training but several weeks are required to cover the frame completely.

Topiary, the art of clipping and training plants to make decorative garden elements, is thought by many to require tremendous skill and artistry. In fact there are many simple but stylish topiary forms, such as clipped box balls, that are quick and easy to make. Ivy topiary, using a frame to create the desired shape, is very straightforward and, given time to grow and fully cover the wire, can rival the look of traditional clipped topiary. Wire frames come in all shapes and sizes from geometric designs such as cones and spirals to figures of animals, birds and so on. As well as covering frames with ivy, you can also set them into the ground and plant up with traditional subjects such as box (*Buxus sempervirens*), **yew** (*Taxus baccata*), **privet** (**Ligustrum**) and **shrubby honeysuckle** (*Lonicera nitida*), clipping growth to fill the frame and keep the desired shape well defined.

1 The antique style bishop's mitre frame is eye-catching in its own right and looks well with the traditional Long Tom clay pot.

2 As with all container plantings, cover the drainage hole with a shard of pottery, a piece of tile or a stone to help prevent clogging and waterlogging.

3 Add a couple of trowel-fulls of gravel to the pot to assist with drainage.

4 Fill the pot to around two thirds of capacity with a good-quality potting mixture, allowing for the ivy to be planted but still leaving a space below the rim of the pot for watering.

5 Take the ivy out of its pot and, using your thumbs, split the circle of cuttings apart to form a row. This will make it easier to distribute the ivy and will encourage it to climb and trail.

6 Plant the ivy round the edge of the pot so that most of the trails hang over the edge; however, point some inwards as well. Fill the pot with more compost and firm the ivy in lightly with your fingers.

7 Place the frame over the pot and begin to push the prongs into the compost. As you do this, pull some of the ivy trails through to the inside of the frame.

8 With each stem in turn, wind around the wires, starting at the base and moving upwards or diagonally.

Caring for Ivy topiary

Water thoroughly and place the topiary in a sheltered, shady spot for a few days so that the ivy can recover. Next move into a reasonably well-lit position on the patio and water and liquid feed regularly to encourage growth. Continue to pinch out new shoot tips and to wind the stems until the frame is covered. Hold any obstinate shoots in place with garden twine. Clip the finished topiary with scissors occasionally. Mist with water in hot dry weather to discourage red spider mite. After a few years the ivy will become too woody and threadbare and the frame will need replanting.

ABOVE: *You can train ivy over a wire grille as well as on a hoop, but water and feed the plants regularly to ensure continued trouble-free growth.*

Making an ornamental bird bath

Tips, tools and materials

SKILL LEVEL
- This is an intermediate level project requiring some DIY skills.

BEST TIME TO DO
- Whenever the weather is reasonably fine and the ground is not too wet or muddy.

TOOLS REQUIRED
- Saw; mitre saw system; lathe (not essential but useful); hand drill; chisel; screwdriver; spirit level; marking gauge; rule; tape measure; pencil.

MATERIALS REQUIRED
- Preservative-treated softwood; plywood; enough exterior cladding to cover the frame (see cutting list opposite), plus odds and ends to make frames, etc.

TIME REQUIRED
- 1–2 days or perhaps a weekend will normally be required to construct this ornamental bird bath.

This project shows you how to make a classically styled stand for an ornamental bird bath. Here it has been finished with a stone effect, but it could be coloured to fit in with your own garden scheme as you wish. The project is designed to provide a pedestal for an independent bird bath vessel. These are available in a host of different shapes, sizes and materials. If you already have a bird bath to hand, then adjust the dimensions of this project to suit. Based on a simple box, this feature is easy to make. The key is getting the size of mouldings in proportion in relationship to the height and overall size of the stand. To make the stand look naturally aged, mix a little water with some yoghurt and dab it on in patches all over the structure. This will encourage algae to grow and will create an effective weathered look quite quickly.

1 This stand is designed to look like a classic column with mouldings on both the top and bottom. Inside the core, four corner posts hold everything together. If you use ready preservative-treated timbers, try to keep the sealed ends for the very bottom of the column.

2 Four equal-sized sheets of exterior grade ply are glued and screwed to the corner posts. Attach one piece of plywood

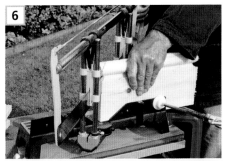

to each post to start leaving about 6mm (¼in) of the post protruding at what will be the bottom end of the stand. This will help lift the sides slightly off the ground, out of the wet.

3 Join all four sides together, with glue and screws, and then check that the finished box section is jointed-up square.

4 Make sure you countersink all your screw heads. Fill any cracks and the recessed screws with an exterior grade filler. The colour is not important; the whole thing should receive several coats of finish to cover it up.

5 Once the filler has hardened, leave it overnight if you can. Sand all the excess back level with the side panel surfaces. Fill and clean back any other gaps found at this stage.

6 The lower base moulding is mitred and fitted to the basic box structure. Use fairly wide pieces if you can. This provides balance once the narrower moulding is fitted to the top.

Cutting list

Component:	Qty:	LENGTH nominal:	WIDTH finished:	THICKNESS finished:
Inner corner posts:	4	600mm/2ft	50mm/2in	50mm/2in
Sides:	4	600mm/2ft	225mm/9in	12mm/½in
Lower base moulding:	4	300mm/1ft	150mm/6in	18mm/¾in
Upper mouldings:	4	300mm1ft	50mm/2in	18mm/¾in
Top:	1	375mm/1ft3in	315mm/12½in	315mm/12½in

Alternative bowls

There are any number of differently styled and coloured bowls to choose from that will serve as an effective bird bath and make a strong decorative feature for the garden. These can be used in conjunction with a stand or simply stood on low feet.

ABOVE: *Several different styles of container that would all serve well as bird baths. The depth of water should always be kept shallow for smaller birds.*

7 Apply plenty of glue to each side face and ends and then clamp the mouldings onto the side panels.

8 Cutting a hole in the centre of the top will provide a useful location seat for any birdbath placed on it.

9 Fit some battens between the posts at the top of the side panels and attach the top piece to these.

10 Decorate the column according to your preference.

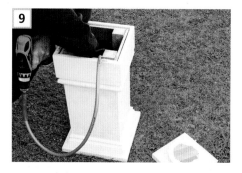

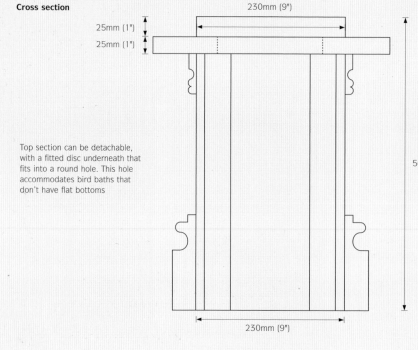

Cross section

230mm (9")

25mm (1")

25mm (1")

The applied mouldings fitted to the top and bottom of the bird bath column are standard items that are readily available

Top section can be detachable, with a fitted disc underneath that fits into a round hole. This hole accommodates bird baths that don't have flat bottoms

560mm (22")

230mm (9")

All measurements are indicative only and should be checked off full-size drawings

OPPOSITE: *The finished article. The stand could be mistaken for stone from a distance.*

PROJECT

Making a traditional wooden dovecote

Making a multi-sided dovecote can be quite challenging if you are to get the angles and proportions exactly right. The beauty of this particular project is that it can be scaled-up to accommodate a whole flock of doves if necessary. This example is designed as a free-standing dovecote, but you could fix it permanently into the ground. If so, allow an extra 45cm (18in) length on the central post. The key to success is getting the hexagonal shapes right from the start. If you are a little uncertain about where to start, work up some full-size drawings on an odd piece of flat-surfaced material. Measurements, shapes and angles can then be taken directly from this. For a dovecote of this size three internal sections provide about the right space for the birds. If you make a larger one it could have multiple layers and more compartments.

Tips, tools and materials

SKILL LEVEL
- This is a fairly advanced project requiring strong DIY skills.

BEST TIME TO DO
- Whenever the weather is reasonably fine and the ground is not too wet or muddy.

TOOLS REQUIRED
- Saw (ideally a powered bandsaw); lathe (not essential but useful); hand drill; chisel; screwdriver; spirit level; marking gauge; rule; tape measure; pencil.

MATERIALS REQUIRED
- Preservative-treated softwood; plywood; enough exterior cladding to cover the frame (see cutting list opposite), plus odds and ends to make frames, etc.

TIME REQUIRED
- 2–3 days or perhaps two weekends will normally be required to construct this wooden dovecote.

1 The key to this project is getting the two hexagonal shapes right. Set out carefully and cut from the plywood to start.

2 As part of the marking out process the centre is found. Using this as the core then mark out each of the square, central stem holes. Cut the squares out so that they are a snug but not too tight fit.

3 Use some equal lengths of 38 x 50mm (1 x 2in) to join the two ply sections together. Turn each one so that the wide face is outwards before fixing. Trim off the excess plywood face points once all have been secured

4 Three internal, ply sections form the partitions. These are simply cut to size, glued and pinned in place.

5 Decide how many access points per compartment you want; two are ideal.

6 The external cladding is laid and fixed on with the holes at alternate levels. A thin strip can be laid down the face of each of the joining pieces to provide a tidy edge.

7 Four brackets are shaped to fix the box structure to the central post. These are cut from 25 x 100mm (1 x 4in) and shaped as desired.

8 The finial for the top of the dovecote being turned on a lathe. Start by creating a hexagonal shape from a block of 100 x 100mm (4 x 4in) timber before mounting in the lathe and shaping.

5

8

6

9

7

10

Cutting list

Component:	Qty:	LENGTH nominal:	WIDTH finished:	THICKNESS finished:
Stem, central pole:	1	2.4m/8ft	75mm/3in	75mm/3in
Cross feet:	2	900mm/3ft	75mm/3in	50mm/2in
Lower braces:	4	600mm/2ft	50mm/2in	50mm/2in
Plywood, (half a standard sheet):	1	1.2m/4ft	1.2m/4ft	12mm/½in
Finial:	1	300mm/12in	100mm/4in	100mm/4in

9 With the main box and finial in place the rafters are fitted and fixed to the top of the unit. You see here how the base, hexagonal shape of the finial determines the positions of the rafters at the top. Additional, pre-coloured, strips are fitted to the rafters to form the tidy edge for each roof section.

10 The retained off-cuts from the access holes can be used to make the perches. These are shaped, platform- and bracket-joined and coloured before fixing to the main structure.

11 A free-standing dovecote needs a set of sturdy, well-balanced feet. Cut cross-halving joints into the two pieces that form these, then glue and fix them together with four screws round the edge of the joint.

12 After painting the feet, bore a recess into the central, lower section of the assembly. This should be deep enough to take the head and a washer of a 100mm (4in) coach screw. Countersink the screw hole.

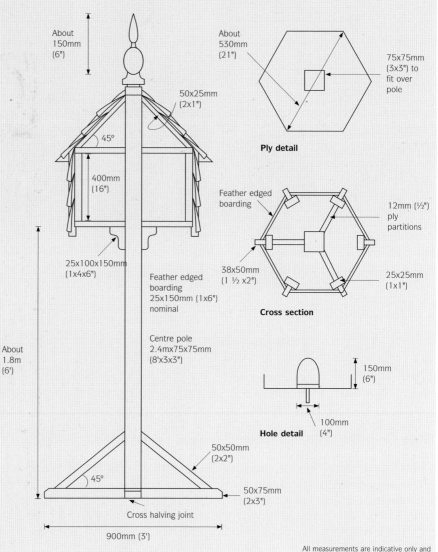

About 150mm (6")

50x25mm (2x1")

45°

400mm (16")

25x100x150mm (1x4x6")

About 1.8m (6')

Feather edged boarding 25x150mm (1x6") nominal

Centre pole 2.4mx75x75mm (8'x3x3")

45°

Cross halving joint

900mm (3')

50x50mm (2x2")

50x75mm (2x3")

About 530mm (21")

75x75mm (3x3") to fit over pole

Ply detail

Feather edged boarding

12mm (½") ply partitions

38x50mm (1 ½x2")

25x25mm (1x1")

Cross section

150mm (6")

100mm (4")

Hole detail

All measurements are indicative only and should be checked off full-size drawings

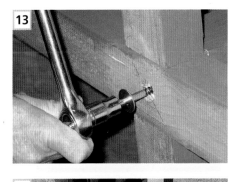

13 The coach bolt is driven up through the feet into the central stem. Drill a pilot hole in the stem once the middle has been found. A little grease or lubrication on the coach screw will make its passage easier. Ensure that it is driven in as tightly as possible, as otherwise the feet assembly will be unstable and will move about.

14 Cut 45 degree angles on the ends of the lower braces and paint these pieces. Fix them on to finish the job off.

ABOVE AND OPPOSITE:
The finished dovecote, in position on a lawn. All that is required now is a few doves! You can buy these from pet stores, but if you are lucky you might be able to attract wild birds by scattering seed on the doorsteps of the compartments.

Constructing a brick or stone barbeque

These days a barbeque grill is an essential item in most gardens. The range and options available are endless, from very simple, home-made versions through to more sophisticated models that run on bottled gas. Make your barbeque grill a feature in the garden or on the patio by using some natural materials for a permanent surround. The most simple of these to use is old bricks. A search through your local directory or on the internet will disclose a number of sources. Try to match the colour to other adjacent structures or just go for the one you like. Unless you want a really rustic effect, ideally try to acquire clean bricks of a regular size. Use recycled materials to create the tray and grill wherever you can. This is a big project, but once your barbeque is built you will really make the most of enjoying outdoor living on warm, sunny days.

Tips, tools and materials

SKILL LEVEL
- This is an intermediate level project requiring some DIY skills.

BEST TIME TO DO
- Whenever the weather is reasonably fine and the ground is not too wet or muddy.

TOOLS REQUIRED
- Bolster chisel; brick hammer; trowel; spirit level; shovel; wheelbarrow. A cement mixer would be useful but is not essential.

MATERIALS REQUIRED
- Bricks and mortar. Depending upon size you will need 150 old bricks or more. Plus sand, a bag or two of cement and aggregate mix for the concrete base.

TIME REQUIRED
- 2–3 days or perhaps a weekend will normally be required to construct this brick barbeque.

1 You can build a barbeque grill from just about anything – stone, concrete blocks or old bricks. The latter can be found all over the place, but try to get them all the same size. This lot is a mixed batch.

2 Some old bricks will have the original mortar still on them. This must be cleaned off before the bricks are re-used. A wide bolster chisel and a brick hammer are useful tools for this.

3 If the barbeque grill is to be incorporated into a decking feature, lay the foundations before the deck. Long nails will key in and support the surrounding joists for the decking. If it is to stand alone, dig out and firm a foundation which is at least 150mm (6in) deep.

4 Check the base for level and get your tools all to hand. A fairly light mix of mortar – say 5 or 6 to 1, sand to cement – will be more than sufficient for this job. Pile up the bricks in sizes near to where you will be working.

Barbeque safety tips

Barbeques can be dangerous, particularly if there are small children or pets around. Once you have constructed your brick or stone barbeque, follow these basic safety tips every time you use it:

- Never use a grill indoors.
- Never leave a grill unattended, particularly when children or animals are present.
- Have a fire extinguisher or garden hose within reach.
- Never wear loose clothing when grilling.
- If your clothes catch fire, remember to 'stop, drop and roll'.
- Use long-handled barbecue tools or flame-resistant mitts.
- Clean your grill regularly and keep it free of grease build-up.
- Keep a water spray bottle ready to reduce flare-ups.

For charcoal grills
- If you use lighter fluid, remove the container from the area before lighting the grill.
- Never add lighter fluid after the coals are lit.
- Leave the used charcoal in the grill until it is cold.
- Never place the used charcoal in a plastic dustbin. Instead, place it in a metal container and douse it with water.

For gas or propane grills
- Periodically clean the venture tubes.
- Always leave the lid open when igniting the grill.
- Never store a gas or propane tank in a garage, or in your home.
- Periodically check the gas or propane tank hose for cracks.
- Check for leaks using sudsy water whenever you replace or refill a gas or propane tank.

5

6

7

5 Lay the first rows of brick with a seam of mortar between them and the foundations. Build on this, overlapping the joints, layer upon layer. Regularly check that the structure is both square and vertical as you go along.

6 To get the joints to stagger, some bricks will need to be halved. A simple thump with a lump hammer and bolster chisel will generally do the job.

7 If walls are to be capped with tiles, check that they are level side to side. A little extra mortar placed underneath makes the job easier.

Charcoal grilling tips

After going to all the trouble of building your own brick barbeque surround, you will want to ensure that you can cook food to a high standard in it! For the best results, buy a decent grill tray and follow these tips when making your selection.

Construction

Look for a grill made of high-grade steel with a porcelain-enamel coating. The coating should be baked on and not just sprayed on. This will prevent rusting, peeling and fading. Leg couplings and grate supports should be welded for added strength. The lid – if it has one – should be heavy and should fit tightly.

Basic features

Cooking and charcoal grates should be nickel-plated or stainless steel. Both of these will clean up very easily and are also rust resistant. Make sure the handles are of wood or plastic. These will stay cool to the touch.

Added features

Easy disposal of ashes is a must. Some grills offer a one-touch system that sweeps the ashes into a disposal pan. A thermometer is always a good idea for keeping an eye on the temperature.

ABOVE: *A high-quality grill tray is an absolute pre-requisite for successful barbeque cooking. It should also be fully height adjustable.*

8

10

9

11

8 Build on beyond the level of the barbeque base. A castellated front makes an attractive feature. Always keep your best bricks for the top, where they are most visible.

9 Throughout the build, rake out the joints with a wooden dowel about 18mm (³/₄in) in diameter. Any gaps need to be carefully re-pointed; then brush off any excess mortar.

10 The barbeque tray itself can be made up from sheet metal and mesh. However, a simple and cheap solution is to use a prefabricated one. This tray has graduated sides to vary the intensity of the cooking heat. For effective grilling, it is vital to be able to adjust the height of the grill above the charcoal.

11 To prolong the life of a cheaper, thinner tray, and to help with heat retention, some bars of mild steel laid in the bottom are useful. Alternatively, you could line the base of the tray with small, flat stones.

Stylish embellishments

There are many ways in which you can embellish the basic brick or stone structure that is demonstrated in this project. For example, you could add stylish wooden slatted shelves, like those pictured here. Alternatively, you could build drinks and utensil holders into your design or maybe a decorative frieze of tiles for a truly personalized finish.

PROJECT: Constructing a brick or stone barbeque

261

12 If the barbeque tray or structure is to stand outside all year round it will need a cover. A simple one can be made from exterior ply and some battens screwed and glued together.

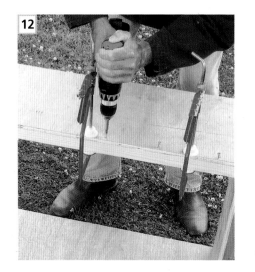

13 Finish the cover off by applying a good quality, exterior finish in a colour of your choice. Fire engine red works well in this case.

RIGHT: *The finished barbeque surround and grill, with the protective cover in place. If you make a cover out of wood, never place it over the barbeque until all the coals are fully extinguished, as otherwise there is a strong risk of it catching fire.*

OPPOSITE: *The finished barbeque surround and grill without the protective cover in place. A barbeque constructed on decking like this makes a stylish and practical feature, but care must be taken that hot coals are not allowed to drop onto the surrounding wooden boards.*

Decorative garden extras

Constructing a garden sundial

This wooden-based sundial is light enough to be moved around or out of the way if it is placed on a lawn. Just remember always to position the twelfth hour in a due north direction and, providing the sun is shining, you will be able to tell the time without a watch! When positioning your sundial don't forget to make allowances for any intercontinental time changes between summer and winter. The critical consideration with any sundial is the relationship between the hour angles and the position and shape of the gnomon (the arrow-like device on the top of the dial). Research is required. Your local library or an internet search will throw up a number of alternative solutions to work these specifics out. The simplest result is probably obtained by finding a reliable internet site with some templates that can be downloaded and printed off.

1 Start the dial construction by marking out a large circle on a planed wooden base. This can be made from any material that will stand continuous exposure to the elements.

2 The gnomon needs to be set exactly in line with the twelfth hour line. With your patterns to hand, cut a trench, 6mm (¼in) wide and about 12mm (½in) deep, slightly shorter than the base of the gnomon.

3 Using a jigsaw, bandsaw or hand saw, cut the actual disc to size and clean up the outer face.

4 Glue your hour angle template to the dial, ensuring that it is precisely in position. With a craft or marking knife scribe each of the hour angles dead centre. The template should also show the position of the gnomon. Strike some marks into the dial so that you can position this correctly later.

5 Using carving chisels, or a wide, straight chisel, cut the hour angle lines. To obtain a sharp result strike a cut down the centre first and then, at about 60 degrees, make the secondary cuts, from each side, to remove the waste wood.

6 Find some examples of Roman numerals and stick them on at the end of each hour angle line. Alternatively, you can draw out your own. Each of these numerals should now be carved out of the dial in a similar way to the hour angle lines. Clean up any waste wood.

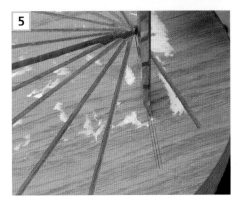

Garden vista stops and 'exclamation marks'

Vertical garden structures – and particularly sundials – have been used for hundreds of years in garden design to serve as end stops or stand-out features – 'exclamation marks', if you will – at the end of long vistas. In the case of a sundial, this makes a lot of sense, as it should not be encumbered by other objects which could cast shadows over it. The effect can be enhanced by mowing or building a long narrow path to the structure, as pictured here. The positioning of the sundial and the extended access to it maximize its effectiveness as a decorative garden feature and make it really stand out.

RIGHT: *This classical stone and lead sundial is not very big, but it makes a huge statement nevertheless, due to its location in the garden.*

7 To ensure that the carved lines and numerals stand out clearly from the base of the dial, apply some dark paint to them. Work it well in with a fine paintbrush. Once the paint is dry, sand or plane off any excess as well as the residues of the paper templates.

8 Having shaped and fitted your gnomon, secure it in exactly the right position vertically, in line with the twelfth hour. A two-part exterior grade epoxy resin adhesive is ideal for this. Leave the gnomon taped in position until the adhesive has set.

9 To start the pyramid base, lay out the framing components on a flat surface. The top of the pyramid must be smaller than the dial.

10 Once the end angles of the rails have been established, cut them all off to length. You will find it useful to draw the frame structure out full size and take your measurements for all parts from this.

Variations on the theme

Sundials come in all shapes and sizes and can be constructed from any number of different materials. If you wanted to adapt the construction process described in this project, you could create a stand with smooth wooden sides as opposed to cladding (see the ornamental bird bath project on pages 250–253) and then use tile adhesive to stick broken tile pieces to it to create a mosaic effect (see the illustration below and the mosaic-making project described on pages 82–85).

11 Make up two sides individually first. A couple of screws and a dab of glue per joint will hold them firm enough. With the last four rails, then join these two sides together.

12 The end stops that give the edge of the pyramid definition sit at right-angles to the corners. To facilitate the fit, take the corner off each post by carefully planing a flat face down each one.

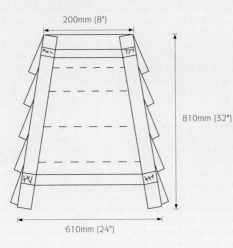

Cross section through stand

After the outside edge of each corner post has been removed, the end stops are fitted

200mm (8")

810mm (32")

610mm (24")

Dial disc and gnomon

32mm (1¼")

355mm (14")

To mark out the hours and the position and size of the gnomon, do some research online or at your local library

All measurements are indicative only and should be checked off full-size drawings

13 Clamp each end stop in place and fix with glue and three or four screws. The top of each should sit flush and level across. The top angle is the same as that on the end of each rail.

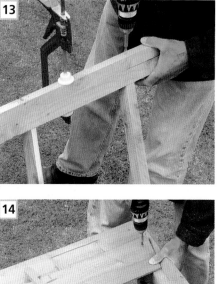

14 Starting at the bottom, and working round, fit the feather-edged boards. Each should be the same length, layer upon layer.

15 If the pyramid base is to be painted, it is a good idea to do this before the sundial itself is fitted on top of the base.

ABOVE: *The key to success with any sundial is getting the position of the gnomon – the part that casts the shadow over the dial – absolutely right. The gnomon should always point north, precisely in line with the twelfth hour.*

OPPOSITE: *The finished sundial. Position it in full sun where plants and trees cannot cast shadows over the dial.*

Garden structure problems/

plant pests and diseases

All gardens require regular maintenance, and perhaps the one downside of building lots of new features into your plot is that they will add to this by inevitably needing repair and renovation. Many of the problems associated with wooden garden structures can be pre-empted through the use of preservative-treated timbers, as recommended throughout this book. However, a little renewal of items will definitely be required at some stage.

By the same token, unfortunately most garden plants are not indestructible and will encounter difficulties at times. Again, by planting carefully in the first place and by maintaining a healthy balance of lots of different plants, many problems can be avoided. However, you need to be aware of a number of potential hazards.

BELOW: *Many of the projects featured in this book are wood-based. Consequently, one of the biggest problems you are likely to face is woodworm.*

Problems with garden structures

Most of the structures demonstrated in this book are based upon preservative-treated softwoods which should last for years if they are properly handled during construction and cared for with a little attention afterwards. The problem you are most likely to encounter will be green mould or mildew covering the

ABOVE: *Death-watch beetle is the scourge of wooden structures in many different climates and situations. Eliminate these pests at all costs.*

surfaces of some of the projects. In most cases this can be easily removed by washing down the structure with soapy water and then applying a fungicide solution.

Regular painting, staining or varnishing of all the wooden projects in this book will prolong their lives and will reduce the risk of woodworm, death-watch beetle or some other form of timber rot taking hold. If you are unfortunate enough to encounter woodworm, eradicate it immediately by cutting out and replacing the affected part of the structure or by applying one of the proprietary solutions that are available from most DIY stores and garden centres.

The wide variety of different garden surfaces featured in this book all require some form of maintenance. Most hard surfaces will normally only need a regular wash-down – ideally with a high-pressure hose – and possibly some re-pointing of joints or re-seating of loose stones and pavers. Most soft surfaces will need regular mowing or trimming as well as fertilizing and frequent watering.

The 10 worst pests

- Aphids – highly invasive.
- Capsid bugs – sap suckers.
- Cutworms – maggot-like.
- Leaf miners – leaf destroyers.
- Mealy bugs – sap suckers.
- Red spider mites – tiny and lethal. Can cause plant death.
- Scale insects – scrape these scaly parasites off plants.
- Slugs and snails – can cause extensive plant damage.
- Vine weevil – voracious leaf-eaters. Larvae damage roots.
- Whitefly – mainly glasshouse pests. Similar to aphids.

The 10 worst diseases

- Blossom end wilt – affects fruit tree blossom and growth.
- Botrytis – also known as grey mould. Causes plant rot.
- Bulb rot – rots and kills bulbs.
- Chlorosis – drains leaf colour.
- Coral spot – affects wood.
- Leaf spot – discolours and marks leaves. A fungal rot.
- Mildew – common disease affecting many plants.
- Rust – fungal disease characterized by orange pustules.
- Sooty mould – smothers leaves.
- Wilt – lethal bacterial infection.

ABOVE: *The aphid is a ubiquitous garden pest which afflicts numerous different plants.*

Plant pests and diseases

Inevitably, any garden will suffer occasional problems that affect the quality and growth of plants and crops. Part of this is due to the very nature of garden plants, many of which are non-native and therefore bring with them their own range of problems that are sometimes exacerbated in a garden setting.

Pests can range from specific insect pests that affect only one group of plants, such as lily beetle, to non-specific pests that might trouble a range of plants – for example, slugs and snails or vine weevil. The latter are ubiquitous and generally more of a problem in most gardens.

The main diseases that plants face are either fungal or viral. Fungal diseases are often associated with weather conditions, either damp and warm or on occasion excessively hot, and can be passed from plant to plant by pollinating insects. Viral conditions are also often passed around by insects. Excessive heat, wind and water-logging are all cultural problems that can damage and kill plants of many different kinds. Poor nutrient levels and inadequate soil cultivation can also have an adverse effect on plant growth and health. Weeds can also exacerbate cultural problems, as they compete with garden plants for nutrients, water, light and space.

Many of the problems that affect plants can be avoided by maintaining a healthy mixture of lots of different species and by regular care and maintenance. So many pest and disease problems are a direct result of improper care and can often be remedied by better cultivation. The use of chemical sprays really should be a last resort rather than routine.

BELOW: *The black vine weevil likes many different plants and causes havoc wherever it becomes established. It is vital to deal with this pest at the first sign of trouble.*

Seasonal maintenance
checklist

If you have gone to the trouble of constructing some of the projects featured in this book, you will now want to take care of them, in order to prolong their lives and maximize the enjoyment that you experience in their daily use.

All natural materials used outdoors are affected by their environment and weather conditions at different times of year. If you have a number of garden features to look after, it will pay to have a plan of action – maybe a seasonal checklist as to what needs doing and when. Some basic tips and advice are provided here, although you should consult the pages on which your particular project is featured for any specific advice. Additionally, an enquiry to an internet search engine will invariably produce all kinds of useful information on how to maintain and care for a particular material or structure.

ABOVE: *All wood used externally contracts and expands according to temperature and weather conditions. For this reason, a little regular maintenance is inevitable.*

BELOW: *Once you have constructed some of the projects in this book, you need to turn your thoughts to maintaining them. A regular lick of paint or preservative is vital.*

Spring

Spring is the season of renewal – a time when the garden is coming back to life after the ravages of the winter. Plants need tending as they waken up and resume their lives, and this is when you should follow the advice given on the tags that come with newly purchased examples. Some will need planting out, some tying up and some potting on. Garden surfaces should be weeded and washed down, or fed and watered as necessary. In late spring it is time to bring out the lawnmower once more and some other soft, organic materials will need trimming or pruning. This is a good time of year to re-paint or stain garden structures, before any plant life growing up them becomes too abundant.

Summer

Long days and, with luck, warm, sunny weather, mean many hours spent working in and enjoying the garden at this time of year. The warmer weather will bring changes to some of your wooden garden structures, as the wood contracts and expands. Consequently, this is a good time to carry out basic maintenance all round. Tighten up loose screws and bolts and hammer back in any nails that might be slipping out. Cut back any overly invasive plant growth that might become too much of a burden on the structure in question. Wash down patios and terraces

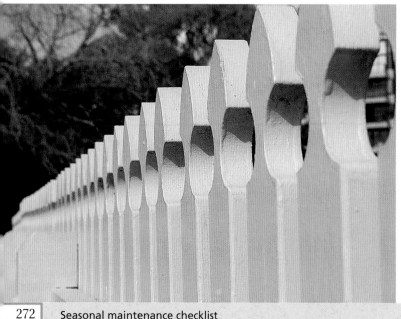

and renew or re-paint tired old pots and containers. Rub away and treat any rust on metal structures. Dead-head faded flowers to promote new blooms and prolong the display.

At this time of year, you should also aerate ponds and water features during still weather to oxygenate the water and keep plants and any fish alive.

Autumn

In the autumn, it is time to begin preparing your garden and its features for the long period of relative dormancy and lack of use that is winter.

Clear away fallen leaves from all surfaces promptly and make leafmould. Clear out summer containers and replant them for winter interest. Protect slightly tender plants by mulching them or by constructing shelters – ensure you do this before the first frosts arrive. Harvest any fruit and vegetables you have grown in containers or on your new structures and store them as appropriate.

Winter

This is the season when your new garden features are most likely to suffer deterioration and damage, so batten down the hatches! Bring smaller, portable features indoors for the duration of winter or cover them with protective sheets and tarpaulins. Take pots and containers indoors or place them in a cold frame or other shelter. Regularly thaw the ice on ponds and water features to prevent toxic gases building up and harming wildlife.

ABOVE: *Some woods benefit from external wood stains and preservatives while others do better with varnish, as pictured here. It all depends which wood you use. In any event, regular maintenance of all wood is essential.*

Cover up for winter

Ideally, put wooden garden furniture away under cover for the winter. However, if you don't have enough storage space, buy covers to protect items or at the very least paint them with wood preservative.

Do's

■ Create a seasonal maintenance schedule so that you keep on top of all your jobs.
■ Keep all wooden structures freshly painted and/or preserved.
■ Regularly re-point mortar joints in hard surfaces.
■ Rub and wash down any brick or stone structures that may attract lichen or algae.
■ Regularly check any electrical connections in the garden.
■ Think about your plants and their well-being in addition to everything you have built.

Don'ts

■ Don't leave tools lying around outside where they will rot and rust in no time at all.
■ Don't leave your structures to take care of themselves – over time, they won't!
■ Don't forget about the wildlife that lives in your garden. The winter months can be very inhospitable for many creatures.
■ Don't use grass under trees or in the shade of buildings.
■ Don't use overly vigorous ground-cover or climbing plants that will swamp your features.

Acid A soil pH value of below 7.0.

AD An abbreviation describing timber that is 'air dried'. Reducing the moisture content of timber to more than this extent has to be done artificially.

Adze A paring tool that is most commonly used for large shaping work, such as chair seats.

Aeration Improving soil air circulation by mechanically loosening the soil.

Aerial root A root that forms above ground on a stem.

Alkaline A soil pH value above 7.0

Alpine A high altitude plant, suitable for rock gardens.

Angiosperms These are hardwoods or 'dicotyledons' generally, deciduous trees with characteristically broad leaves and seeds enclosed in a seed case.

Annual A plant completing its life cycle within one growing season.

Aquatic plant A plant that grows in or floats on water.

Auger A long twist bit for boring large holes by hand. Most twist bits used in powered tools are called augers.

Awl A pointed tool used for boring small lead holes. It should also be sharp enough to use as a marking tool.

Back saw A tenon, dovetail or similar thin-bladed saw that has been stiffened along the top edge for added strength, helping to produce a straight cut.

Balk or Baulk A square lump of timber, sawn or hewn, which is at least 225mm (9in) square.

Bare When timber is measured undersize or a measurement is taken to fit and needs to be underside by a fraction that is not measurable.

Basal At the base of a structure or organ, e.g. leaf or stem.

Berry The fruit surrounding a seed or seeds.

Biennial A plant that completes its lifecycle in two years by growing in the first year and flowering in the second.

Biological control A naturally occurring or introduced control for pests, normally in the form of nematodes or insect predators.

Bloom Flower or blossom, or a white, powdery coating found on some plants.

Blue stain A bluish staining of sapwood created by a fungi attack.

Bog garden A waterlogged area suitable for plants that thrive in permanently moist soil.

Bottom heat A method employed in propagation, heating provided at the root zone to encourage rooting.

Bract A modified leaf at the base of a flower designed to look like a large flower or petal.

Bud The organ enclosing the immature stage of a leaf, flower, shoot.

Bulb A modified bud growing below ground.

Bulblet A small bulb formed at the side of the parent.

Burrs Odd-shaped growths that occur on the sides of some trees. Twig burr is sought after and valued for the production of fancy veneers.

Cabinet maker This is the skill that

is used to make fine furniture.

Carpenter The art of 'carpentry' is related to the structural use of wood in buildings. A carpenter is a practitioner of carpentry.

Catkin A form of inflorescence consisting of bracts and tiny flowers, usually arranged in a pendant form.

Caulk A joint that has been filled to make it watertight is 'caulked'. A boat building practice that fills the deck joints with tar or a similar substance.

Centre matched A term used to describe a method of veneering in which a number of pieces have a central meeting point.

Chalky A soil with a high level of calcium carbonate (chalk) or magnesium carbonate.

Check A small split in the surface of a board that does not go right through.

Chlorophyll The green pigment that absorbs energy from sunlight.

Chlorosis The loss of chlorophyll leading to leaf discolouration; yellowing caused by mineral deficiency, disease or low light levels.

Clay Fertile, heavy soil that is moisture retentive and prone to compaction and capping.

Cleft This term refers to when a block of wood is split rather than sawn.

Climber A plant that climbs or climbs by using modified stems, leaves, roots or leaf stalks.

Coniferous Refers to a conifer tree; softwoods, which are generally, but not always, evergreen.

Coppice To prune shrubs or trees to ground level to promote strong regeneration.

Cordon This term refers to a plant that is trained and restricted to only one stem.

Corm A below-ground storage organ.

Cross Interbreeding, hybridization between two or more plants.

Cross-cut Cutting across the width of a plank or board, involving a cut across the grain.

Crown The growing point of a plant from which new stems grow, or, the upper foliage and framework of a tree or large shrub.

Cultivar A cultivated variety of a species.

Cupping A distortion in the width of a board when the edges curl up to create a cup effect.

Curl This refers to a veneer that has been cut from the fork of a tree. Also known as fan, crotch or crutch veneers.

Cut nails These are flat nails that are cut or stamped out of a sheet of metal.

Cutting A section of stem, leaf or root used for propagation.

Damp down Wetting the floor of a greenhouse or conservatory to boost humidity and reduce temperatures.

Damping off A fungal disease causing the rotting and collapse of seedlings.

Dead-head Removing old and spent flowers/flower heads to promote further flowering or prevent seed setting.

Deciduous This term applies to trees that shed their leaves annually.

Deep cut This is the long cut through the width and down the length of a board as opposed to through the thickness (see Rip cut).

Density Timber density is arrived at by comparing the weight of a constant volume with specific moisture content.

Divide Propagation of plants (usually perennials) by dividing the parent crown into several sections.

Dote A type of wood rot caused by fungal decay. Timber affected will smell of mould and become discoloured on the surface. Also referred to as doty, dosy and dozy.

Dressed This term is used to describe timber that has been planed on one or more sides.

Durability The factors affecting durability are things like density, hardness, oil or mineral content and so on.

Dwarf A small or slow-growing form of plant.

Earlywood This is the layers of growth that trees in temperate climates put on rapidly at the start of the growing season in spring; also known as springwood.

End check Or 'split'. The small splits in the end of a board that naturally occur during drying.

End matched Usually refers to flooring. The matching occurs when the end is square-cut, so that there is no gap in the joint.

Epiphyte A plant that grows on another without acting as a parasite by taking food, water.

Equilibrium Moisture Content Wood is hygroscopic – it has the ability to take up and give off moisture. When the wood's moisture content has become equal to that of its environment, it is said to have reached its EMC.

Ericaceous Acid-loving plant/compost, plant from the family Ericaceae.

Espalier A method of training fruit into a tree with pairs of horizontal branches from a main trunk.

Evergreen A plant that retains its leaves over more than one season, or which retains most of its leaves over that period.

Family The primary category in plant classification, coming between order and genus.

Feathered (as in feathered maiden) A tree with a main trunk and lateral branches furnished to the ground.

Fern A non-flowering vascular plant, frequently with feathery fronds.

Fertilization The sexual fusion of male and female plant elements that initiates the development of seed.

Fertilizer Organic or inorganic compounds added to the growing media to improve/alter nutrient levels.

Flight hole The exit hole created when a wood-boring beetle bores its way to the surface.

Flower The reproductive structure of flowering plants.

Frass Wood boring beetle droppings. Each type of beetle produces a different textured dropping. Examination under a microscope will help determine which it is.

Frond The leaf of a fern.

Fuming The darkening of oak, and some other timbers, by the use of ammonia.

Glossary

Fungus Non-photosynthetic, non-vascular organism including mushrooms, moulds.

Garden origin Applies to plants that have been artificially bred or selected.

Gash A piece or pieces of waste or spare wood that can be used in a secondary position and not as the primary show wood.

Genus The primary category in plant classification, ranked between family and species.

Germination The change that occurs when a seed develops into a young plant.

Girdling This is the technique of cutting right through the bark of a standing, live tree, to the wood underneath. It effectively kills the tree, stopping the flow of sap and allowing the tree to dry before felling.

Girth This is the outside measurement around a log or tree the circumference.

Glaucous Covered with a blue/green or blue/grey bloom.

Green Often used to describe freshly felled timber that has high moisture content.

Grow on The stage after propagation when plants have been potted on and are grown for a further period before planting.

Growing season The part of the year in which active plant growth occurs.

Habit The appearance or growing tendency of a plant that gives it its characteristic form.

Hammering The use of a veneer hammer to press down on a veneer

and squeeze the excess glue out.

Hand Left- or right-handed. Can refer to a variety of subjects, including doors and door furniture.

Harden off To gradually acclimatize plants that have been raised in a greenhouse to the external environment.

Hardiness The measure of reliance to frosts displayed by plants.

Hardwood A conventional term used to denote timber of broad-leaved trees with porous wood belonging to the botanical group known as Angiosperms.

Hardwood Mature wood used for cutting material.

Herb A plant with practical applications such as culinary or medicinal, or in botany any herbaceous plant.

Herbaceous A plant that dies back to ground level at the end of the growing season and regenerates from the crown the following season.

Herbicide Chemicals used in weed control.

Honeycombing Another drying defect in wood. Similar to collapse, it is difficult to spot until the wood is cut.

Humidity The measure of air moisture content.

Humus Decomposed organic matter found in or introduced into soil/growing media.

Hybrid A natural or artificially produced plant with two genetically distinct parents.

Hygroscopic All wood has the ability to take on and give off moisture like a sponge; this is known as 'hygroscopic'.

Incipient decay The initial stages of fungal decay. Associated signs are a discoloration of the wood.

Indigenous Native wood or plant of a particular country.

Infertile Soil low in nutrients or plants that do not flower due to cultural problems, disease or pests.

Inflorescence Arrangement of flowers on a single stem or axis.

Insecticide Chemical used to control insect pests.

Internode A section of stem between two nodes.

Invasive An aggressive plant that invades or overwhelms other plants.

Joinery This is the art of making and fixing wooden items in buildings, such as windows and doors.

Joint This is the generic term relating to the junction between timbers; the act of jointing wood together.

KD The abbreviation for 'kiln dried'. KD does not always mean that the timber is dry enough for the purpose that you intend.

Kerf The width of a saw cut. Also used to describe the width at which the teeth of a saw are set to cut.

Late wood The growth layer of wood laid down later in the annual cycle.

Lateral Side shoot from the stem of the main plant.

Layering A method of propagation in which an attached stem is encouraged to root by laying and fixing on the soil.

Leader The main growing stem of a plant.

Leaf Plant organ that is the primary organ in photosynthesis.

Linear measure The length measure of timber, either as an individual piece or as a cumulative total.

Liquid feed A fertilizer diluted in water for application.

Loam Fertile, well-drained but moisture-retentive soil.

Lumber A phrase used mostly in North America that refers to converted wood.

m2/m3 The surface area and volume abbreviations of 'square metre' and 'cubic metre'.

Marginal A plant requiring permanently moist conditions, as found at the edge of a water course.

MDF This is the abbreviation of 'medium density fibreboard'.

Mist A method of increasing humidity by spraying fine droplets of water into the atmosphere or on to a plant.

Moisture content The weight of moisture contained in wood expressed as a percentage. In some cases it is possible for the moisture content of timber to exceed 100 per cent.

Moisture gradient Because timber is hygroscopic, it tends to dry quicker on the outside than it does in the middle.

Mulch A layer of material spread on the soil surface to suppress weeds and/or improve fertility.

Native An endemic plant that occurs naturally in an area/country.

Naturalized Introduced plants that grow as if native.

Nectar Sugary liquid secreted by some plants to attract pollinators.

Neutral A pH of 7.0, i.e. neither acid nor alkaline.

Node The point on a stem at which leaves, leaf buds and shoots arise.

Nominal size This refers to timber sizes before they have been dressed to a 'finished size'.

Non-porous wood Timbers that contain no pores in their structure; usually softwoods.

Nut Dry fruit surrounding a single seed.

Nutrients The minerals needed for healthy plant growth.

Offset A small plant that forms naturally as part of a plant's vegetative growth.

Oxygenator A fully submerged aquatic plant that releases oxygen into the water.

Pan A shallow dish used for growing alpines.

Panicle Term applied to plants with freely branched inflorescences.

PAR The abbreviation that refers to 'planed all round'.

Parasite A plant that derives nutrients from another plant.

Patina The deep gloss or lustre finish that a piece of furniture acquires over years of polishing and handling.

Peat Humus-rich, moisture-retentive decayed organic matter with a pH below 6.5.

Perennial A plant that lives for more than two growing seasons.

Pesticide Chemicals used to control insect pests.

Petal A modified leaf that makes up part of the flower.

pH measure of acidity or alkalinity.

Photosynthesis The complex series of chemical reactions in which energy from sunlight is absorbed by chlorophyll and carbon dioxide and water converted into sugars and oxygen.

Plain-sawn Any timber that is not 'quarter-sawn'.

Plantlet A young, small plant that develops alongside an older one.

Pollard To cut branches back hard to a framework or to the main trunk of a tree to restrict growth.

Pollen Grains containing the male element needed for fertilization.

Pores The pores, or 'vessels', are the principle water/food conduction elements in the structure of hardwoods. Their size, shape and distribution, along with other factors, helps with the identification of specific timbers.

Prick out The transfer of seedlings or small cuttings into larger pots or containers.

Prime The best possible grade available for that particular timber species; the highest quality.

Propagate To increase plants by seed, cuttings, etc.

Prostrate A plant with stems that trail or lie flat against the ground.

Quarter-sawn The best cut to produce planks from a log, but not always the most economical.

Rays Correctly called 'medullary' rays, in hardwoods. These are the cells that when cut on the quarter produce the figure seen in quarter-sawn material.

Redwood A trade term that refers to the pine group of timbers.

Regularized Pieces of wood of a given size that have been sawn or partly planed to a consistent size.

Resaw This is a bandsaw, or larger circular saw, used to cut and produce a number of pieces from larger stock.

Respiration Absorption of oxygen and breakdown of carbohydrates, releasing carbon dioxide and water and providing energy for the plant.

Rhizome Horizontal, branching or fleshy stem growing underground or at ground level.

Rip cut Also known as flatting, cutting down the length of the wood. The cuts are made through the thickness rather than through the width.

Rock garden Area for growing alpine plants.

Root Part of the plant that anchors it and absorbs water and nutrients from the soil or to successfully strike cuttings.

Rootball A mass of roots and the compost or soil attached to them.

Rootstock The underground part of a plant or the plant onto which another is grafted, as in fruit trees, roses, etc.

Rosette The dense whorl of leaves arising from a central point or crown of a plant.

Rough timber Rough timber is lumber that is sawn only not planed, dressed or even moulded.

Round timber These are logs ready for conversion into lumber. They may be referred to as 'in the round'.

Sap The watery fluid that runs through the conductive tissue of plants.

Sapwood The layer of growing wood just underneath the bark of a tree.

Scarify Removal of moss, weeds and thatch from a lawn by mechanical abrasion.

Seed head The dried fruits of, for example, perennials.

Seedling A young plant raised from seed.

Shake Any split, cleavage or partial separation between adjacent layers of wood fibres.

Shoot Side growth, branch, twig or stem.

Show wood Literally the wood that is showing as opposed to hidden.

Any polished wooden surface showing on upholstered furniture is called show wood.

Shrinkage As wood dries it shrinks, because the cellular structure reduces in size as moisture is lost.

Shrub A deciduous or evergreen woody plant with multiple stems.

Silt Moderately fertile, moisture-retentive soil prone to capping and compaction.

Softwood The soft, young unripened wood of trees and shrubs.

Softwood trees Gymnosperms, coniferous or needle-leaved trees that have a non-porous wood structure.

Species A basic category of plant classification, ranked below genus.

Specification A listing of requirements.

Specimen plant A plant grown in a prominent position, alone or with a low planting, which can be viewed from multiple angles.

Spur Short branches or branchlets along the main stem on which flowers and fruit are produced.

Square-edged This is effectively lumber, planks or boards with both edges sawn square and straight.

Standard A tree or shrub that has been trained with a clear stem and head of foliage.

Stem The main part of a plant, from which side stems form.

Sterile A flower that cannot produce seeds or soil that is lacking in nutrients or has been treated to kill weed seeds.

Sticker stain Or 'shadow'. This is when there has been some sort of chemical reaction between the sticker and the stock being dried.

Stickers These are the regular sized strips of wood used to separate layers of boards or planks when in the air and kiln drying process; sometimes called 'strips'.

Succulent A plant with fleshy leaves and stems which is often native to dry areas.

Surfaced When one or both wider faces of a board have been planed or dressed.

T & G The abbreviation of tongued and grooved; a machined profile usually used as floor boarding.

Tally The record of timber sizes picked and prepared against an order.

Tap root A primary root, often swollen, from which the secondary root system develops.

Terminal The end point of a stem, or shoot, on a plant.

Terrestrial A plant that grows in soil.

Thicknesser A powered planing machine that can plane wood to a regular thickness.

Through and through The most commonly used method of cutting logs to produce lumber.

To cut Timber, machined or sawn, supplied so that the customer is able to cut his or her specific requirements from it.

Topiary The clipping and training of plants into architectural or representational forms.

Train The pruning and shaping of a tree or shrub.

Transpiration The evaporation of water from the leaves of a plant.

Tree A woody perennial with a crown of branches developing from a single trunk.

Tyloses Found in porous hardwoods, this is a thin, bubble-like obstruction within the vessel cell structure, in the pore cavity.

Variegation The irregular pigmentation in a leaf caused by mutation or disease.

Variety A naturally occurring variation of a species.

Vascular Containing conductive tissue that enable the passage of sap in a plant.

Veneers Thin slices of decorative wood used to face up a cheaper, plainer wood.

Wane The outer, uneven edge or edges of timber planks that have been cut 'through and through'.

Warp This term refers to any distortion in a board when it is not flat and straight.

Waterlogged Soil that is saturated with water.

Weed Vigorous, invasive plant or any plant growing where it is not wanted.

Whitewood The general classification that covers softwood species such as spruces and firs.

Worm holes This is the common name for the flight hole of a mature wood-boring beetle.

Yield The amount of timber products of value that is cut or produced from logs. The amount of yield depends both on the timber that is being cut and the method that is employed.

Index

Index

Acknowledgements

The authors and publishers would like to thank the following companies for their assistance and co-operation in the making of this book: the staff at **Coolings Nurseries** for their assistance with the commissioned photography, including the loan of tools, plants and specialist equipment. Coolings Nurseries Ltd., Rushmore Hill, Knockholt, Kent, TN14 7NN, UK; Tel: 00 44 1959 532269; Email: rushmorehill@coolings.co.uk ; and Coolings Outdoor Inspirations, Main Road, Knockholt, Kent, TN14 7LJ, UK; Tel: 00 44 1959 534386; Email: mainroad@coolings.co.uk; Website: www.coolings.co.uk; the staff at **Silverland Stone** for the loan of all hard landscaping materials: Silverland Stone, Main Road, Knockholt, Sevenoaks, Kent, TN14 7LJ, UK; Tel: 00 44 1959 532244; Email; enquiries@silverlandstone.co.uk; **Forest Garden Ltd**., for supplying much of the timber used in the projects; Units 291 & 296 Hartlebury Trading Estate, Hartlebury, Worcestershire, DY10 4JB; Tel: 0844 248 9800; E-mail; info@forestgarden.co.uk; website www.forestgarden.co.uk.

The publishers would like to thank the following individuals and agencies for contributing images to this book:
BigStockPhoto.com: prelims 'Flower bed garden soil close up' © Stephen Rees; p6; 'Birdhouses' © Regina Chayer; p7 'Water curves' © John Wallace; p8 'Backyard flowers' © Joseph Wentzel; p11 'Ramada' © Allison Brown; p12 'Buddah and blooms' © John Sartin; p21 'Garden path' © Lisa Turay; p56 'Succulent garden' © Ellen Henneke; p56 'Birdhouse among the flowers' © Darren Baker; p57 'Sidewalk zen garden' © Ramona D'Viola; p58 'Lizard out of pebble' © Musat Christian; p59 'Wet stones' © Caroline Hedges; p88 'Fence' © Anna Karwowska; p89 'Floats' © Robert Hackett; p90 'English ivy on bright red painted wall' © Mark Stahl; p91 'Curved walkway trellis' © Darryl Brooks; p95 'Climbing red roses' © Bonnie Watton; p103 'Flowers on the fence' © C L Triplett; p131; p146 'Dining outdoors' © Barbara Speckart; p147 'Hammock' © Juan J Gutierree; p174 'Children in garden' © Marzanna Syncerz; p174 'Childrens hand with watering can' © Darryl Sleath; p176 'Picnic bears' © Len Green; p176 'Big chess match' © Lance Bellers; p177 'Children's playhouse' © Rony Zmiri; p204 'Garden water falls' © Heng Kong Chen; p228 'Bicycle in the garden' © Jiri Vaclavek; p228 'Secret garden' © Tracy Hebden; p234 'Exterior living space' © Brenda A Smith; p232 'Hanging Basket' © David Huges; p236 'Al fresco eating' © David Hilcher; p236 'Garden chairs' © Jyothi Joshi; p236 'Outside night light' © John Casey; p268 'Sun Dial' © Steve Mann; **Garden World Images:** pp 6 (T, B); 8 (L); 9 (T, B); 10; 11; 12 (B); 13 (TL, BR); 14; 15 (T, C, B); 16 (T, B); 17 (T, B); 18 (T, B); 19 (T, B); 20 (T); 22; 23 (TL, TC, TR, BC, BR); 24 (T, B); 25 (TL, TR, BL, BR); 26 (T, B); 27 (B); 28 (BL, BR); 29 (TR, B); 30 (T, B); 31 (T, B); 32 (C, B); 33 (TL, TR); 34 (T, B); 35 (T, B); 36; 37(T, C, B); 39 (BR); 52 (BR); 53; 54 (T, C, BL); 55 (TL, TR, BR); 58 (B); 59 (T); 63 (B); 65 (B); 67 (BL); 69; 78 (BR); 79; 83 (TR); 87 (T, CL, CR); 88 (B); 89 (T, BL); 90 (CR, B); 91 (B); 93 (BR); 102 (BR); 114 (C, B); 116 (B); 117 (L, TR, BR); 118 (T, B); 119 (T); 120; 121 (TL, TR); 126 (TR); 142 (BR); 144 (C, B); 146 (T, BL); 147 (T); 148 (T, B); 149 (T, B); 170 (BL); 173 (TL); 175 (B); 203 (C, BL); 205 (T, C, B); 206 (T); 207 (T, B); 218 (B); 223; 225 (BL); 229 (TL, R); 230 (T, B); 231 (T, B); 232 (CL, CR, BL, BR); 233 (T, CL, CR, BL, BR); 234 (T); 235 (TL, TR, B); 237 (TL, TR); 245 (B); 249 (B); Hozelock p.28 (TR); 29; **Peter Bishop:** pp 42–43; 70–75; 92–114; 122–136; 138–143; 150–152; 154–162; 164–170; 178–194; 196–201; 252–269; **Chris and Jenny Hendy:** pp 238–251; **Focus Publishing:** pp 44–45; 62–63; 66–68; 76–78; **Tim Sandall** pp 2; 21; 27 (T); 38–41; 46–52; 60–61; 64–65; 73; 77; 80–85; 105; 109; 111; 127; 131; 133; 137(B); 153; 163; 167; 171; 174 (C); 175 (T); 179 (B); 189; 195; 208–222; 224–227; 239; 251; 287; **Stock Xchange:** 1; 4; 7 (T, BL); 32; 33 (BL; BR); 43 (C, BR); 51 (T, BR); 55 (C); 67 (BR); 68 (TR, CR, BR); 71(BL, BR); 75 (B); 76 (L); 81 (BR); 83 (TL); 86 (T, C, B); 87 (B); 93 (BR); 97 (BR); 100 (BL); 102 (TR); 107 (BR); 109 (R); 113 (B); 115; 116 (T, C); 119 (B); 125 (B); 126 (BR); 127; 137 (TL, TR); 141 (BL, BR); 144 (T); 145 (L, TR); 161 (TR, BR); 170 (TR); 172 (T, C, B); 173 (TR, B, BR); 177 (T); 199 (BR); 202 (T, C, B); 203 (T, BR); 204 (T); 206 (B); 207 (C); 210 (BR); 214 (C, BC, BR); 221 (TR, TC, BR); 222 (TR, BL, BR); 225 (BC, BR); 227 (B); 228(T); 236 (BR); 270 (T, B); 271 (T, B); 272 (T, B); 273 (T, B); 277; 280; 284; StockXpertcom: p.81 (BL); 90 (TL); 121 (B); 218 (TR).

Key: T = Top, B = Bottom, C = Centre, TL = Top Left, TR = Top Right, BL = Bottom Left, BR = Bottom Right, CL = Centre Left, CR = Centre Right, BC= Bottom Centre